GETTIN'
HOME

GETTIN' HOME

An Odyssey Through The '60s

An Illustrated Memoir By

Steve Nelson

Massaemett Media

ISBN 978-1717358158

A production of
Massaemett Media

This is dedicated
to the one I love.

Life can never be
Exactly like we want it to be
But I can be satisfied
Just knowing you love me.

The "5" Royales

covered by
The Shirelles
and
The Mamas & The Papas

INTRO

THERE'S A SAYING THAT, "If you can remember the '60s, you weren't there." Or is it that, "If you were there in the '60s, you can't remember it." I forget which.

But I was there, and I remember a lot. Some of what happened then was unforgettable, some of it forgettable, some of it I wish I could forget but can't.

This is not a book about the '60s as an historical era, but a personal account of a young man's journey through that time. I've tried my best to tell it like it was, as I lived it. My son Nate told me, "You've got to be honest." I always kept that in mind as I wrote.

Why write this at all after so many years? Partly it was because once the idea of doing it crossed my mind, it became a challenge I had to face. Partly it was because if I didn't do it now, I might not remember as much later, or might not still be around. And partly it was because I felt I had a tale to tell which might be of interest to some people, and add to the record of a remarkable time.

When I began this project, I thought I knew my own story well. But I was surprised how the process of writing released memories I didn't know were there, how the joy and pain I'd experienced in the '60s became so real the second time around.

Somehow, half a century later, you still can't avoid taking sides when talking about such a groundbreaking, controversial and divisive era. So let me confess that in many ways I'm an unrepentant child of the '60s. It was an exciting time of unprecedented creativity, one that gave rise to political, social and cultural changes that people are still embracing, or resisting. Sure, there were things which seemed groovy then but silly later. Well, that's just background noise, not the essence of what the '60s were.

To all the young and not so young people in the '60s who put their hearts and souls into living what they believed and dreamed, I'll just say: I love you. Yeah yeah yeah.

Odyssey

1: a long wandering or voyage usually marked by many changes of fortune
2: an intellectual or spiritual wandering or quest; an odyssey of self-discovery

(The Merriam-Webster Dictionary)

El Condor Pasa

"It is not the mountain we conquer but ourselves."
Edmund Hillary, first man to summit Mount Everest

PART ONE

1. The Journey Begins

MY FLIGHT WAS DELAYED. Again.

I was on a layover in the Miami airport on the morning of June 19, 1961. I'd left LaGuardia at midnight on Eastern Airlines and arrived about 3 a.m., at age 20 my first time on an airplane. The connection to my destination of Lima, Peru had been due to depart at 7 a.m., now hours ago. Shaky after the first leg of the journey, I was glad for the reprieve to settle my stomach and my nerves, facing a 12-hour flight on a prop-driven DC-6 flown by Aerolineas Peruanas, the Peruvian national airline.

I'd been up all night, but was too restless to sit still for long or to doze off in the uncomfortable waiting area chairs, and wandered aimlessly around the airport. Hoping for a breath of fresh air, I stepped outside the terminal, but was hit by a blast of Florida heat and humidity that quickly sent me back inside. Suspended in time and space, I had little to do but think about the journey that was taking me to Vicos, a remote village high in the Peruvian Andes. Assuming that the plane ever left and that I was still willing to get on it, despite my anxiety at what lay ahead.

The East Coast of the U.S. was in the same time zone as Peru on the West Coast of South America, so I wouldn't have to reset my watch. But I was about to travel back in time to a place totally removed from the middle-class life I knew as a teenager in the suburbs of Long Island and as a college student at Cornell University.

In the world I was leaving behind, a crisis was brewing over Soviet demands that the U.S. and its allies withdraw from East Berlin, which they'd occupied since defeating Germany sixteen years ago. Ex-Nazi Adolph Eichmann was testifying in Israel in defense of his role in the murder of millions of Jews. The U.S. Supreme Court was handing down a landmark ruling, *Mapp v. Ohio*, that illegally-obtained evidence could not be used in a state criminal trial. In sports, Roger Maris and Mickey Mantle were chasing Babe Ruth's hallowed record of 60 home runs in a season, set in 1927. On the radio, Gary U.S. Bonds was dancin' till a "Quarter to

Three," Bobby Lewis was "Tossin' and Turnin'," and Roy Orbison was "Running Scared."

The flight to Lima finally departed at 2 p.m., seven hours late. I was on it. So was my Cornell classmate Harold Skalka. We were among six students chosen for a program to spend the summer in Vicos doing anthropological field work. I only had a vague idea of what lay ahead in the mountains, and we had no formal training to prepare for what we might encounter living there. You just got on a plane and showed up.

The two of us were the only *norteamericanos* on board, surrounded by Peruvians before we even arrived in Peru. The DC-6 plodded along to the loud drone of its propellers on a flight that seemed endless. After a refueling stop in Panama, it soon got dark and there was nothing to see out the windows, no way of knowing where we were, over land or over sea. For food service we were handed a ham sandwich.

Lima was often under a dense cloud cover, so when we reached its airspace, we circled for what must have been two hours, waiting to land. There was no radar to guide us in. The pilot had to wait until he could see the lights of the city through an opening in the clouds, then dive down through it. When he finally did, we had no warning. I fumbled for the airsick bag. Too late. My body dropped and the partially-digested remains of the ham sandwich rose, only to land on my lap. The Peruvians did their best to ignore me.

We touched down at 2 a.m., 26 hours after leaving New York. When we disembarked down stairs directly onto the tarmac, I was struck by the foreign smell of the moist tropical air, all the stranger in my state of fatigue. Going through customs, with my chinos emitting their own distinct odor from my air disaster, I presented my passport along with the immunization record of the multiple shots I needed for the trip. Peru and Vietnam were the only two places in the world where to enter the country you had to be vaccinated for bubonic plague, the Black Death which decimated Europe in the 14th century, killing 50 million people. I was glad to have made it to Peru, but had no reason to think I might ever go to Vietnam.

Hal and I were picked up and taken to a *pencion* (inn) where all the students in the program were staying. In the morning we were awakened to a breakfast of rolls and potent black coffee called *tinto*, almost like hot coffee syrup to which you added hot milk to taste. It sure beat the watery brown liquid with creamer and sugar I was used to drinking at the Cornell Student Union. I managed to make a collect call home to my parents, to let them know I had arrived safely. It was much harder to speak my rudimentary Spanish with the telephone operator than it had been in Spanish class at Cornell.

The capital of Peru, Lima was founded by the Spanish *conquistador* (conqueror) Francisco Pizarro in 1535, shortly after he overthrew the Inca Empire. Our student group spent two days there acclimating and getting to know each other. The main daily newspaper *La Prensa* ran a story about what these *universitarios norteamericanos* (American college students) were doing in Peru. Exploring the city, we sampled the fare from the many street food vendors. I particularly liked the *anticuchos*, pieces of beef heart grilled over charcoal on a skewer and basted with a spicy sauce.

For dinner one night we went to a gourmet Chinese restaurant. In the late 19th and early 20th century indentured Chinese workers were brought to Peru to work on the railroads, just as they did in the American West. The food prepared by their descendants was a tasty mix of their ancestral cooking and Peruvian spices and ingredients, with fresh fish from the Pacific Ocean at Lima's doorstep. I also had my first taste of *ceviche*, the signature Peruvian dish of raw seafood marinated in lime juice.

Lima was growing rapidly due to the influx of indigenous Andeans coming down from the mountains to seek a better life than the hardscrabble existence they eked out in their homelands. But economic opportunity was elusive. They lived in *barriadas* (shantytowns) on the outskirts of the city. Our student group visited one on the edge of a giant garbage dump, where the inhabitants built shacks out of anything they could find – sheet metal, scrap wood, cardboard – and foraged for scraps of leftover food.

As we walked through the dump, I noticed the partial carcass of a pig, its rear quarters missing. Strangely, it was wobbling and shaking. The cause of this eerie phenomenon was revealed when a scrawny dog backed out of the body cavity after scavenging what it could from the innards. There were quite a few dogs wandering around in search of food, not pets and definitely not to be approached. At the edge of the dump I looked down into enclosures holding hundreds if not thousands of pigs. Crammed together, they were waiting to be slaughtered, squealing and grunting, emitting an overpowering stench, steam rising from their bodies, a porcine purgatory. We'd seen enough of the city. It was time to head for the mountains.

2. ON (AND OFF) THE ROAD

THE PAN-AMERICAN HIGHWAY runs nearly 20,000 miles from Prudhoe Bay, Alaska, north of the Arctic Circle, to Argentina in southern South America. It hugs the Pacific coastline in Peru. Our route would take the highway north for several hours, then head east over a mountain pass before descending into the Callejon de Huaylas, the high Andean valley where Vicos was located.

Leaving Lima, we all piled into a Jeep station wagon driven by Paul Doughty, a Cornell graduate student who was working in Vicos. We made a stop at the ruins of Pachacamac, which was first settled around 200 A.D. and fell under the control of the Inca Empire in the 15th century. It was not like the great stone ruins of Machu Picchu, but built of smaller stones and adobe, its numerous buildings and temples slowly eroding like crumbling sand castles.

Mummification had been a highly-evolved art there, and there were extensive burial grounds, the mummies well-preserved in the extremely arid climate. Most of them had already been removed from the site, either by archaeologists or grave robbers. Among the remains which had been found there were those of several young women, human sacrifices with cotton garrotes still looped around their necks.

After exploring the windblown ruins for a while, we came upon a shallow pit with pieces of bones and remnants of cloth scattered around. Paul reached down, brushed away some sand, and lifted a skull which he held up, like Hamlet contemplating Yorick. The bits of cloth were amazingly well preserved, because it hadn't rained at Pachacamac for centuries.

We encountered a different scene of death on the Pan-American Highway. The road is built into a sandy slope, with a steep drop to the ocean. A southbound bus on the ocean side of the road had been swept over the edge by a sand slide from the uphill side. All the passengers were killed, which had been headline news while we were in Lima. As we neared the scene of the accident, the road narrowed to a single lane where the slide had occurred, with the wreckage of the bus lying far below at the edge of the Pacific. The bodies had been removed, but it was still an unsettling sight. We were well aware before coming to Peru that it was prone to epic disasters such as massive floods and powerful earthquakes. Here was another one to think about, as we faced a long journey up the coast with the steep hillside looming above.

Our mood was lightened when we stopped for lunch in a village along the highway, at another Peruvian Chinese restaurant, a local café with home cooking. They served the best wonton soup, a big pottery bowl loaded with vegetables and seafood. It was the last Chinese meal I ate in Peru. About 200 miles north of Lima, at Casma, we turned east toward the mountains and left the coast behind. Where we were going, they didn't serve Chinese food, or even have restaurants.

The road into the mountains was one switchback after another as we gained elevation. Just when we thought we were finally seeing the top of the mountain range, we'd come around a bend and see even higher mountains ahead. The road was unpaved, not really two full lanes wide, with no guardrails. As we climbed on its outside lane, a bus or truck coming down in the other lane would

Paul Doughty holding skull he unearthed at Pachacamac

Bulldozer clearing sandslide on the Pan-American Highway

Switchbacks on the road from Casma into the Andes

*At the pass over the Cordillera Negra before descending into
the Callejon de Huaylas, with the Cordillera Blanca behind me*

have to squeeze up against the hillside to get by, as we hugged the edge. Sitting by the window in the Jeep, I looked down at a drop-off of hundreds of feet, pretending not to worry that we might make headlines.

We finally reached a mountain pass, at about 14,000 feet, and could see snow-capped peaks in the distance across a deep valley. We got out of the Jeep to look around and breathe the thin air. The land was rock-strewn and barren of vegetation, like I imagined the surface of the moon might be. One of the students complained of chest pains from the altitude. But we were all relieved when they subsided as we descended into the valley below, the Callejon de Huaylas, toward our destination of Vicos, at about 10,000 feet.

Callejon means "alley," and it is just that, a passageway from south to north between the Cordillera Negra, or Black Mountain Range, to its west and the Cordillera Blanca, White Mountain Range, to its east. The latter, about 125 miles long, includes 33 glacial peaks over 18,000 feet high, crowned by Huascaran, at 22,200 feet the tallest mountain in the Earth's tropical zone (the highest peak in the Rockies is only 14,440 feet). The Cordillera Negra, relatively lower and exposed to mild prevailing winds from the Pacific Ocean, is bare of snow. The floor of the Callejon is about 13,000 feet above sea level at its southern end and slopes down to about 6,500 feet at its northern end. The Santa River runs through its middle, arising from a high mountain lake and flowing north toward the Equator until, at the end of the Callejon, it turns west toward the Pacific.

In the late 1940's the Peruvian government proposed to dam the river to produce hydroelectric power. This caught the attention of Peruvian anthropologist and Cornell graduate student Mario Vazquez as an ideal opportunity to study the impact of rural electrification on people without electric power. As it turned out, the dam was not built, due to an avalanche, but the *hacienda* of Vicos in the valley became the focus of an even more interesting project.

Descendants of the Incas, the Vicosinos had, for centuries since the Spanish conquest of Peru, been subjugated under a system of feudal servitude. In exchange for living on the land and farming it, they owed the *hacendado* (landlord) three days a week of their labor, enforced with a whip by an overseer on horseback. Every five years the corporation which owned the 30,000+ acres of land offered up the lease on the Vicos *hacienda* for renewal, for about $600 per year. That entitled the leaseholder to the labors of the 2,000 people living there, and their animals too.

Cornell Professor Allan R. Holmberg saw in Vicos an opportunity to put into practice his view on the role of anthropologists as working with a community toward its betterment, not merely studying it and writing papers. So in 1952 Holmberg and Vazquez founded the Cornell-Peru Project in Vicos, a landmark experiment in activist anthropology and land reform. Cornell University put up the money to become the leaseholder of the *hacienda*, and Cornell and Peruvian anthropologists set about on a revolutionary course of social change. Its focus was on improving health care, education, farming practices and the self-worth of the Vicosinos, who were always closely involved by Cornell in these efforts and by 1957 had become self-governing.

The Cornell team worked with the Vicosinos to create a community-owned agricultural cooperative. They saved up money from the sale of their communal crops, primarily potatoes, which had formerly belonged to the *hacienda* owner. This enabled them to buy a truck to bring their produce to Lima, where they could get a better price. They even were able to lend money to their neighbors in nearby haciendas. By 1960 they had enough funds on hand to realize a daring dream, to buy the Vicos *hacienda* and liberate themselves from servitude. But negotiations stalled when the corporate landowner suddenly jacked up the price more than 10x.

That summer a police contingent entered a neighboring *hacienda* and shot three men dead while wounding many others. Their crime? Attempting to sell produce from *hacienda* land to raise money to build a school. The massacre raised tensions throughout the Andes. And a year later there was still no deal on the table for Vicos. That's where matters stood when we arrived.

Loading sacks of potatoes on the Vicos community-owned truck

3. FROM AN ISLAND TO A LAKE

THREE YEARS EARLIER, in 1958, I could not have imagined myself in the Andes. I was living on Long Island with my father, mother, two brothers and a dachshund. We'd followed the station wagon train to the new American frontier. Our ranch house in Roslyn Heights was built by the man who created Levittown, the ultimate post-war suburb of look-alike houses in neat rows on small plots of well-groomed lawns. I'd just graduated from high school, where my life had revolved around girls, cars, sports, TV, comic books, sci-fi and rock 'n' roll.

Especially rock 'n' roll, and rockabilly, and doo wop, and rhythm and blues. This music spoke to me in a way other kinds of music did not, despite my parents efforts to turn me into a classical music lover like them. It was my literature, it was my poetry, it was the movie playing in my head. I kept the radio on when I was in my room and knew hundreds of songs by heart. A math whiz, I loved doing my homework to the great disk jockey Alan Freed's "Rock 'n' Roll Party" on WINS 1010. Math + Music = Double the Pleasure, Double the Fun, in the words of the Doublemint gum jingle.

Quiet, shy and studious, I wasn't big or strong enough to make varsity sports, but was agile and athletic enough to be a really good dancer, uninhibited moving my body to the beat. That was my hall pass for admission to the "in crowd" of jocks and cheerleaders. In the summer we hung out at the community pool or went to the beach. In our Fifties clothes and hair styles, some people called us "juvenile delinquents." But in the lingo of Long Island we called ourselves "rocks."

We were living the middle-class American dream. But we'd grown up doing "duck-and-cover" air raid drills, and beneath the placid surface of our suburban lives lurked the fear of nuclear war between the USA and the USSR. The main conflict in our day-to-day lives was between Yankee and Dodger fans. Mickey Mantle was my boyhood hero. He was a muscular blue-eyed blond Adonis

A "rock" in our backyard on Long Island, 1956

from Oklahoma, I was a skinny brown-eyed Jewish kid born in the Bronx not far from Yankee Stadium.

As valedictorian of my high school class, I had hoped to get into Harvard, but only made the waiting list. And I couldn't afford to pass up two scholarships to go to Cornell. The university is famously "far above Cayuga's waters," in the rural and rolling Finger Lakes region in upstate New York. I arrived there as a freshman in 1958, the cloistered campus so unlike Long Island. Social life at Cornell was dominated by the 50+ fraternities, whose members dressed in the preppy style called "tweedy" for their de rigueur costume of tweed sport jackets, chinos and penny loafers.

There was also a very different group of guys who wore blue denim jackets proclaiming their membership in the "Future Farmers of America." They were attending Cornell's aggie school, the only one among the eight Ivy League universities. If there was a chapter of FFA on the Island, I'd never heard of it. Still, I enjoyed discovering Cornell's vast agricultural lands at the far reaches of the campus, a pastoral setting for experimental livestock herds. I was fascinated by massive pigs that looked as big as the hippos at the Bronx Zoo.

The era of space travel had dawned in 1957 with the launch of Sputnik, the Soviet satellite which was the first to orbit the Earth. I entered Cornell as a physics major, perhaps aspiring to become an astrophysicist. The physics classrooms and labs were in Rockefeller Hall, named for the family which donated the money for it. Apparently the Cornell administration at the time decided to skimp on the building and put most of the money into its facilities and equipment, a decision that was scientifically sound, if not politically so. The resulting structure was pretty drab looking, not the gleaming monument which the Rockefellers may have envisioned their name on. That was the last time they gave any money to Cornell.

I found the building rather gloomy myself, nor did I take to the lab work. So by my sophomore year I switched my major to math. There was something particularly satisfying about solving a math problem, that "aha!" moment when I got it. To balance the abstractness of math, I took electives in the humanities, including several anthropology courses. One was on pre-Columbian civilizations: the Incas, the Mayas, the Aztecs, and many others which rose and fell before them. One day the professor mentioned that there were applications for the Columbia-Cornell-Harvard Summer Field Studies Program on a table at the back of the room. Out of curiosity, I picked one up on the way out.

The three universities were doing anthropological field work in Ecuador, Peru and Mexico, respectively. An undergraduate at those universities could apply for the Program and choose one of the three locations to work in the field for a summer. I was not very adventurous, but became increasingly fascinated by the idea of spending two months in a faraway exotic land, and decided to apply. Even though I aced my anthro courses, I didn't think that as a math major my odds were all that good for being selected. But I figured that if I were, I might as well go to the most remote place, so I checked the box for Peru. I knew about the Incas and their great stoneworks, but had little idea what it would be like living among their descendants high in the Andes.

Professor Holmberg taught the pre-Columbian course I took. I was intrigued by the mystery of the Mayas, who suddenly disappeared at the height of their culture, renowned for its pyramids, art and astronomical calendars. That was the subject of my paper required for the course. It became my ticket to Peru when Holmberg praised it and recommended me as one of six students to go to Vicos. I was excited when I got the word that I was chosen. Despite feeling uncertain about what I might be getting myself into, there was no way I was going to pass up the opportunity.

Each of the students received a $1200 grant, and was required to write a paper based on field research. There were no restrictions on how the money was spent, or not. To fly to Lima on Pan-American would have cost the entire amount of the grant, twice the fare on Aerolineas Peruanas. The $600 difference was about half of the annual tuition at Cornell. To supplement my scholarships, I usually had a summer job, and during my junior year I'd waited tables at a fraternity, a job arranged by house member and old family friend Mickey Schwerner. I needed to save the money, so I went for the cheap flight.

Shortly before I left for Peru, on May 29, 1961, my 20th birthday, "Travelin' Man" by Ricky Nelson reached #1 on the Billboard Hot 100 record charts. He sang of finding romance all over the world. I would be travelin' too, not to look for romance, but to leave the cocoon of my life in Ithaca and Long Island, and spread my wings in the Andes.

4. IN VICOS

OUR GROUP OF FIELD STUDIES PROGRAM students included Hal Skalka and me from Cornell, Richard Price from Harvard, Jane Fearer from Radcliffe, and David Barkin and William Tuohy from Columbia. Brenda Beck, a student at the University of Chicago, was not part of the Program but joined us in Vicos for the summer. I was the odd man out, a math guy among students of anthropology, economic development and other more relevant disciplines. Not that I ever felt I didn't belong or was ever treated that way. I had proven myself to Professor Holmberg.

Unfortunately, it turned out that he was not able to join us that summer, due to a serious illness. This was a big disappointment, especially to those of us from Cornell who knew and admired him. A native Minnesotan of Scandinavian roots, Holmberg was a great teacher, innovator and leader, a soft-spoken man not afraid to stand up to those members of the anthropology establishment who took a dim view of his social activism. His innate empathy and caring was essential to engaging the Vicosinos in the Cornell-Peru Project, and to its success.

In his absence, we looked forward to working with Mario Vazquez, Field Director for the Project. He spoke fluent Quechua, the native language of the Andes, and would be tutoring us

The guys "at work": (L-R) Bill Tuohy, Dave Barkin, Paul Doughty, me, Hal Skalka (in pit), Rich Price

Jane Fearer

Brenda Beck (L) and Polly Doughty

in speaking it. Paul Doughty was the supervisor of our student group, as he had been the previous summer when the first group of Field Studies students came to Peru. Working for his doctorate, he had been living in Vicos with his wife Polly, and they were friends as well as mentors to us. We were in very good hands.

Paul's Jeep, a couple of trucks and a clunky generator at Cornell headquarters were the only electrical devices in Vicos – no lights, no refrigerators, no radio. The summer program was intended to expose us to the hardships of life in the field, and we knew there'd be no electricity. Growing up, I'd avidly read about those primitive societies in the National Geographics my parents subscribed to. But now, in the words of a popular 1950s TV show hosted by Walter Cronkite, *You Are There*. So there I was, de-electrified. In all of human history the single greatest change, since our primitive ancestors stood upright, developed language and began using tools, was the advent of electricity. There was the time before electricity, for many thousands of years, and there was the time after, less than a century since Edison invented the light bulb. When we arrived in Vicos and stepped out of the Jeep, we stepped backwards across a great divide.

The Field Studies Program required each student to write a paper. Most of our time would be spent out in the field, but we would regularly meet and type up our field notes in the *hacienda* building where the Cornell-Peru Project was headquartered, on the central plaza in Vicos. That's where the new school was, built by Vicosinos with guidance from Project staff, as well as a clinic, a community center, a small mortuary and a Catholic church.

Inside it hung portraits of two leading Catholics, Pope Pius XII and President John F. Kennedy. While Kennedy was new to the office, Pius had been dead for three years. A picture of the current Pope, John XXIII, had not yet arrived from the Vatican. Just who actually was the Pope seemed of little concern to the Vicosinos. Catholicism had been brought to Peru by the Spaniards, and enforced among the indigenous peoples by an often-brutal clergy. Over time

Festivalgoers at Recuayhuanca

The crowd in Recuayhuanca plaza

the Andeans reverted to many of their native beliefs. The Church counted millions of native Latin Americans as parishioners, but they didn't count on the Church for their spiritual sustenance.

5. PARTY TIME

ON OUR FIRST FULL DAY in Vicos, Friday, June 23, we could see fires burning on the hillsides. They signaled the start of the fiesta of San Juan, a major three-day annual event about to begin that evening on the plaza at Recuayhuanca, a neighboring *hacienda* about a mile from Vicos. By late afternoon, we heard sounds of the festival echoing around the hills, and in the early evening several of us walked over there. The plaza was filled with several hundred people. We could see from their clothing, the blue-black wool and brilliant colors typical of the Vicosinos and their neighbors, that it was largely local people who had come to party. Parents arrived with their children and wandered around in the crowd, not always staying together during the evening. Some of the men and women got too drunk to keep close watch on their kids, who were perfectly safe among their communally-minded neighbors. The kids were unconcerned about being separated from their parents, enjoying a night out on their own.

Two bands were playing, sometimes first one and then the other, sometimes both at the same time playing different songs within earshot of each other. Either way, it was a cacophony. They played a musical style called *huayno*, which dated back to the flute and drum music of the Incas, before the *conquistadores* unsuccessfully banned it for a while. The modernized version might include a fiddle, a trumpet, a saxophone, a guitar, a traditional small 10-stringed instrument called a *charango*, and even a harp. [*Huayno* gained a brief worldwide audience a few years later in the Simon and Garfunkel megahit *El Condor Pasa* (The Condor Passes). Simon first heard it in Paris from a group of Peruvian buskers called

Los Incas, who wound up playing instrumental backing on the record, to which Simon added lyrics. The Los Incas street version, without lyrics, was actually written in 1903 by a composer in Lima of Spanish descent, based on Andean folk music. Quite a lineage for so simple a tune.]

Wooden flutes provided the characteristic haunting sound of Andean music. It was easy to imagine centuries ago their wistful notes echoing through the mountains to the pounding of a drum made of wood and animal skin. In its simplest form, one man could play a flute with one hand and the drum with the other. But on the Recuayhuanca plaza the bands played multiple instruments to deliver a raucous and rhythmic sound for dancing, which along with drinking was the main activity of the fiesta. To get a partner, a man would tap a woman on the shoulder or even grab her arm and half-drag her into the dancing area, but the women seemed to regard this as an acceptable form of invitation. Couples did not hold each other, but danced next to and around each other, holding up and twirling a white handkerchief in one hand with the other resting on a hip. They even drifted from one partner to another in their group jubilation.

Aside from the handkerchief, no-touch dancing had its counterpart in the U.S. with some of the rock 'n' roll dance styles of the late '50s and early '60s which I knew well. To the delight of the locals I fell right in with the dancers in Recuayhuanca, as did a few others in our student group. Once we *gringos* started dancing, the locals were reluctant to let us stop. Not being used to the altitude, I couldn't dance for hours like I could at sea level. They passed us a bottle of *washcu*, a high-proof alcohol made from cane sugar. You couldn't just sip it politely, but had to take a big swig.

I managed to stay fairly sober for the walk home, and came back the following night when the crowd was even bigger and if anything more inebriated. Yet I never saw any violence, which you might expect in a large drunken crowd. Walking around the back of a building on the plaza, I came upon a small crowd circling and cheering a couple on the ground having, or trying to have, sex.

They both seemed totally drunk, and the many layers of heavy wool skirts worn by the woman, the typical local costume, proved to be impenetrable.

On the second night of the fiesta I noticed more men in western style of dress, even suits and ties, not just locals in their typical handmade wool outfits. They were Mestizos, of mixed Spanish-Andean blood, visitors for the most part from the nearby towns of Marcara and Carhuaz. They tended to be more noisy and ostentatious than the indigenous Andeans, maybe to set themselves apart. In Peru, as elsewhere in Latin America, there were three principal ethnic groups: those of pure Andean descent, those of pure descent from the conquistadores and the Spanish and European settlers who followed them, and the mixed-blood Mestizos. There were rigid social divisions among the three groups.

Mestizos were keenly sensitive about distinguishing themselves from the native Andeans, whom they considered their inferiors, although obviously someone of Spanish descent couldn't have become a Mestizo had not one of their ancestors crossed that social barrier. Vicosino men adopted some of the clothing of the Mestizos, like button-front dress shirts and fedoras. But style never went the other way -- if you wore native clothes, you were a native. The indigenous women always wore native dress, and unlike some of the men, spoke no Spanish whatsoever, only Quechua.

Another mark of ethnic distinction was chewing coca leaves, which indigenous Andean men had done for centuries. A paper written by one of the field study program students the previous summer concluded that chewing was not so much about getting high from the cocaine in the leaves, but rather as a stimulant and a means to cope with hunger. Vicosino men normally didn't eat during the day while they were out working, but took regular breaks to chew, usually in small groups.

Coca plants grew wild in the area. They dried the leaves and carried them in a small leather pouch or cloth bag with a strap slung over the shoulder. They also carried a small long-necked gourd, filled with powdered lime, which had a stopper with a heavy wire attached. After working up a good chaw of leaves in your cheek, you wet the wire in your mouth and then stuck it back into the gourd. When you removed the wire it was covered with the powdered lime, which you then poked into the chaw. The lime reacted chemically to release the cocaine from the leaves, but in a weak form.

I found that the immediate effect of chewing was to numb your mouth. As you did enough, it overcame hunger pangs and boosted your energy. Chewing was very much a social activity and very common during the fiesta. Combined with alcohol, which they didn't drink while working, it induced a feeling of euphoria. For me, the altitude and the alcohol was more than enough for my system to contend with that night.

Hanging from a tall pole over the fiesta plaza was the carcass of a pig, split open lengthwise. Roast pork was for sale in the market-place. Vendors also sold rolls shaped like babies (probably fertility objects), shaved ice with syrup (familiar to any New Yorker), veg-etables and of course alcohol. In addition to the bands, groups of flutists and drummers wandered around marching to their own tunes. Adding to the general chaos, small fireworks – rockets and pinwheels – were set off intermittently, with little concern for who might be standing nearby. Some men were pushing around a bull-shaped wooden frame covered with more fireworks, again uncon-cerned with who might be in the way.

On the final day of the fiesta, Sunday afternoon was the time for live bulls. The plaza was fenced off to form a bull ring, with a hundred or more people lingering inside to participate in the *corrida* (bull fight). They were either a little drunk or a little foolhardy, but in fact it wasn't much of a fight. The crowd -- which included some women, children and me -- was in no real danger, and some of the "bulls" were cows. They were let loose to run around and butt anyone who got in the way. But they were pretty lethargic, and it took a lot of yelling and waiving of jackets and *ponchos* to get any response from them at all. This was nothing like the pro-fessional bullring in Lima, the oldest in the western Hemisphere.

6. MOVING IN

ON OUR FIRST FEW NIGHTS in Vicos, we stayed at Cornell's headquarters building on the plaza, but each of us would soon move in with a Vicosino family. To pick up a few things we needed, on the Sunday morning of the fiesta Paul drove some of us to the outdoor market about 20 miles away, in the small city which was the commercial center of the Callejon de Huaylas. Its name, Huaraz, means sunrise in Quechua; Huascaran looms over it. In 1941 much of the northern end and center of the city were destroyed when a small earthquake triggered an avalanche on Huascaran which sent water and debris rushing into the reservoir above the city, bursting its dam. Twenty years later, boulders and debris were still strewn about the north side of town, where many of the destroyed buildings had not yet been rebuilt.

When we arrived at 9:30, the market had been open for several hours. Vendors were selling food, cloth and clothing, and small hardware items. Andean women sat cross-legged with their produce, like different kinds of hot peppers, arrayed in front of them on a blanket. Prices in the market were determined by bargaining, and a merchant would deadpan a buyer's lowball first offer for his deliberately overpriced goods. One Mestizo vendor was selling enameled plates for 7.5 *soles* each, about 25 cents. We bid 7 *soles*, or 49 *soles* for seven plates, but he refused to go below 52 for the lot. So we simply handed him a 50 *sol* note and walked off with the plates. He gave no sign of accepting our offer, but neither did he protest when we left. Paul assured us that it was a done deal.

I was going to be living with the family of Nestor Sanchez Bautista, a respected Vicos elder, and Carmela Tafur Copitan. They'd both been born in the 19th century; he was in his seventies, she in her sixties. They were not married, each of them having been married previously to spouses who died. They were what was called *convivientes* (living together), a normal practice for older couples with second partners. The Vicosinos viewed the marriage ritual as something you did once, and didn't have to repeat later with a

(top) Nestor and me; Carmela, at home with piglet;
(middle) Agustin, with pot for dying wool;
(bottom) Urbano and Pancho striking a pose

second partner. There may have been a practical reason for this, not undergoing the expense of a second wedding. But more than that, they saw no issue of morality in living together, whatever the Catholic Church might think.

Nestor and Carmela had four sons. I was not aware of any other children of theirs who might be deceased, but that would not have been surprising, given high child mortality rates and short life expectancy. Their oldest son Agustin lived with the extended family of his wife-to-be Rosa Reyes, and their two children. This kind of trial marriage, or *watanaki*, was a common practice. Their second oldest, Donato, had served in the Peruvian Army and moved to Lima afterwards, where he wore western-style clothing and worked as a car mechanic. The third son was Urbano, a teenager attending *colegio* (high school) in Carhuaz, the only indigenous Andean in the school and the first Vicosino to go there. The youngest was Pancho. While Urbano was more serious and committed to his studies, Pancho was a playful and friendly kid of 12 who attended the school in Vicos. As best I could guess, he was born when Carmela was in her early fifties, which showed how altitude can affect a woman's fertility cycle.

So far my travels had taken me on my late-night first flight from New York to Miami, on the prop-driven connection from Miami through Panama to Lima, and on the drive from Lima up the coast and over the Cordillera Negra to Vicos, arduous journeys all. Now I was about to depart on the final leg of my trip, from the Vicos plaza to the Sanchez *casa*, only about 1/3 of a mile but the biggest leap of all, beyond western civilization. Of course, I knew when I signed up for the Field Studies Program that I would be staying with a Vicosino family, but now I was faced with the reality. The men only spoke a little Spanish, as did I, the women none -- how would we be able to relate to one another? It's not that I was setting out into the wilderness all alone, cut off from my American colleagues. I'd regularly be walking back to Cornell headquarters to type up my field notes and see some of my fellow students and the Cornell staff. But I would be living in the world of the Vicosinos.

On Wednesday, June 28, Nestor showed up with Agustin at about 8:30 a.m. to help move me. Nestor tied my cot and a thin mattress to his back, Agustin carried my cooking utensils and small supply of canned food in a burlap bag tied to his back, and I lugged my duffel bag. Nestor led the way down the road, and when we got to the house, he made me wait while he and Carmela made a last-minute check of my room. It was one of several small abutting adobe structures with tiled roofs which opened onto a common area. Formerly a storage space, my windowless room had been freshly whitewashed for my arrival, with some wooden pegs for my clothes set into the walls.

Agustin and Nestor moved the cot in, put the mattress and my sleeping bag on it, and carried in my luggage. The two of them disappeared for a few minutes, and then returned with a table for my room. I hadn't asked for one, but they anticipated that I could use it. Dusting it off, they put it on the uneven dirt floor in the room, and slid some stones under the legs to keep it from tipping. Nestor also swept the floor with a bundle of twigs, and collected the excess dirt in an animal skin. While all this was going on, they wouldn't let me do any of the work. Only after the room was set up to their satisfaction and ready for their guest, could I move in.

7. WATER AND FOOD

THE WATER WE DRANK came from a stream which originated in the glaciers of the Cordillera Blanca. It seemed it hardly could have been more pure, but the Cornell staff warned us not to drink it without boiling it first, because it could have been contaminated upstream by bacteria, animal waste or a dead carcass. I had a portable burner in my room, but no way to cool off boiled water other than to let it sit around at room temperature. I missed ice cubes.

Hiking up into the hills one day I got incredibly thirsty from the exertion and strong sun. I had carried some water with me but finished it off. I needed a drink really badly, so I took my chances and drank from a stream. What wonderful water, refreshingly cool. Fortunately I didn't get sick. But not to push my luck, I continued to boil drinking water back in my room.

I also had a pan in which I could fry an occasional egg, as well as heat up a few cans of beans I had brought with me, but for the most part I ate with the family. Meals were prepared and eaten in another small adobe structure which opened on the central area. It had an open cooking fire and a hole in the ceiling for smoke to escape. There was no table or chairs; people either squatted on the ground or sat on a log. Their diet was mainly boiled potatoes, often served in a watery soup. There was a huge variety of potatoes: white, yellow, red, blue, purple. Some you ate raw, crunchy and sweet.

The potato had a long history as a staple in the Peruvian diet. It was thought to have originated in southern Peru and adjoining northern Bolivia about 10,000 years ago. As cultivation of potatoes spread from the sea coast up into the mountains, certain strains thrived there. Even living at 10,000 feet, Vicosinos cultivated potatoes at higher altitudes.

Corn was another ancient food from Latin America, originating in Mexico about 10,000 years ago and then spreading throughout Central and South America. Vicosinos grew some corn, but it was a minor part of their diet. One thing they did with it was roasting corn kernels, which turned them crispy although they didn't pop. Fun and tasty to eat, even without the salt I would have liked to sprinkle on it. At times they served me a hot bowl of another ancient cereal-like grain which they grew there called *kinuwa* or *quinua* in Quechua. First cultivated in the Peruvian Andes but basically unknown outside of Peru, it had the highest protein content of any grain in the world.

I got a taste of another protein at dinner early in my stay, when I bit into a potato and tasted something bitter. It was a worm, although I didn't actually see it in the dimly-lit eating area. They'd saved that special potato for me, with its bit of protein, and everyone watched me and smiled encouragingly while I ate it. I tried my best not to show my distaste. But they must have sensed that I didn't enjoy what they considered to be a treat, and never served me a wormy potato again.

Meat was a rarity. Vicosino families typically kept livestock like cows, sheep, goats and pigs. They were the principal wealth of the household, and were slaughtered for food only on very special occasions. *Cuy* (guinea pig) was another source of meat we ate once in a while. Nestor and Carmela kept several of them in an enclosure where they had plenty of room to scurry around, looking just like the fuzzy little critters some people had as pets back home. I tried not to think about that when served a piece of roasted guinea pig. I really craved the protein, since I was so undernourished from the steady diet of potatoes. It tasted like -- what else? – chicken. I had no hesitation about eating a real pig the one time during the summer when they slaughtered and roasted one. I was happy to pig out on pork.

The day after I moved into my new home was a very special occasion in Vicos, a fiesta celebrating the induction of the new members of the communal governing council. After I finished unpacking and organizing my room, I met Paul, Polly and several of the students in the plaza to watch as four goats were slaughtered by two Vicosinos. One of the men dragged a goat down, pressing its back to the ground while holding its legs to immobilize it. The other grabbed the goat's beard, pulled its head back to expose its neck, and slit its throat. The animal bleated loudly but briefly, then struggled for a minute or so before it died. The blood was caught in a bucket and put aside. Not being a Future Farmer of America, I had never seen an animal slaughtered, and found it difficult to watch. The two Vicosinos went about their job silently and showed no emotion.

The goats were then hung up by their hind legs to be skinned. One man held the carcass and kept the skin taut, while the other sliced up the abdomen and chest, being careful not to slit the underlying membrane which held the innards in place. The hide was removed almost intact, except for a small piece around each hoof.

One of the goats slaughtered for the pachamanca

Vicosina preparing the entrails

With great effort they then broke the collar and pelvic bones to get at the marrow, cut open the membrane, and spilled the entrails and marrow into a large tub. During this process the men chatted, smiled and even laughed a bit, even as they sweated from the difficulty of the work, carried out with great zest. They had done the killing with a quiet respect for the lives they were taking, but now were enjoying the prospect of eating the fruits of their labor.

The next day for the fiesta they cooked the goat meat with a technique used since the days of the Incas, a *pachamanca* (*pacha* in Quechua meant "earth," *manca* "pot"). Several Vicosinos dug a pit in the ground, about 4-5 feet in diameter and 1½-2 feet deep, and built a dome of rocks over it. They filled the space with wood and built a fire. After it heated the rocks and burned down to hot coals, they collapsed some of the rocks into the pit and added a layer of potatoes. Then they collapsed more rocks on top of the potatoes. The goat meat had been marinating overnight in *aji*, a spicy sauce with *chiles* used in traditional Andean cooking. The meat was wrapped in large fragrant leaves and placed on the rocks, audibly sizzling. They added more layers of meat and rocks until the contents of the pit were about level with the ground. At this point they covered it all with leafy branches and then with burlap bags, which they had on hand for packing up potatoes. Then they covered the bags with loose dirt, taking care that no smoke was escaping. With this insulation, there was enough heat retained in the pile to roast the potatoes and meat in less than an hour.

The blood they had collected when slaughtering the goats was cooked in a large pot with hot peppers and other spices, making a thick gravy. When I got to taste the goat meat, it was somewhat chewy but with the gravy made for a really tasty Andean barbecue. The entrails became a large pot of tripe soup with, of course, potatoes.

8. BEGGARS BANQUET

THE FIESTA BEGAN WITH a morning volleyball tournament, and our student group was asked to be one of the teams. None of us were experienced players but we were willing and it seemed like it would be fun. We did have one thing going for us, since we were considerably taller than the Peruvians. A second team was made up of teachers at the Vicos school, both men and women. Our first clue that people took the games seriously was when the other two teams showed up, all-female squads from Marcara and Carhuaz, in nifty white and blue satin uniforms. They were obviously not pickup squads like us, and ran around the field in their practiced pregame routine, warming up and hollering to boost team spirit.

Fortunately, we were paired against the teachers in the first semi-final, and did not have to embarrass ourselves against one of the girls teams, who played each other in the other semi. From the start we were frustrated at being repeatedly called for violations of ball-handling rules which we didn't understand but the referees strictly enforced against us. We did take advantage of our height to score some points spiking the ball at the net, but when we missed a spike, it drew loud derisive applause from the spectators. There was evident satisfaction in the crowd when the *Americanos* lost to the teachers, who then lost to the girls from Carhuaz in the final.

Beyond the rules, we were also handicapped by playing at that altitude, to which we were far from acclimated after less than a week in Vicos. It was just as well that we lost our game, because I don't think we had it in us to play another, especially against one of the skilled girls teams. Some of us occasionally played informal soccer games with the elementary school boys. Although much smaller than us, they were more agile, had greater stamina, and ran rings around us.

Following volleyball, the main business of the day began. Cornell had run the Vicos *hacienda* during the first five-year lease, from 1952 to 1957. But by 1961, although technically Cornell still held the lease, the Vicosinos were self-governing. The fiesta was to mark the milestone of their local officials taking office, and to showcase the status of Vicos to the dignitaries and residents from nearby towns who were invited to witness the ceremony and participate in the celebration. Their local pride was not shared by the visitors, who were there for the party, just as they had been at Recuayhuanca the week before. A rowdy crowd, they drank and talked throughout the ceremony. There was a band for the occasion, a seven-piece outfit from Huaraz uniformed in bright orange vests and American-style chinos. From what I could overhear as they talked among themselves in Spanish, they too looked down on the Vicosinos, even though they had paid the band to play.

When lunch was about to be served the "guests" began moving tables and benches into the community function room even before the council inductions were over. To "reserve" a place at a table, some of them hopped on the benches even before they were put down on the ground, and grabbed utensils from the hands of the volunteer waiters, which included us students. When hot bowls of goat entrail soup were carried out two at a time to be served, people wouldn't get out of the way, just to make sure they got theirs, and not necessarily just one helping. They ate so fast, it was impossible to keep track of who had eaten and who hadn't, with some people licking their bowls and spoons clean and then clamoring that they didn't get any.

When it was time to serve the main course, Rich was unfortunate to be the first one out of the kitchen carrying plates of goat meat. He never got past the first table. People fell all over each other trying to get at the food, shouting "Gringo!" to attract his attention, in an obviously patronizing and hostile manner. As I carried out a plate of meat, a "gentleman" avidly gnawing on a meaty bone grabbed the plate as I passed his table and immediately began eating the meat on it before I grabbed it back. Once again, people licked their plates and utensils clean in a ploy to get seconds before others had eaten at all.

It was obvious which partakers of this beggars' banquet were the greediest and most hostile toward the Vicosinos. They were the ones most conspicuously dressed in western style clothing: suits and ties, dresses, even sunglasses. One guy flaunted his Mexican-style sombrero, anything to avoid being mistaken for a lowly Andean peasant. The mestizos came not out of respect for the meaning of the event, for which they didn't give a damn, but to gorge on free food and enjoy the novelty of being served by gringos, while the band played on. The Vicosinos did the work to make the fiesta happen, but they were marginalized and disrespected at their own event, which emphasized to our student group the depth of the class divide. We had been treated discourteously as we served the guests, which embarrassed our Vicosino hosts.

9. DEATH IN VICOS

THE NEXT DAY I ATTENDED a more somber event. Or at least that's what I expected it to be, when David Barkin and I came upon the conclusion of a funeral, which can be a day-long affair. When we showed up in the late afternoon it was obvious that it had been going on for some time, because the thirty or so members of the funeral party were drunkenly struggling to carry the coffin to the cemetery chapel. They followed a path strewn with small red flowers, accompanied by flute and drum music.

An argument broke out next to the open grave. Since it was in Quechua I couldn't understand it, but from their gestures it seemed the issue was whether the hole had been dug too close to a mausoleum. The dispute ended when the coffin was lowered into the ground, with some difficulty but little formality. Up until this point I had not seen the outbursts of grief, expressions of respect for the dead, or religious formalities you'd expect at a funeral. Some of the drunkards were carrying on rather jovially, their antics providing comic relief. When someone threw a handful of dirt on the coffin, a woman suddenly hurried away crying loudly, helped off by a teenage girl at her side, probably her daughter. I

Musicians playing in front of the mortuary

assumed it was their husband and father who had died, because the other women remained at the site, preoccupied with looking after their drunk husbands.

The funeral-goers then gathered around the grave to throw dirt on the coffin as well. Many of them carried a cup or small pot, filled with a clear liquid which they sprinkled on the casket. It could have been water, but I suspected it was the *washcu* so eagerly consumed during the day, perhaps to help the deceased forget his anguish at dying, as it helped the living to forget theirs. As each of them performed the dirt and liquid ritual, the women gathered their menfolk and left, leaving fewer than ten people to complete the burial. At this point a cantor (singer) appeared and chanted some verses in Quechua, sprinkled liquid and helped fill in the grave. He was dressed in Vicosino clothing, but atypically neat and clean. He had not been part of the funeral proceedings until then, arriving in time to perform his service and complete the burial.

Life in Vicos could be "poor, nasty, brutish and short" as the philosopher Thomas Hobbes famously said. Death from disease and disaster was an ever-present threat, arriving sometimes on an almost incomprehensible scale in a land prone to massive earthquakes, landslides and floods. But it would be wrong to conclude from the drunken carryings on and the gravesite argument that Vicosinos did not value life and cherish their loved ones. I always felt a warmth within Vicosino families and among their friends, which embraced me too as I became part of their community.

All cultures have institutionalized ways of coping with death. Sometimes they involve great public displays of grief, yet in New Orleans, funeral processions march down the streets to some of the most joyous music you'll ever hear. In the Andes, the indigenous Incan culture had been stamped out by the Spanish invaders. The Andean people were forcibly converted to Catholicism, with the brutal methods of the Inquisition to impose orthodoxy. Churches were built on the intricate stone foundations of Inca temples which the conquerors tore down. The native Peruvians became forced laborers, initially to exploit the rich gold and silver deposits, but later to farm the land, as in Vicos. With the repression of their pre-conquest society, the deadly epidemics from diseases brought to Peru by the Spanish, and the imposition of a feudal economic structure, many Andeans subsisted for centuries as serfs with little hope and lacking cultural traditions such as funerary rites.

10. Living in Vicos

With the fiestas over, I began to settle into a more regular routine. Most of my time was spent with Nestor and the family, primarily as an observer, but occasionally pitching in and trying to be useful, or at least getting the feel for their manual labor in the fields, rather than just standing around watching. When I walked back up the road to the *hacienda* building to type up my field notes, what a walk it was, with Huascaran and the Cordillera Blanca gleaming in the distance, usually under a brilliant blue sky. The scenery was even more spectacular than I had imagined it would be, and I often found myself thinking how lucky I was to be there.

For the first few days Pancho or Agustin would come up to the plaza to fetch me for dinner back at the house. Not that I could have gotten lost on my own, because the road from the plaza went right past the house. Still, they wanted to be sure I was OK getting around. This was just one example of how Nestor and family took pains to make me feel at home. A couple of days after moving in, I came back to my room late one afternoon to find that they'd cleaned the carbon black off my kerosene lantern and hung up a shelf for my suitcase, which I'd been keeping on the dirt floor under my bed.

One evening, when Nestor offered me a piece of some food he'd already bitten into. I ate it, *muchas gracias* (many thanks), in respect for their kindness to me, despite exposing myself to who knew what kind of germs. If I was going to participate in the social life of the family and the village, then I was not going to be able to maintain my "normal" standards of hygiene. So be it, I was a healthy guy with a strong stomach – well, maybe not in airplanes – so I decided to take my chances and live as the Vicosinos did. I didn't come this far to hold myself back.

Nestor was a short wiry man, but then, all the Vicosinos were well short of my 5' 10". I never did see a fat Vicosino male. With the women it was harder to tell, since they wore so many thick wool skirts, but they did seem generally more heavyset than the men. Few Vicosinos lived to be as old as Nestor, whose age showed in his deeply lined face, missing teeth and slight stoop. He had a serene presence about him, from having survived such an arduous life for so long, and was friendly and chatty, with a wry sense of humor. He began to call me *Don Esteban*, using the Spanish honorific "Don" as an expression of respect, but not totally serious about the deference it implied. There was no getting around the fact that I was a white *Norteamericano*, of a higher social caste in his eyes, but I didn't want this title to be a barrier in our relationship. So to reciprocate and play along, I called him *Don Nestor*. He got a kick out of that, because I doubt anyone had ever bestowed that title on him, a man at the bottom of the Peruvian social order.

A few days after moving in, Pancho came to my room after dinner with his cousin Pedro Aurelio Coleto, who had eaten with us. I was surprised to see that he brought an egg and some grease on a spoon to cook it. I lit the Primus camp stove, and after making the egg, offered some to Pancho. He was hesitant at first, not expecting my offer, but he and Aurelio sat on the edge of the cot with me and shared half of the egg, a treat for them. At one point they both burst into giggles from their delight at the novelty of the situation. As he was leaving to take our plates back to Carmela to be washed, we shook hands and he said *"Buenas noches*, Doctor," good night. "Don," "Doctor," they had a reflexive reaction to acknowledge what they viewed as my higher station in life, while I just wanted to be their house guest "Esteban."

The next night Nestor came to my room after dinner to chat, as he often did. This time he had some big news to share: Agustin and Rosa Reyes were going to be married in August. Living together in a trial marriage with her family, they had two very young children. Nestor was very excited about the wedding, which was to take place in Marcara, with all their friends and relatives invited. Two bands will play, a cow will be slaughtered, and there will be plenty to drink: *washcu*, *chicha* (a homebrewed corn-based beer) and bottled Peruvian beer. I could look forward to it as well, since it would happen just before the Field Studies Program students were due to depart.

After his evening visits, Nestor retired to his and Carmela's quarters next door. Sometimes there'd be a little party going on, with other family members and friends. I could hear some flute-and-drum music, and I assumed they were drinking and chewing. For whatever reason, I was never invited to join them. I guess this was private time for them, and I didn't push it. Anyhow, I was too tired by then, needing ten to twelve hours of sleep, while back home I normally slept for about seven. It was of course due to the altitude. At 10,000 feet, the air is about one-third thinner, so you have to breathe faster and deeper. But even so, you still get less oxygen than at sea level.

Adapting to the altitude was a lengthy and complex process, as I learned from Dr. Marshall T. Newman and Dr. William J. Tobin, physical anthropologists from the Smithsonian Institution working in Vicos that summer. In his earlier work there, Newman found that compared to someone living at sea level, Vicosinos had larger chests, lungs, hearts and red blood cells to facilitate oxygen absorption and circulation, along with an additional two quarts of blood. They told me that of the twenty or so known internal human parasites, all but two of them had been found among the Vicosinos, who seemed able to cope with this horde of aliens which invaded their bodies.

As for the bodies of outsiders like me coping with the altitude, they explained that certain biological functions slowed or shut down for a period of time to allow the body to focus on what was necessary for immediate survival. Production of testosterone was one of those functions not essential in the short term. Losing my sex drive was convenient as far as I was concerned. Sex within our student group would have been very disruptive, sex with a Vicosina absolutely taboo (although there was one young woman I sometimes saw around the Sanchez household whose exotic beauty intrigued me, but strictly from a distance). It could take many weeks for the body to complete the adjustment process and return to normal functioning. Sex could wait.

I had promised Pancho that he could come up to Cornell headquarters to try using a typewriter. He showed up after school with two classmates, and they took turns banging out their names. With a little encouragement, they began typing the names of various people to whom they were related. This was a big help to me in trying to figure out who was related to whom, to get their names spelled right, and much easier to read than if they had written them out by hand. In addition to the four brothers I was aware of, I learned that there was another older brother, Cesar Sanchez, the son of Nestor and his first wife. I realized that using the typewriter as an incentive would be a good tool for the interviews I was planning to do with Urbano about his experiences attending the *colegio* in Carhuaz, research for my paper in fulfillment of the grant.

July 2 was national census day in Peru. Just after lunch a census taker from Marcara showed up at the Sanchez household, which piqued a lot of curiosity in the family. Nestor offered him a seat on a log, with a goatskin placed on it for the comfort of their guest, and squatted on the ground near him. I sat on the other end of the log, without a goatskin. Nestor busied himself peeling corn cobs and tossing the kernels into a basket, while the census man went through the questions on the form slowly and carefully, translating from Spanish to Quechua, which he spoke with ease. The two conducted this process at a very leisurely pace, apparently engaging in a lot of small talk unrelated to the business at hand -- how do you say kibitzing in Quechua? -- before anything got recorded on the form.

The census asked the usual things, such as who lived there, the kind of structure they lived in, what they grew, etc. One question struck me as particularly amusing, about the hygienic facilities. Answer: none. When I moved in, Nestor took me around to the rear of the house, and explained that I was to pick out a place in the field to use as my personal bathroom. I had brought toilet paper with me. They used corncobs.

The census also asked about their animals. The Sanchez family had relatively sizable livestock holdings for Vicosinos: over twenty head of cattle, four horses, a large flock of sheep and goats, several chickens, a sow with seven piglets, and twenty or so guinea pigs. Nestor made no mention of the dogs which hung around, much like dogs once did at early human settlements, foraging and eventually becoming domesticated. In Vicos they were not considered pets and were somewhat wild.

One day Hal Skalka and I went for a long walk, when a pack of dogs started barking at us and then charged. We were carrying big walking sticks, partly for protection in such a situation, well aware that the summer before a student was bitten and sent home for precautionary rabies shots. As the dogs came running toward us, I picked up a flat rock with sharp edges and threw it sidearm toward them, which made it spin. It hit the lead dog in the leg. He jumped in the air yelping in pain and then ran away, with the others pausing and then following him. My many hours throwing sidearm pitches in stickball games on Long Island had paid off.

11. THE PUNA

THE *puna* IS A HIGH GRASSLAND above the tree line and below the permanent snow line, ranging in altitude from about 12,000 to 16,000 feet, and extending from central Peru south to Argentina. The combination of soil nutrients and adequate moisture in the central Andes makes it well suited for growing potatoes. In early

July Nestor and a small contingent of Vicosinos were preparing to leave for the *puna* to harvest their potato crops there.

The day before, Mario Vazquez was riding on horseback up to the *puna*. As his horse crossed an area of smooth flat rock, it lost its footing and fell over on him, shattering his leg. Several Vicosino men used a *poncho* as a makeshift stretcher and ran with him for a couple of hours back down the rough mountain trail to Vicos, from where he was driven to the small hospital in Huaraz and then airlifted to Lima. The horse was unhurt, but Mario's excruciating-ly painful accident meant that he could not return to Vicos that summer. He was fluent in Quechua and was to have tutored our student group, so that left us only able to pick up a few words and phrases here and there.

The next morning Dave Barkin and I were to leave for the *puna* with Nestor. Although trips there normally got underway at 6 a.m., we didn't start out until about 9. This confirmed my obser-vation that the Sanchez family tended to be late risers compared to their neighbors, although Pancho did get up earlier to go to school. It wasn't that they were lazy, because they worked hard. Maybe at their age they needed more sleep, especially after staying up late for their little evening socials. And I was certainly glad not to get up at the break of dawn, but instead to be on "Nestor time."

The three of us went on horseback. I had been on a horse briefly a couple of times before, but in very tame circumstances. I was really apprehensive after what had happened to Mario. So was Dave. Growing up in the Bronx and going to college in Manhattan, he was no seasoned horseman either. But we both put on brave faces and went along for the ride, mostly uphill at a very slow pace. At times the horses balked at going any further, given the uneven footing, which only made us all the more uneasy. But we kept them moving ahead, Dave and I hanging on to our mounts as best we could. At least we had simple saddles. Nestor rode with some blankets and padding thrown over his horse's back.

As we plodded along, we met people in transit to and from the *puna*. Vicosinos typically were not on horseback and walked, sometimes in family groups, with or without their men. They led burros or drove herds of livestock up to the rich grazing lands. Those on the way back down had large sacks of potatoes loaded on the burros. But some men carried them strapped to their backs, with another strap across the chest to secure the load. The sacks must have weighed 50 pounds or more, which was enormous in relation to their body size. Human beasts of burden shod in sandals, they typically descended in small groups, moving in an odd mincing side-to-side trot so as not to be pitched forward by the weight. Of course, they made frequent stops to chew coca, the pause that refreshes.

During the first part of the trip Nestor tried to keep up a conversation with me and Dave, but we couldn't communicate that well with everyone's limited Spanish and our precarious perch on horseback demanding our attention. Nestor was a talkative guy, so when some Vicosinos came along whom he seemed to know, they fell in with our little caravan, chatting nonstop with Nestor while we rode in silence. We arrived at our destination in mid-afternoon.

We met up there with Agustin, his older half-brother Cesar Sanchez and his wife, several other relatives and friends, and five very young children, about fifteen of us in all. There was also a flock of about thirty sheep, seven dogs and three large pigs. Dave and I left our sleeping bags under the spacious cavelike rock overhang which provided shelter, as it probably had for many years, if not centuries. The center of the roof dropped down in the middle to form a "V" shape from front to back, creating a natural partition between the men's sleeping area and that of the women and children.

A cooking area had been set up toward the front of the women's section. The food as usual was almost entirely potatoes, no different from what I was getting accustomed to at "home." Mostly it was prepared in the form of soups, and as guests we were served first and continually urged to have more. The heat from soup was welcome. In Vicos, days were typically very sunny, with a high of perhaps 70 and a low in the 40s or 50s, with a pleasant cool breeze. At the higher altitude of the *puna* the sun was even stronger, but because we were closer to the mountains than in the more open valley in Vicos, it only appeared in the morning around 9 and disappeared by 4 in the afternoon. When the sun shone during the day it was very warming, but after sunset it got cold fast and the temperature dropped below freezing.

Drinking was the main pastime for the men after dinner. We sat in a circle at the front of the overhang and Agustin passed around a bottle of *washcu*. I'd participated in this ritual at the festival in Recuayhuanca, so when the bottle came to me I wanted to show how macho I was and took a big swig. Big mistake. This *washcu* was much stronger, almost pure cane alcohol. As soon as I swallowed, my mouth and throat began to burn intensely. I was gasping, barely able to breathe. So much for being macho. When the bottle came back around my way again, I didn't refuse, which would have been socially difficult, but only took a tiny sip. The Vicosinos, however, had no trouble drinking it, and more.

The conversation turned to Mario's accident the day before. It was obvious to everyone at the scene that his leg was badly broken, and Dave and I confirmed that the doctor who treated him in Huaraz agreed. But we were taken aback when Agustin insisted that his leg was not broken and that "the doctors don't know." Dave and I patiently tried to explain, with support from Cesar, that it really was, but Agustin would have none of it. We weren't sure whether it was because he was drunk, which he certainly was, or reacting out of a personal conflict with Cesar, who was the village bone setter in Vicos, or just rejecting Western ways. Dave and I eventually eased ourselves out of the argument, saying that maybe doctors were good for us but not for other people.

When we retreated to our sleeping bags toward the back of the space, we found that the three big pigs had been driven to the very back. The other men slept closer to the front, with the sheep just outside. They bleated off and on all night, which made sleep difficult, but that wasn't the worst of it. Seeking warmth, the pigs gradually moved over and snuggled up against me. I wasn't flattered. Whenever one of them would shift around in its sleep, it invariably would disrupt the other two, setting off a round of squealing and more shifting. The sound was jarring, and I was really afraid they would roll over on me. But in the dark of the shelter, there was no way to pick my way around the other sleeping bodies and bed down in another spot. Stuck with the pigs, I fell into an exhausted but too brief sleep.

When I began to stir in the dim light of early morning, the pigs were gone, and people were up and about. Oddly, Nestor was sitting at the foot of my sleeping bag chewing coca, which was what he was doing with the other men when I had tumbled off to sleep. He was not normally a heavy chewer, but on the *puna*, he never seemed to be without coca leaves in his mouth. All the men were drinking and chewing more than usual. Even though they'd come to the *puna* to work harvesting potatoes, the trip was also a bit of a holiday away from home.

The women, on the other hand, kept to their chores, stoking up the fire that morning to cook breakfast -- potatoes of course -- in simple round metal pots they brought from home. Dave and I provided some oatmeal we had brought, which they cooked for us but with the consistency of soup. After eating the women took care to make sure our dishes and spoons were cleaned well, using boiling water, and kept separated from the other utensils, just as they did back in Vicos. We also had brought a can of salmon and some rice, which became the makings of a casserole for lunch cooked out in the potato fields. We made a point of sharing it, and while the Vicosinos liked it, they still left most of it for me and Dave. The salmon and rice, and the oatmeal, were the last of the food we'd brought with us to Peru. There was no way we could have carried more than several days' worth on the plane, so in a sense it was pointless. Maybe we just needed the comfort of having some of our own food on hand. But it was soon gone and we were on a totally local diet.

Despite getting up at first light, we didn't leave for the potato fields until about 9:00. Until then, when the sun finally rose above the wall of mountains surrounding us, it was just too cold to work.

We gathered the horses and burros to lead them up to the field. Although the harvest would not be packed out until the following day, the rich *puna* grasslands provided excellent forage for the animals. Besides Dave and me, our party included Nestor, Agustin, Cesar, two women and a very young child. We followed a circuitous route, crossing and recrossing a river, climbing about 500 feet to the fields, and warming up as the sun rose higher. Judging from the snow line, which was at about 16,000 feet, the field was probably at about 14,000 feet. By now Dave and I were gradually acclimating to the altitude and not having any major difficulty.

At first glance, the field hardly seemed a likely place to cultivate a crop. The potatoes were planted in scattered patches between rock outcroppings and tall wild grasses. Although the land in Vicos was owned communally, families maintained small individual plots like this in the *puna*. The men and women worked together gathering the crop, although from what I saw, the women did so far more efficiently than the men, who spent a lot of time on coca breaks. In fact, the first thing the men did when arriving at the field was to take a break. True, after the hike up a breather was in order, but not a full scale social event of chewing, talking, smoking cigarettes and even drinking. The women as usual did not participate, but I did notice them taking a nip occasionally from a bottle.

The harvesting was done with a small hoe-like tool, with a wooden handle about a yard long and a metal blade about 6" wide and 3" deep. The digger stood half bent over the spot where he was working, with legs spread to keep his balance as he used the tool with one hand to loosen the dirt around a plant and reached with the other to pick up potatoes and toss them onto a burlap sack. Very few were rejected by the digger, although the women later sifted through them and discarded some.

Dave and I tried our hand at harvesting, although with no tools available for two extra workers, we improvised with some sticks we found. This was not only inefficient, but backbreaking work which quickly tired us out. Our efforts yielded few potatoes but provided some amusement for the rest of the group. We decided instead to

Harvesting potatoes on the puna, Nestor standing top middle

Running with sacks of potatoes to the storehouse in Vicos

busy ourselves with picture-taking, and waiting for lunch. We were frequently asked the time, so preparation of lunch began punctually at 11:00.

When Vicosino men worked in the fields, the women did not usually accompany them. Instead of lunch, they chewed coca to ward off the hunger. Now in the *puna*, even though preparing lunch did not involve the men, they slacked off in anticipation of eating, only occasionally feeling an urge to dig and unearth a few potatoes here and there. Nestor proved to be far and away the most steadfast relaxer in the group. At the slightest provocation, or even none, he plopped down and began chewing, while watching the others at work. But as an elder in the community of Vicos, and by far the oldest of the group on the *puna*, he got no complaints.

Finally, after a leisurely lunch and a coca break following it, the men settled down to a routine of steady hard work. Dave and I again tried our hand with our improvised digging sticks, only to get ourselves totally pooped. Nestor showed us how comfortable it could be to lie down in the tall grass, if you knew how to do it in a certain way. Over the next couple of hours the two of us mastered the art of lounging in the grass, every fifteen minutes or so declaring ourselves to be on a new break lest we become stale from the last one. By 4:00 Nestor decided to make himself useful by leading Dave and me back to the rock shelter. The rest of the men did not return for another hour or so, by which time it was getting dark. The yield for the day was four burlap sacks of potatoes, which were left in the field overnight.

Our departure from the *puna* in the morning had to wait until the men went back up to the potato field to round up the animals and load the sacks of potatoes on the burros. Agustin had insisted that we leave for Vicos by 7:00, and Dave and I were more than willing to get going early, but it was 8:30 when we finally headed off. At first we kept up a good pace, but the final steep descent into the valley slowed us considerably. Mario Vazquez's accident was still very much on our minds. Riding horseback downhill was even more unnerving than it had been going uphill, perched higher off the ground sloping down in front of us. The horses picked their way slowly and carefully, as we swayed in the saddle with their movements, pushing back in the stirrups against gravity pulling us forward. The trip took about 5½ hours, as it had on the way up. I was warmly greeted by my family when we reached Vicos. It was a relief to be back on more level ground.

Nestor had stayed behind on the *puna* for another day. During dinner he usually kept up a running conversation, but that role more or less fell to me, in my halting Spanish, since I brought news of our trip. Pancho in particular was glad to hear about his father, but I said nothing about his lounging and carousing. Carmela usually didn't pay close attention to the mealtime chatter, staying focused on cooking and cleaning, and of course she couldn't understand what I had to say unless someone was inclined to repeat something in Quechua. But this time Pancho provided a running translation of my report from the *puna*, which she followed with interest. Being the bearer of news and at the center of the conversation in Nestor's absence enhanced my rapport with her and my place in the family.

12. THE U.S. COMES TO VICOS

ON SUNDAY, JULY 9, the U.S. Ambassador to Peru, James I. Loeb, visited Vicos with a delegation from the American Embassy in Lima. Loeb had been a teacher, a political advisor in Washington, and a co-founder of the liberal advocacy group Americans for Democratic Action, before moving to the Adirondack Mountains in 1953 as a newspaper publisher and editor. In 1961 President Kennedy tapped him for the Ambassadorship. Loeb, who resembled Lincoln without a beard, came to Vicos to learn more about the plight of the native Andeans and the stalled Vicosino effort to buy themselves out of servitude. Most people would see such a democratic and capitalist solution as totally consistent with "the American way." Loeb certainly did. But I overheard a couple of old hands from the embassy grousing to one another that the cooperative formed by the Vicosinos to market their produce was nothing but Communism. It didn't occur to them that communal forms of ownership in the Andes predated Karl Marx by many centuries.

The visit was the occasion for another *pachamanca*, this time with eight goats and two cooking pits. About forty Vicosino men were involved in the process, but many of them contributed more moral support than actual labor to the few men who worked busily by the hot stone pile under the strong midday sun. Our watches kept track of the cooking time, which they followed carefully. How they did it when we weren't there I don't know. After 45 minutes, they cut off a couple of chunks of meat to taste, and satisfied that it was ready, took the meat to the serving table. The food was accompanied by *chicha* which had been fermenting for three days. But several people preferred bottled beer which had been brought in for the occasion, or bottled soda, either local (Inca Kola) or American. Coca Cola was so widely distributed around the world that supposedly you were never more than a few miles from a Coke, even somewhere as remote as Vicos.

The following Thursday another representative from the U.S. arrived in Vicos, this time in the form of mail. There was no direct delivery to Vicos. Mail got as far as Marcara, where Paul Doughty usually picked it up at the post office. That day there was a manila envelope addressed to me, from my mom. Judging from the cancellations, she'd sent it by "air mail" from Long Island on Monday morning, and somehow it arrived in the Andes three days later. Opening it, I was surprised to find the "Sports" and "News of the Week in Review" sections from the Sunday *New York Times*. My mom knew that I'd be hungry for news of the U.S. and the world. She was a great cook of traditional Eastern European Jewish foods like matzo ball soup and stuffed cabbage. It was just as well that she didn't know much about my diet in Vicos.

I went and sat down by myself in the Vicos plaza, astonished to be holding the *Times* in my hands. I checked the sports section first, to catch up with Maris and Mantle's home run chase.

From The New York Times, Sunday, July 9: Mickey hit his 29th the day before, and Roger now had 32. With 81 games played, exactly half-way through the 162-game season, the Babe's record of 60 was still in sight. • *In world news, East-West tension was growing over the status of Berlin, with Soviet Premier Nikita Khrushchev announcing the cancellation of a planned troop reduction.*

13. VICOSINO CLOTHES

ONE EVENING AGUSTIN came to my room and showed me two photos of his younger brother Donato, taken in Lima. Dressed in a suit and tie, he looked very much Mestizoized. Earlier in the year, Agustin and Urbano had gone to Lima to visit him. Agustin left after a week but Urbano stayed for a month. I wondered what kind of impression living in the "big city" had made on him. Like Donato, Agustin served in the Army but resumed life as a Vicosino, wearing the typical handmade wool clothing and raising a family. Urbano dressed in western-style clothes not only at school but at home as well. He bridged both worlds.

I was eager to get a Vicosino *poncho*, and asked Agustin how I might buy one. He smiled, left my room and went into the storeroom next door, returning with a brand-new *poncho* which still needed a little finishing, only lacking a cloth border to be sewn around the neck opening. *Ponchos* can be of elaborate design, but typically in Vicos they had a more minimalist look. This one was black with three narrow hot pink vertical stripes, very sharp. He handed it to me, and I was surprised how heavy it was, easily ten pounds or more, its dense wool tightly woven to keep out the cold. Agustin said he'd talk over the purchase price with Nestor, and later told me that they wanted 350 *soles* for it, about 12 or 13 bucks. I took it.

A few days after doing the *poncho* deal, Nestor came into my room after dinner and suggested that I also get a suit. He was excited when I told him that's just what I'd been thinking. He explained the various items I'd need: pants, belt (a woven sash, actually), jacket and a vest. He said it would cost about 200 *soles* to have a suit made, a reasonable price considering the work that would go into it: shearing sheep, spinning the raw wool, weaving it, dying the cloth, then cutting and assembling all the pieces. From their sheep to my shoulders. To go with it I'd need *llanquis*, sandals with soles cut from old tires and laced on with strips of rubber. The tire treads provided better traction than leather-soled sandals.

Nestor got a big kick out of the idea of me wearing Vicosino clothes, and taking them home to the U.S. and wearing them there as a good way to remember Vicos. He and Agustin wondered if I would return to Vicos sometime. I said that I hoped to but that it wouldn't be for a long time, because I had to finish school. They asked me to write when I got home and send a picture of my family, since I was taking photos of their family. I said I would. Sometimes when we were sitting around chatting in the evening, Nestor would sigh "Ah, Don Esteban!," a prelude to talking about my departure. We had formed a bond, the Sanchezes and I. While never saying so, I wondered whether in fact I ever would come back.

From The New York Times, Sunday, July 16: Roger Maris had 35 home runs, Mickey Mantle 31, through 86 games. That put Roger on a pace to hit 66 over the 162-game season. But debate was growing over whether he would truly break Babe Ruth's record if he did it in 162 games, when in the Babe's day the season was only 154 games. • In his three-month old trial in Israel, Adolf Eichmann, who had steadfastly refused to express any regret for his role as the head of the Gestapo's Jewish Affairs Bureau, finally admitted that: "I saw in the murder of Jews – in the extermination of Jews – one of the most hideous crimes in the history of mankind." • In

Germany, the crisis with the Soviet Union intensified over access to West Berlin by the U.S., Britain and France.

14. SCHOOL

BY NOW I'D BEEN IN VICOS almost a month, and settled into a routine of observing, writing up field notes and living the life. One afternoon Jane Fearer and I went over to the school to sit in on a fifth year class of 15 boys. The teacher Alejandro Alegre was expecting us but had not yet arrived when we showed up a few minutes before 2:00. Entering the classroom, we were surprised at how quiet it was, not what you'd expect from a bunch of young boys just back from a two-hour lunch break and with no one in charge. Seeing us, they all quickly stood at attention, but we told them to sit down while we took seats at an empty double desk at the back of the room.

When Senor Alegre arrived, the students began reading their lessons from textbooks in Spanish. He walked around the room checking on their progress and correcting poor posture. Jane and I found ourselves sitting very erect in our seats so as not so set a bad example. When the reading was done, he began questioning them on what they had read, with the students required to answer in Spanish. If they wanted to continue their education at colegio, as Urbano Sanchez was doing, speaking Spanish was essential, as it also would be in dealing with most Peruvians outside Vicos.

I was interested in observing the class for my paper about Urbano's pursuit of a secondary education. Although he had a bicycle, Carhuaz was about 8 miles away, much too far to go back and forth every day. That meant staying in a *pencion* in Carhuaz, coming home Saturday noon and going back on Sunday afternoon. Mario Vazquez encouraged him to attend and paid his room and board, with the Sanchez family chipping in what very little they could afford.

Urbano was not simply attending the *colegio* in Carhuaz, he was integrating it as the first indigenous Andean to go there. This was of more than academic interest to me. In the spring of 1959, my freshman year at Cornell, I was among a group of about twenty white students who took a chartered bus from Ithaca to Washington, D.C. to participate in the second "Youth March for Integrated Schools." The first one had been held the previous fall, but Dr. Martin Luther King Jr., one of its principal organizers, had been unable to attend, recovering from a near-fatal knife wound. It drew 10,000 marchers, the second one 25,000, largely black high school and college students, but also many mostly-white delegations from prestigious colleges. We carried signs identifying our schools, which drew applause from spectators along the route.

The march ended at the Washington Monument, where the speakers included Dr. King and other prominent civil rights leaders, as well as Jackie Robinson and Harry Belafonte. In his speech King called the gathering "this great historic assembly, this unprecedented gathering of young people," and said: "As I stand here and look out upon the thousands of Negro faces, and the thousands of white faces, intermingled like the waters of a river, I see only one face — the face of the future." Two years later, a few weeks before I left for Peru, I followed the news in the Times and on TV as black and white Freedom Riders set out to desegregate transportation and public facilities in the South. Among them were several Cornell students, including Peter Sterling, my next-door neighbor in our freshman dorm.

15. A Visit and Some Visitors

Chavin de Huantar is an ancient site about two hours from Vicos, on the far (eastern) side of the Cordillera Blanca. Occupied as early as 3000 BC, construction of buildings there began around 1200 BC. It was a center for religious ceremonies and events for the Chavin, an important pre-Inca society whose influence spread throughout the highlands and out to the coast. They

Stone head on a wall at Chavin de Huantar

developed the first noteworthy artistic style in the Andes. Chavin works exhibited in Europe influenced Pablo Picasso, who said: "Of all of the ancient cultures I admire, that of Chavin amazes me the most. Actually, it has been the inspiration behind most of my art."

One notable expression of Chavin style is the large stone heads which protrude from the walls of a temple. They had fangs like a jaguar, a frequent image in Chavin art. The Chavin people must have been well traveled. Jaguars are jungle animals not found in that mountainous environment, nor are some of the tropical plants which were design elements in their art. Some of the stone used in the buildings is not found there either, and was transported a long distance to the site.

I'd learned about the Chavin culture in Professor Holmberg's course on pre-Columbian civilizations, so I was eager to visit the ruins when Paul drove several of our group there. The trip took us across the *altiplano*, a "high plain" dotted with rocks and barren of vegetation, very unlike the lush *puna*. It was an unusually dark cloudy day, which made the harsh landscape all the more foreboding. The Cordillera, so radiant in sunshine, appeared cold, gray and oppressive as it towered above us.

Nearing Chavin, the mountains were too rugged to build a road up and over to the east side where the ruins were, at about 10,000 feet. Instead, a long rough-hewn tunnel had been cut through the granite. It was only a single lane, and you could barely see a spot of light at the far end, half a mile or so away. From there, the mountains eventually sloped down to the Amazon basin. The ruins were slated to be restored but had not yet been, with rubble strewn about from rains which washed through. A unique feature of the site is the system of tunnels created by its ancient builders to channel the flow of rain water.

We were the only ones there. Paul led us down to a dark central chamber in the main temple to behold *El Lanzon*, the main deity of the Chavin, represented by a 15-foot high vertical stone carving with fantastical creatures and images. Its shape resembled a knife, with the handle at the top and the point of its blade resting on the floor. An opening in the ceiling admitted a shaft of light down into the chamber which highlighted the object and its imagery. Paul explained that some archaeologists believed it was an instrument of ritual sacrifice. The victim, perhaps a prisoner of war, was taken to the roof by the opening. His throat was slit, and his blood ran down the blade.

On our return trip to Vicos, it was dark by the time we reached the dirt road nearing the plaza. Suddenly, from the right side of the road a very large animal jumped in front of the Jeep and ran ahead of us in the headlights, before cutting to the left off the road and disappearing into the darkness. This was no phantasmagorical creature from Chavin, but a flesh-and-blood *puma* (mountain lion), clearly visible in the lights. *Pumas* normally stayed at higher altitudes, but sometimes descended in search of food. When I went to use the "facilities" behind the house later that night, wondering if our visitor was still in the area, I was scared shitless. In fact, for the rest of the summer I never quite got over the *puma* sighting when I went out back at night. I usually tried to hold off going until it was dawn. Fortunately, I had a large bladder.

Not long after the *puma* sighting, I was jolted awake in the middle of the night by something moving around under my cot, pushing against me from underneath as it shifted around. An animal had wandered into my room, there being no door to close off the entrance. Despite my initial fear and pounding heart, I quickly realized that it wasn't a lion, which would not likely have entered the Sanchez compound, but if it did, would make quick work of me. I lay still, too afraid to move, until the animal settled down and went to sleep, which I eventually did too. My visitor was gone by the morning, and I never figured out what it was. Too big for a dog, maybe it was another pig come to share my bed.

16. TWO BROTHERS

AGUSTIN AND URBANO, though brothers, were very different people. Agustin could be moody and contradictory, like when he insisted Mario Vazquez's leg was not broken. While this episode may have him look bad to me and Dave Barkin, he was usually very sensitive about the image he presented to other people, especially the *norteamericanos* with the Cornell-Peru Project.

Returning from the market in Huaraz one Sunday, some of us were riding with Agustin in the back of a pickup truck driven by Dr. Henry Dobyns, the research director for the Project. Along the way we picked up a Vicosino to give him a ride back. The man was very drunk and we began joking around with him. Agustin was trying hard to ignore him, staring fixedly out the side of the truck. The drunkard was speaking so indistinctly we weren't even sure whether it was in Spanish or Quechua, so we asked Agustin what he was saying. He answered with an abrupt *"No se"* (I don't know), although we had no doubt he understood him well enough. He just didn't want to be associated with the man in our eyes, and was clearly very uncomfortable to be there in the truck with him. Of course, Dave and I had been with Agustin in the *puna* when it was he who was totally blotto.

Perhaps as a result of having been in the army, where chewing coca was forbidden, Agustin rarely did it. This could be socially awkward for him. Chewing was considered a mark of manhood, and Agustin was sometimes teased by his male peers as being womanly for not chewing. Rich was with him in the *puna* once and did see him chew. Agustin begged him not to tell the other students.

Urbano never drank or chewed, at least as far as I knew. Whatever the rules were for being old enough to indulge – he was seventeen -- they seemed widely respected, and it was unlikely kids could get away with it in such a close-knit community. In any event, it was the kind of typical Vicosino behavior Urbano would want to avoid. Although still quite close with his family, he was moving beyond the local culture. Wider horizons were opening for him, and he was serious about pursuing his education and a likely career as a teacher.

Yet he was still a teenage boy whom I saw get embarrassed and run from the room when teased about having a girlfriend. Although somewhat shy by nature, he had gained a degree of self-assurance from his success at school. Agustin had not, despite successfully completing his military service. I wondered if some experience in the army, perhaps related to his ethnicity, fed his insecurity and led him to re-embrace a traditional Vicosino lifestyle, unlike his older brother Donato.

Urbano was easygoing and level-headed, while his older brother was temperamental. Pancho once made an offhand remark needling Agustin, who reacted by grabbing a bamboo pole and beating him with it. Nestor, yelling and uncharacteristically angry, came running over and drove him off with a big stick he kept handy to chase off stray dogs. The fuss brought Carmela out of the kitchen to calm Pancho, who had burst into tears. She was typically unperturbed by goings-on around her. As she passed me she smiled knowingly and muttered *"borracho"* (drunk), as if telling me not to take this family spat too seriously. It was the first word I heard her say in Spanish.

From The New York Times, Sunday, July 23: Mickey Mantle edged ahead of Roger Maris, with 37 home runs to 36 through 93 games. At that pace over a 162-game season, they would both top the 60 home run mark; projected over 154 games, Mick would still make it, with Roger barely missing. • *Tensions continued to escalate in Berlin. Soviet Premier Nikita Khrushchev threatened to sign a treaty with East Germany giving it control over access to West Berlin, and to back the East Germans with military force.* • *Competition between the two superpowers heated up as well in the space race. Virgil Grissom made the second U.S. suborbital manned space flight, reaching an altitude of 118 miles during his 16-minute journey, after a similar flight by Alan Shepard in May. The Soviet's Yuri Gagarin still held the record. In April he had flown 188 miles high in a 108-minute orbit completely around the earth.*

17. URBANO

SCHOOLS LET OUT on Friday, July 28 for the annual two-week patriotic holidays, marking Peru's declaration of its independence from Spain on that date in 1821. I looked forward to spending time with Urbano, who would be home then, and learning more about his school experiences for my research paper. I told Urbano that I was interested in learning some Quechua from him. In return, I would help him with English, which he was studying at school, with an exam coming up right after vacation.

Urbano at home eating sugar cane

He was eager to get started with our lessons right away, even though it was his first day of vacation. So while we were waiting for dinner, he showed me the Quechua numbering system, and I showed him the English equivalents. His pronunciation of English was much better than mine of Quechua. After a break for dinner, we resumed the lessons, with the names of several animals and some other common words. Pancho joined us, as did their cousin Felix Sanchez, who had eaten dinner with us. So I had a chorus of teachers eager to help me learn.

The next morning Urbano and I got up at 5:00 am to go to Huaraz to buy some parts for his bicycle, without which he could not get to Carhuaz for *colegio*. First we walked to Marcara, then took one of the open-bed trucks which provided public transportation. There were a few seats inside, but like most of the passengers, we sat out back. I was shivering from the cold walk without breakfast and the open-air ride, so it was a relief to feel the strong warm rays of the sun when it rose over the mountains.

I wasn't looking to buy anything, but I wanted to spend the time with Urbano and see how he handled himself among Mestizos. Agustin, dressed as a Vicosino, was always somewhat unsure of himself in a Mestizo environment and aware of his outsider status. But Urbano would have no trouble passing for Mestizo, dressed in a sport jacket, slacks, shoes, socks, dress shirt and a hat of the sort commonly worn by the men there. We rode with Tomas Ramirez, a Mestizo from Marcara, the three of us looking more like three Mestizos than a Mestizo, a Vicosino and a gringo. In fact, none of the other passengers seemed to notice me, although a gringo riding in the back of the truck, and not upfront, would normally attract attention. It wasn't until we got to Huaraz that people realized I wasn't Peruvian, since the driver had to take down the names of the passengers for the police. He noted me as an *extranjero* (foreigner), not a *gringo*.

The night before I had paid Nestor the balance I owed for my room and board, 220 *soles* (with the 150 *soles* I already gave him, all told it came to about $53). Nestor handed the money over to Urbano, trusting him as to how he would spend it in Huaraz. He bought a tire pump, tires, inner tubes and wrenches, all from different stores, while I stood to the side and let him do all the talking. But when he tested the pump by trying to inflate an inner tube, it turned out to have a leaky hose. Urbano was prepared to accept this defect, saying he'd just hold his fingers over the hole. But I convinced him to go exchange it.

When the Mestiza storekeeper who sold him the pump gave him a hard time about returning it, trying to sell him a more expensive one, he wavered. I encouraged him not to do it, and he finally persuaded her to give his money back, 18 *soles*. Shopping around, we found the same pump at another store for 17 *soles*, a lesson learned in standing up for himself. The storekeeper had no change, so he told Urbano he could have the pump for 15. This brought a big smile to his face.

One thing I noticed with Agustin was that he never offered to repay small favors, like when I bought him breakfast once in Huaraz. Of course, money was an issue, but even when I saw Agustin with money, he never made an offer to buy me anything. The same was true of other Vicosinos. It did not seem to be the Vicos way. With Urbano that day, I had paid for the truck ride as well as breakfast and lunch. As we were waiting for the truck back to Marcara, my attention was briefly diverted. When I turned back to Urbano, he handed me an ice cream he had just bought, a much appreciated surprise, standing around in the hot sun. On the walk back from Marcara to Vicos, he shared with me some peanuts he had bought in Huaraz. He was becoming a "mensch" as my mom would say in Yiddish, someone returning generosity.

When Urbano had come home from school, I asked him about his plans for the vacation. He said he was going to study and not work in the fields. At dinner a couple of days after our trip to Huaraz, Pancho asked if he was going to come with him to help plant potatoes. When he said no, Pancho seemed hurt and replied sarcastically, "Do you want to eat potatoes?" The next morning Urbano was glum, not his usual self. Nestor had laid down the law, Urbano was going to help plant. He and I were the first to leave for the field. He hitched up the two oxen and, joined by Nestor and Pancho, we all began plowing and planting. Despite his reluctance, Urbano worked the hardest of all. Maybe this was to be expected, when the other three

Urbano plowing, with help from Pancho

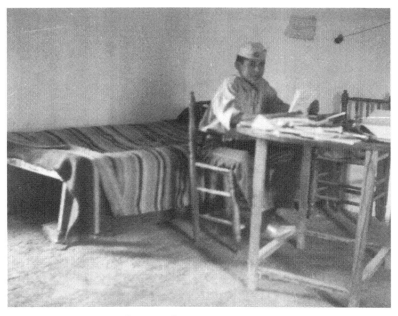

Urbano in his room in Carhuaz

were an old man, a young boy and an inexperienced gringo. He'd brought his notebook along, and we did find some time to get in a little English practice.

There were other people out in the fields at work. At one point Nestor brought me over to meet a young woman named Rosa. His idea, he told me, was that I could marry her and live in Vicos. I'll admit, she was cute, maybe all of 4'6" tall. He must have said something to her in Quechua, because she was smiling. Of course I wasn't going to marry her, but I smiled too, touched by his desire for me to stay.

From The New York Times, Sunday, July 30: Roger Maris had regained the lead over Mickey Mantle in their home run derby, 40 to 39, after 100 games. But baseball Commissioner Ford Frick decreed that Roger and Mick would have to beat the Bambino in 154 games. Otherwise, their home run totals would be marked with an asterisk, and not recognized as the record. • In a televised address to the Nation, President Kennedy proposed several steps to address the Berlin crisis, including increasing the Selective Service draft from 8,000 to 20,000 a month. Among those still eligible for deferments were students "in good standing." At the same time, he expressed a willingness to negotiate with the Soviets.

Urbano and I did find time over the holiday for me to get my research done. The typewriter tactic worked again. He was glad to come to the administration building and type out information. What enabled Urbano to attend *colegio* and succeed was his determination. At first he was uncomfortable there and taunted by the other students for being a Vicosino. But he persevered, and made friends. Entering his second year, two other Vicosino boys joined him, but one dropped out. Money of course was the big barrier for Vicosinos attending *colegio*. They were considering setting up group housing for them in Carhuaz, with mothers taking turns spending weekdays there cooking and overseeing the household. A very Vicosino communal solution.

One day during the vacation period we all took a break from our routines. Urbano and Pancho led me, Rich and Hal on a long uphill hike to a mountain pond, just below the snow line. The water was a brilliant green from algae which thrived under the intense sun. We three gringos stripped down to our underwear and basked in the sun for a while, not quite like being at Jones Beach on Long Island. Urbano and Pancho made no comment about this behavior, leaving their clothes on.

As we started back down, a shadow flickered across us. We looked up to see a condor drifting overhead. It's the largest flying bird in the world, when taking into account wingspan and weight: its wings up to 10½ feet across, its body up to 33 pounds and up to 50 inches long. This awesome creature has long been a symbol of power in Andean culture. It nests at altitudes up to 16,000 feet, so we were in its habitat. Condors are vultures which usually feed on large dead animals, but can also catch small live animals like rodents and rabbits by pecking them with their massive beaks. It was probably checking us out to see what was moving around on the mountainside. We were too alive and too big to become food. So the condor passed.

18. THE TWO SIDES OF TED KENNEDY

IN THE SUMMER OF 1961, President Kennedy sent his 29 year-old youngest brother Ted on a goodwill tour to meet with heads of state in South America. This was intended in part to repair relations with those leaders after the disastrous invasion of Cuba at the Bay of Pigs in April. Yet in his inaugural address Kennedy had said: "To our sister republics south of our border, we offer a special pledge–to convert our good words into good deeds–in a new alliance for progress–to assist free men and free governments in casting off the chains of poverty."

That was the same speech in which he also said: "Ask not what your country can do for you, ask what you can do for your country." Then in March he announced the formation of the Peace Corps, whose mission of volunteers assisting development in un-developed countries was like what Cornell had been doing in Vicos for almost ten years. And in May Kennedy set a goal for landing a man on the moon before the end of the decade. For me and my fellow students, here for the first time in our lives was a President who made concern for Latin America a policy of his Administration, and spoke to our higher aspirations, on earth and beyond.

At the urging of U.S. Ambassador Loeb, Ted and an entourage from the Embassy came to Vicos on August 10th. This was of course an exciting event for us, and for the Vicosinos as well. They had only a vague grasp of who JFK was, or for that matter the United States. But because of the work of the Cornell-Peru Project, they held Americans in high regard. Family relations being very important among the Vicosinos, for them that made Ted the most important person ever to visit Vicos.

Of course there was a *pachamanca*, an 8-goater. But the most important part of the day for the Vicosinos took place in a make-shift "hearing room," where for several hours Ted listened intently and asked questions with great interest about their living conditions and the stalled deal to buy their freedom. The Kennedy contingent also visited a Vicosino household, which because it was so near the plaza, was the *casa* of Nestor and Carmela. This was Ted Kennedy, the young, dedicated, caring public servant.

But we also saw another Ted Kennedy. As he and his traveling pal Claude Hooton, an old Harvard buddy, were getting ready to fly back to Lima, Ted tried to persuade Jane Fearer to leave with him. Not out of sight whispering in her ear, but right in front of all of us, with Claude adding his encouragement in his heavy Texas drawl. I think they'd worked this routine before, and I don't think that touring Inca ruins with Jane was what Ted had in mind. He even tried to sweeten the offer by giving her one of the JFK inaugural medallions he brought with him as gifts from his brother to

Ted Kennedy with Vicosinos and Henry Dobyns of Cornell

Ted Kennedy hearing local delegation; Claude Hooton (white shirt) behind him; at rear wall: (L-R) me, Hal, Rich, Jane obscured by Bill

heads of state. The rest of us had to settle for one of the PT109 tie pins which JFK gave out during his Presidential campaign to remind voters of his naval heroism.

Jane was no doubt flattered by Ted's attentions. His brother was the President of the United States, and Ted was a handsome and charming guy. But she smilingly brushed aside his proposition, probably not the first one she'd heard from a smooth-talking Harvard man. During the course of the summer I was not aware of any personal conflicts within our student group. We lived separately and didn't spend a lot of time together, but became friends through the experience we shared of being in Vicos. Our reaction to Jane's getting a medallion, instead of a tie clip, was more amusement at the situation, not resentment. But the next day word got around that her medallion had disappeared overnight. Did she lose it? Was it stolen? No one knew, but it seemed like a fitting ending to the episode.

Kennedy went on to Lima to meet with the president of Peru, Manuel Prado, as part of his tour. Word came back to us that Vicos was a major topic in their talk. Kennedy read him the riot act, telling him to get the deal done with the Vicosinos or risk losing American foreign aid. Ted did not have the power to block that aid, but Prado didn't know that.

From The New York Times, Sunday, August 6: After 106 games, Roger Maris had 41 home runs, Mickey Mantle 40. They were still ahead of Babe Ruth, who at that point had hit 35. Projected over a 162-game season they would both top the Babe, but not in 154 games. • East-West tensions eased somewhat as Soviet Premier Khrushchev suggested a willingness to negotiate a resolution to the Berlin crisis. • On the other side of the globe, delegates from Latin-American nations were meeting in Uruguay at an economic conference seeking to turn President Kennedy's slogan "The Alliance for Progress" into "a working proposition." Cuba was represented by Che Guevara. The Times noted that Peru "is facing a new drought and food shortages while pressure for land reform increases."

In my Vicosino suit with Pancho

Two "Vicosinos" (me and Cesar Sanchez)

19. THE SUMMER NEARS AN END

AFTER KENNEDY'S VISIT, school vacation ended and Urbano went back to Carhuaz. I still didn't have a Vicosino suit, although I'd paid 200 *soles* to have a new one made. I was hoping to wear it at Agustin's wedding on August 26, the day before leaving Vicos. The situation was resolved when Nestor gave me one which had been made for Donato. He had never worn it, and likely never would. But I knew that Nestor's giving me this particular suit, intended for his son, was an expression of affection. I was excited to put it on, Pancho maybe even more so when he saw me in it. The sleeves and pants were a bit short, since I was taller than Donato, but otherwise it fit pretty well. I could see how the heavy dense wool would keep you warm in the cool evenings, yet I didn't feel hot wearing it under the midday sun. Well, maybe a bit itchy.

By then I already had a white felt hat like the men wore, as well as rubber *llanquis* for sandals. Wearing Vicosino clothing made me feel more connected to the people and the place. All dressed up, I had somewhere to go: Cornell headquarters in the plaza, where I was expected for a group meeting that afternoon. It was not unusual for a Vicosino or two to wander into such a meeting and wait silently off to the side, perhaps to ask a question or make a request. So that's what I did, standing there unobtrusively with the brim of my hat pulled down low. For several minutes no one took notice of me. Then Jane suddenly yelled, "Steve! Is that you?"

Everyone turned toward me, shocked to realize that yes, it was me. For a short while, aided by my clothes and abetted by my tan, I had experienced how it felt to be on the other side of the cultural and racial divide between the North Americans and the Andeans. The Cornell people took me for a Vicosino, and ignored me as they would have any Vicosino. This was not racism, which was totally lacking in people so dedicated to their work with the Vicosinos, just a matter of the situation, focused on their meeting. But for that brief time I was not one of them, not a white man.

From The New York Times, Sunday, August 13: Mickey Mantle took the home-run lead back from Roger Maris, 44 to 43, after 114 games, versus Babe Ruth's 37 in that time span. They were both on pace to hit more than 60 by season's end, although not in 154 games. • As the West pondered whether Khrushchev would negotiate in good faith, East German troops blocked streets and trains from East Germany into Berlin to halt the growing flight of refugees to the West. • In the space race, the Soviets took a giant step forward when Cosmonaut Gherman Titov flew for 25 hours while circling the earth 17 times. That prompted Congress to approve funding for the moon mission Kennedy had announced in May.

With Urbano back in *colegio*, I spent some time at the school in Vicos to finish up the research for my paper. I wanted to learn more about the boys in the fifth grade, their last in the Vicos elementary school before possibly following in Urbano's footsteps. One of the interesting innovations to prepare them for that was the formation of a *Club de Aula* ("classroom club"), now only in its second year and only open to fifth graders. Without any teacher supervision, they nominate and elect club officers, hold regular meetings, set rules of conduct (e.g., "attend school punctually every day") and assign various classroom tasks (e.g., cleaning the blackboard). The purpose of the club is to help them learn to function in the Mestizo world. But it underscored for me the communal nature of Vicosino culture, that these young boys could work so well together on a cooperative basis, with no adult involved.

I interviewed each of the boys about their background, their families, whether they wanted to go to *colegio*, and whether their parents wanted them to. All but two of fifteen said they wanted to go. But their teacher told me it was more likely that only about half of them would. Their fathers wanted them working in the fields, their mothers didn't want them to be away from home, and of course there was the problem of no *plata* ("money").

Still, it had been less than a year and a half since Urbano left for school in Carhuaz, in April 1960. Now *colegio* was a near-universal aspiration in Vicos, if not always a practical reality. Many

Vicosino parents had come to accept it as a necessary and valuable extension of their children's education, with some even hoping they could go on to university and become professionals. For his part, after *colegio* Urbano planned to attend the normal (teachers) school in Tingua, a few miles beyond Carhuaz, and then return to Vicos to teach. He told me he enjoyed living in Carhuaz in his own room, and having electricity so he could study at night. He wanted to build *una casa buena* ("a good house") in Vicos. I imagined that someday he'd have electricity there too.

After my school visit, I picked up my last newspaper delivery in Vicos.

From The New York Times, Sunday, August 20: Roger Maris now has 48 home runs and Mickey Mantle 45, after 121 games. By that point Babe Ruth only had 40. Maris was still on track to top 60 in 154 games; Mantle would need 162 games to do it. • In Uruguay, representatives of the U.S. and every Latin American nation except Cuba signed the charter for the Alliance for Progress. • In Germany, the Soviets shut down East Berlin with concrete barriers and barbed wire, although some border crossings remained open for official business. The flood of refugees, once as many as 2000 a day, slowed to a trickle. President Kennedy sent Vice President Lyndon Johnson to West Berlin in a show of solidarity with our allies, while reinforcing the U.S. military presence there and putting Army reserve units on alert for possible callup.

It was the most serious confrontation between the U.S. and the Soviet Union since the start of the Cold War. I found myself thinking the unthinkable, what if there was a nuclear war? With the certain devastation of the metropolitan New York area, there'd be nothing for me to go home to. I'd just stay in Vicos, which had become like home. I knew I could survive there.

Nestor brewing chicha for the wedding

Nestor leading the wedding procession into Marcara

20. THE BIG DAY

SATURDAY, AUGUST 26. Wedding day for Agustin Sanchez and Rosa Reyes. On Friday afternoon I moved back into Cornell headquarters, leaving some things behind with the Sanchez family, clothes and kitchen implements. Saturday would be a busy day, so now I was ready to take off with Rich and Hal at the crack of dawn on Sunday, in a car we hired to take us to Lima. As I was going to sleep Friday night, looking forward to the wedding and my last day in Vicos, the church bells started ringing furiously. I joined people congregating in the plaza, and looking up, we saw that "the moon is dying," turning red. It was a near total lunar eclipse.

The festivities on Saturday morning began with a procession of the wedding party and guests, from Vicos to Marcara, where the marriage ceremony was to be performed by the Mayor of the town, not by a priest. Several dozen of us followed the band down the road to Marcara, walking and dancing. Bottles of *washcu* were passed around before we even got there. Nestor and Carmela, happy and proud, were dressed up in their Vicosino finest, as I'd never seen them. It was the first time she was comfortable with me taking her picture, and the first time I felt comfortable taking it.

Rosa was beautifully dressed as a Vicosina bride, but Agustin wore Mestizo-style clothing. He obviously felt this was more appropriate for a ceremony in Marcara. I wore my Vicosino suit, as did Rich, who got it from Rosa's family, with whom he had been living. Dancing and drinking were the order of the day, which Rich and I wholeheartedly participated in, even dancing with Carmela.

My body decided that day to resume production of testosterone, so I was finally fully acclimated to the altitude just as I was about to leave. As a result I was ragingly horny from the rush of hormones in my body. I'd been dancing with a Mestiza from Marcara, and at one point we slipped away and she led me to a field, where we lay down and began making out heavily. When I reached down into her pants and started stroking her, she suddenly sat up, pushed me away and yelled angrily, *"Estas Judio?"* ("Are

The wedding party: (L-R) Carmela, Nestor, Augustin, Rosa,
the Mayor of Marcara and his wife

Carmela (center) in her wedding finery

you a Jew?"). I was shocked, she had no way to know that I was, my pants were still on. But maybe it was her way of labeling me as an outsider. And maybe the men in Marcara didn't go in much for foreplay, that was for *los judios*, and that's all women expected. She stormed off, leaving me confused by her reaction.

I honestly can't say how I managed to follow the parade back to Vicos, where the party continued well into the night. I was already *muy borracho* ("very drunk"), and a bottle kept coming around. I managed somehow to get to my bed at headquarters and pass out. Rich was sharing the room, and I don't know how he got there either. Suddenly we were awakened by Agustin standing in the doorway, now wearing his everyday Vicosino clothes and ranting angrily. He was too drunk to speak clearly, and I was too drunk and half-asleep to fully understand what he was saying. It had something to do with my having Donato's suit. Was he jealous of my relationship with his family, symbolized by the suit? Did he feel awkward to be seen in Marcara with two gringos who had come to his wedding dressed as Vicosinos? Was he embarrassed by our carrying on during his wedding, drunk and attracting attention? Probably all of the above. He finally left, it was his wedding night after all, although he and Rosa had long been living together as man and wife. I collapsed for a few hours.

21. HOMEWARD BOUND

IT WAS BARELY LIGHT when the car came for us in the morning. By then I was more than a little hung over, and seriously sick to my stomach. It was a bumpy ride, and it wasn't long before I opened my window, stuck my head out to get some fresh cool air, and began throwing up as we drove along. I suppose this was an appropriate bookend to my visit, along with my episode in the plane arriving in Lima. It was of course a physical response to the excesses of the day before, but also an emotional response to the late-night confrontation with Agustin, a sour note on which to leave Vicos. I'd acclimated to more than just the altitude, but to a way of life. For what it lacked in modern amenities, it made up with the bonds I'd formed with my family, other Vicosinos and the people of the Cornell-Peru Project. I went there as a student to do field studies. I left enriched and changed by what I learned, what I saw, what I felt, what I experienced, how I lived in a place of awe-inspiring beauty. I had first survived and then thrived there, and felt the pain of leaving.

Before going home, Rich, Hal and I were going to take a few days to do some sightseeing around Peru. How could we not see Machu Picchu? After staying the night in Lima, and having my first bath in two months, we flew in the morning to Cuzco, the capital of the Inca empire. The cabin of our DC-3 was not pressurized. In the seat-back in front of each passenger was a plastic hose for breathing oxygen during the flight. We must have flown at least 18,000 feet high, because out the window I was looking down at snowcapped mountains, which we skirted around. But I found I didn't need the oxygen, and had no trouble breathing, or keeping my stomach down.

In Cuzco we got hotel rooms and set out to see some of the fabled Inca stonework around the city. We also saw our first llamas, which had once been found in the Callejon de Huaylas but no longer were. We also hiked up to Sacsayhuaman, an Inca citadel of massive and intricately fitted stones, overlooking Cuzco. No one else was there. The next morning we took a train, the only way to get to Machu Picchu, with very few other passengers on board. Partway through the trip the train turned around and continued the rest of the way backwards, as though heading back in time to one of the wonders of the ancient world. The end of the line, a stop but hardly a station, was along the banks of the Urubamba River, which flowed 2,000 feet below Machu Picchu. From there we boarded a shuttle bus to take us up to the ruins.

We got off the bus and got our first breathtaking view of the site, even more spectacular than in photos we'd seen: its commanding location on a saddle between two towering peaks, the massive

Hal and Rich on the throne of the sun god in Machu Picchu

Stonework at Machu Picchu

terracing creating level areas for agriculture, the numerous structures, the millions of stones they were made of. It was hard to take it all in, the views unspoiled with only a handful of other visitors there. 50 years ago that summer, Hiram Bingham, an explorer from Yale, found the "Lost City of the Incas" he'd been searching for, covered with tropical vegetation. When the time came for us to get the train back to Cuzco, we started to walk down a path through the underbrush, rather than take the bus. Realizing that we were in danger of missing the train, we began to run, laughing on the way down. Machu Picchu was "only" at 8,000 feet. No big deal.

Having seen the Pacific Coast, the desert, and the high mountains, we decided to visit the jungle before going home. No other country in the world has so many extreme varieties of terrain, much less the ancient ruins which bejewel them. We took a flight from Cuzco, an old military DC-3. Instead of seats it had canvas slings parallel to the fuselage, for transporting troops. We noticed a number of burlap sacks on the floor at the back of the plane. They stayed there when it was climbing, nose up. When it began to descend, nose down, the sacks slid down the aisle, with an outburst of oinking and squawking from the pigs and chickens inside them.

Our destination was Puerto Maldonado, on the Madre de Dios River in far eastern Peru near the Bolivian border. "Maldonado" means "ill-favored", sometimes referring to a bad guy. The name was appropriate. The town was a notorious center for smuggling. It was hot there, it was humid. We mostly sat around sweating and drinking warm soft drinks – there was no ice. Nor was there a shower where we were staying. We tried to cool down with a dip in the river, stripping to our underwear. We looked like three pale scarecrows. During the summer all the male students had lost 10-20 pounds on our carbohydrate diet, while the women gained 10-20 pounds eating the same food.

The river water was wet but unpleasantly warm. Wooden dugout canoes were tied up along the banks, used to ferry goods across the border. We didn't stay in long, because we heard there were parasites which would swim up a certain warm orifice in the lower human abdomen. Whether this was true or not, that was it for the river. We were also advised to stay off the streets after dark, and to sleep under mosquito netting. In our hammocks that night, under the netting, we heard raucous carryings on around the town, and gunfire. It was Peru's Wild East. In the morning the wooden floor of our shelter was covered with hundreds of dead insects, small and large, whose life span in this tropical climate was brief. There was no way to walk around them, just put on shoes and crunch your way across the floor.

If we could have, we would have flown back to Cuzco that day. But the plane only went every other day, so we were stuck there to spend another day much as we had the first, minus the dip in the river. From Cuzco it was back to Lima. My flight to Miami on Aerolineas Peruanas was due to depart about midnight. I got a cab and told him to take me to the airport where I'd arrived in June. When we pulled up, the place looked deserted. I got out and walked into a cavernous empty terminal, my footsteps echoing.

I was totally confused, until the cabbie told me that over the summer they'd opened a new international airport in Lima. Fortunately it wasn't far away, he drove like crazy, and I just made my plane. Looking out my window, I wished for a moment that I'd missed it. There was the captain, holding up a drunk copilot and leading him to the plane. Many of the pilots in South America were ex-U.S. Air Force guys who couldn't get a job flying in the States for one reason or another, like having a drinking problem. Down here they were less scrupulous about checking pilot qualifications.

I guess he slept it off while the captain flew us to Tegucigalpa, Honduras, our one stop on the way to the U.S. By now my innards were roiled from the food in the jungle and the long flight to Honduras. I was dismayed to discover that the "toilet" in the men's room was just a hole in the middle of the floor. My "place" out back of the Sanchez *casa* was more sanitary than these facilities in the capital of Honduras. I was only too happy when we departed on time for Miami, where we arrived about mid-day, back in the USA.

Now I was faced with getting through customs, with a bag of coca leaves and a bottle of *washcu* in my duffel bag. I had crammed them all the way on the bottom, under two months' worth of really rancid dirty clothes. The problem was, I looked like someone who might well be carrying contraband, with my scraggly beard and longish hair. My plan was to get on the line for a female customs agent, hoping she'd be disinclined to search through my smelly clothes too closely. She was. I cleared customs and was safely back in the U.S.

My cousin Sandy, the daughter of my Mom's youngest sister, lived in Miami. She was my age and growing up we'd spent a lot of time together. Since I had a long layover, I called her on a pay phone, after getting American coins at the currency exchange. Half an hour later I saw her walking toward me in the terminal. At first she didn't recognize me as I approached her, until I smiled and greeted her. When it suddenly dawned on her who this disreputable looking person was, she screamed. Not the warm welcome I expected, but still, it was nice to see family after two months.

On the Eastern Airlines flight home to New York, due in that evening, I thought about where I'd been and what I'd done. Vicos was an epicenter of social change, and living there had changed me, a middle-class kid from the suburbs, in ways I had yet to fully understand. I thought about seeing my parents and brothers again. Would I seem changed to them? I thought about listening to the radio and watching the Yankees on TV. And I thought about having a big steak, but no potatoes please.

The plane landed and I got off, glad to be home.

POSTSCRIPT

PROFESSOR ALLAN HOLMBERG returned to Peru in April 1962 for a ceremony in Lima, attended by the Prime Minister of Peru, at which the Vicosinos made a down payment of one half million *soles* toward their purchase of the Vicos hacienda. To celebrate their liberation after the sale was finalized in July, they bought a new truck on which they painted "Vicos Communal Property" and "Cry of Reform." Walter Cronkite hosted a documentary about Vicos, *So That Men Are Free*, which aired on CBS in 1963 and can be viewed online. While Holmberg lived to see the culmination of his pioneering work, he succumbed to his disease and died in 1966.

Closing the sale of Vicos in Lima; Professor Holmberg smiling

Paul Doughty became a distinguished anthropologist. In 2005 he received a prestigious lifetime achievement award from the Society for Applied Anthropology in recognition of "a career dedicated to the goal of solving human problems through the application of concepts and tools from the social sciences."

Mario Vazquez recovered from his broken leg and continued in a leadership role with the Cornell-Peru Project until it ended in 1966.

Urbano Sanchez graduated from *colegio* in 1964, ranked fifth in his class of 27. He became the first Vicosino to get a post-secondary school education when he attended normal school, and then became a teacher in Vicos.

My fellow field studies students went on to respected careers in anthropology, economic development, arts administration and medicine.

As for me? Well, that's a long story.

School Days

*"A mind that is stretched by a new experience
can never go back to its old dimensions."*
Oliver Wendell Holmes, Jr., Supreme Court Justice

1. You Can't Go Home Again

MY PARENTS PICKED ME UP at LaGuardia Airport. They didn't make a big deal about my appearance. Maybe they expected worse, maybe they were just happy to see me, as I was to see them. Leaving the terminal and carrying my duffel bag to their car, I smelled the air of a Long Island summer night, familiar not exotic. In a letter over the summer they told me they were selling the house in Roslyn Heights and moving to Great Neck, further west on Long Island. This made sense for my father, because it would shorten his daily commute into Manhattan and back.

But it didn't make sense for me. In the car they talked about the new house, especially my Mom enthusiastically telling me how much I was going to like it. But I was not feeling enthusiastic. I'd lived in our old house since I was nine years old. In my mind that was still home, where I'd grown up and spent so many hours listening to the radio in my room. That's where I wanted to go home to from Peru. Now I could never go home there again, just when I was so close after coming so far. Sitting in the back seat of the car in the dark, heading somewhere unfamiliar, I felt disoriented.

My mom also casually mentioned that in the course of moving she got rid of those piles of old comic books and magazines in my closet. That really pissed me off, but to avoid an angry scene, all too common in our family, I held my tongue. I had every issue of Mad from #2 on (I missed the first one, which came out when I was 11), every issue of Sports Illustrated (I became a charter subscriber at 13). At least she didn't find any copies of Playboy under the bed.

The new house was nice, oddly enough somewhat Spanish in style, with stucco walls and a tiled roof. But in a way it seemed less like home than *mi casa* in Vicos had become. Sure, in Peru I missed family and friends, food and electricity, and my suburban life, especially the radio. But I'd become used to day-to-day life in Vicos. I'd been a stranger in a strange land when I arrived there. Now I was back in what should have been a familiar land, but in a strange place.

My feelings of dislocation were put aside when my mom served me a big steak dinner, even though it was going on midnight. My parents and two brothers – Peter had just graduated from high school, Rich was in junior high – wanted to hear "all about it." I was happy to share my experiences with them over the next few days, but at that moment I wanted to eat, not talk. They watched me like it was feeding time at the Bronx Zoo and they'd thrown a slab of meat in a lion's cage. I devoured it. Because I'd never changed time zones in the trip from Lima to New York, I had no problem getting right to sleep with a full stomach. At least my bed was familiar from the old house.

Before leaving Peru I tried to clean up in a hotel bathtub (there was no shower), but the water got filthy too quickly from two months of accumulated grime. When I arrived home my mom commented that I smelled strange. Maybe two months of an Andean diet and living at 10,000 feet had affected my body chemistry and odor, even beyond the layer of dirt. The next morning I had a long hot shower. Very long, very hot. Late to reach puberty, my body hadn't fully matured when I went to Peru. Now in the mirror I could see that my chest had expanded from acclimating to breathing the thin air. With plenty of hot water and hot food – real chicken soup! – my foreign aroma soon disappeared.

I was eager to catch up on the news. Now I could read the full Sunday Times the same day it came out, rather than having to wait for my Thursday delivery in Vicos.

From The New York Times, Sunday, September 3: Roger Maris hit two home runs in game 134 to bring his total for the season to 53, on pace to top Babe Ruth's 60 by game 154. Mickey Mantle was close behind at 50, but left the game with an injury. • The Soviet Union broke a moratorium by resuming nuclear weapons tests, bringing the Berlin crisis near "the boiling point." The U.S. sent 72 jet fighters to Europe to participate in NATO war games, suggesting that they might stay there.

I could follow the news and watch Yankees games on my parents' black-and-white TV. But the radio was still special to me. My teen idol Alan Freed was long gone from the air, caught up in the payola scandal – record companies paying DJs to spin their records. The great wave of rock 'n' roll in the '50s had ebbed, and now was even a source for nostalgia with the Top Ten record "Those Oldies but Goodies (Remind Me of You)" by Little Caesar & The Romans. Most of Top 40 airtime was filled with soft schlock from the likes of Bobby Vee. But Elvis was still doing it, his latest the two-sided hit "Little Sister" and "(Marie's The Name) His Latest Flame." Gary U.S. Bonds rocked "School is Out" up the charts just as school was about to be back in.

2. To Be or Not To Be Me

On the road to Ithaca, I was elated to be in my car again, a Triumph Herald, a sporty compact sedan from the same company that made the famed TR2 and TR3 sports cars. It had an Italian design, four-on-the-floor stick shift and lots of glass providing a panoramic view. I settled in for the five-hour drive, radio on, thinking about the year ahead. By then most people in my senior class had a pretty good idea of what they wanted to do after college, become a doctor or a lawyer, an engineer or a teacher. I didn't. And when they came back to school that fall, they'd pretty much be who they were when they'd left in the spring. I wasn't. Living in Vicos was a profound experience that made me think differently about who I was – no longer a typical college student who took for granted the comforts of the middle-class and the freedom of living in the U.S.A.

It was not only a question of who I'd become, but who I would appear to be around the Cornell campus. Passing for a Vicosino in my new suit of clothes was not something new to me. I'd been manipulating my appearance since my freshman year at Mineola High School. There were some tough kids there, like in the movie

Home in Great Neck, ready to drive to Cornell in my Triumph Herald

"The Blackboard Jungle" (its opening credits song, Bill Haley & His Comets' "Rock Around the Clock," went to #1 on the charts). To get by and not get picked on as a smarty-pants Jew from Roslyn Heights (the gym teacher called the boys "no-necks"), you had to look tough (even though I wasn't) and dress like a "rock." So I did, my pompadour greased up, wearing Levis or pink-and-black pegged pants (they were tapered or "pegged" to be narrow at the ankles). The girls wore long tight skirts and pointy bras.

In my junior year, my class moved to a new high school built in 1956 to serve kids in Roslyn Heights and neighboring towns, as the population of Long Island was growing rapidly. The school administration wanted their new school to be noticed by college admissions officers, so instead of calling it Wheatley High School, they named it The Wheatley School, like it was some kind of prep school. They also had an idea of what a proper Wheatley student should look like, a clean-cut teenager, and it wasn't me.

As a top student, I got interviewed by two teachers for a small scholarship. Apparently my style of dress was an issue with the faculty and administration, because their first question to me was, "Do clothes make the man?" I guess they wanted to give me the opportunity to say "No" and disavow my appearance, don't judge my book by my cover. But I said "Yes" and talked about how clothes did make the man, in the sense of the image I chose to project and how people perceived me. Ironically, the two teachers didn't get what I was saying about creating your image, even though the Wheatley administration was doing the much the same thing with the school's name, trying to project a certain image. I didn't win the scholarship, but I did get a watch as a consolation prize. It was the one I wore in Vicos.

When I went off to Cornell for my freshman year, I tried to look collegiate, to fit in with a social life dominated by fraternities and sororities. The first few days of school were rush period. Fraternity members would come around to your dorm room and knock on the door. You'd tell them to come in, so they could look over the nervous freshmen as potential pledges. Two guys, very

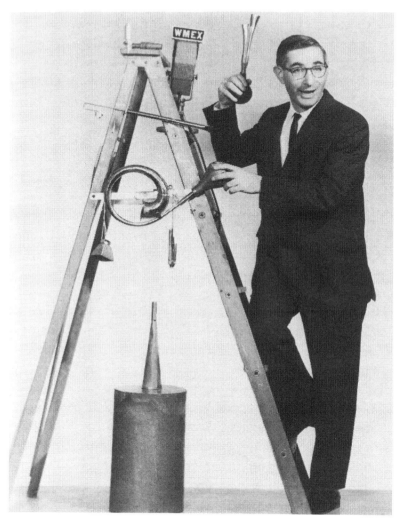

Arnie "Woo Woo" Ginsburg

preppy and snobby, showed up from Zeta Beta Tau, the top Jewish house on campus for the financially well-off and those striving to be. They weren't impressed by me or my roommate Phil as potential ZBTs. One of them was smoking a cigarette, which he tossed on the tile floor and crushed out with his penny loafer, before they left snickering to themselves.

I did pledge a fraternity, Phi Alpha, a house of bohemians and misfits, at least compared to the typical Cornell frat guys. Peter Yarrow was a senior member. I'd seen him strolling around campus with his long haired, shoeless beatnik girlfriend "Baby." He also "taught" a class that was very popular, despite meeting on Saturday mornings. Known popularly as "Romp and Stomp," it mostly involved his leading the packed lecture hall crowd in group folk sing-along. Another freshman at Phi Alpha, Lenny Lipton, wrote a child's poem which Yarrow adopted as the lyrics for the classic hit "Puff the Magic Dragon" by his folk trio Peter, Paul & Mary.

But the idea that rejects from more conventional fraternities could find a home together in Phi Alpha didn't really work for me. Its members were not social climbers like the ZBTs, but there was still an inherent element of group regimentation in fraternity life, like showing up for dinner every night at 6:00 to eat lousy food. So I never completed my pledge to become a member. Besides, I found a much better place to eat, at the School of Hotel Administration. As part of their schoolwork, the Hotelies cooked international foods which were served for dinner at the school's cafeteria. Those student chefs put a lot of effort into their dishes, because they were graded on them. The food was really good, and it was cheap. If it were up to me, I'd give them an A.

I became what the fraternity boys called a "GDI", a "God Damn Independent." Meant as a term of derision, some of us took it as a badge of honor. In my sophomore year I lived in an off-campus apartment with three other GDIs: Bill Pagell and Michael Baker from the Boston area, and Dave Scudellari from Long Island. Knowing my love of rock 'n' roll, Bill and Mike told me all about the big D.J. in Boston, Arnie Ginsburg, known as "Woo

Woo" for the sound effects he made with whistles and horns during his show, the "Night Train." They regaled me with their rendition of the jingle for the Adventure Car Hop, a roadside drive-in which Arnie made popular and which featured the "Ginsburger," for its debut served on a record.

Freed of the need to fit in the fraternity world, I reverted to my natural rock 'n' roll style. This was the early '60s "continental" look, not Fifties greaser, featuring narrow black slacks and pointy-toed black shoes, "rat stabbers." I didn't shop for clothes in Ithaca, but at some stores around Times Square which catered to a mixed-race clientele of sharp and flamboyant dressers. That's where I found two sweaters I loved, not the crew-neck Shetlands popular around campus, but v-neck fuzzy mohairs. Their silky goat hair could take bright-colored dyes – one sweater was a brilliant grape, the other an electric blue. I certainly stood out at Cornell, and quietly enjoyed the notoriety. When I walked by, the ivy on the old buildings just about shriveled up and died.

But getting ready for my senior year, I decided to reinvent my image to pass for a typical Cornellian. For three years, like an anthropologist in the field, I'd observed the customs and culture of the "tweed" tribe in their native habitat on campus. So I adopted their costume, my new clothes already packed in a suitcase in the trunk of the Herald: Harris tweed sport jacket, chinos, button-down shirt, penny loafers, and white wool socks. And not bright white wool socks, which would have been seen as cheesy by the arbiters of preppy fashion. The trick was to wash new ones with bleach, so that they turned an ivory color, looking like old socks that had been handed down in the family, like old money.

From The New York Times, Sunday, September 10: Roger Maris blasted his 56th homer of the season in game #142, with Mickey Mantle having hit his 52nd in the previous game. Babe Ruth didn't get his 56th until game #149. • Soviet Premier Khrushchev rejected a proposal by the U.S. and Britain to ban atmospheric testing of nuclear weapons unless the West agreed to a treaty permanently dividing Germany. The U.S.

was speeding deployment of 40,000 troops to Europe, while the Soviets announced it would "further strengthen" its defenses to counter what it perceived as threats by NATO of going to war over Berlin.

3. OH SUSIE Q

THE ROUTE TO ITHACA was a nostalgic one for me. It passed Monticello, a village of about 5,000 people in the Catskills. My father's father, sister and brother all lived there with their families. Since I was little, my parents packed the kids in the car every spring to go to Monticello for Passover. I loved being with the whole family, and the ritual of the seder. You ate harsh and bitter food to remember the Jews' lives as slaves in Egypt. Nothing was harsher than Grandpa's home-grown horseradish. But I savored it all.

As I'd grown up and lived on my own, my Jewishness faded in its importance as to how I defined myself, and how others saw a guy with the un-Jewish name of "Nelson" (it had been shortened from the historical family name "Katznelson"). I was proud of my heritage as a Jew but by this time no longer practiced Judaism as a religion or participated in its rituals, other than Passover. Now, after Vicos, the seder message of enduring and escaping servitude, of the quest for freedom, was more relevant to me than ever. The Vicosinos and I had this in common: our ancestors built massive stone monuments.

When I arrived in Ithaca, I was glad to see my roommate Bill again. He'd been a steady friend. Not at all a flashy guy himself, he was never bothered by my sometimes outrageous appearance. I got to know him freshman year during compulsory ROTC drills, when we all dressed alike in our Army uniforms. Bill was heading for graduate school in psychology, and had a steady girlfriend. Unlike me, not knowing what I'd be doing after Cornell, and without a girlfriend.

Even with my new Ivy League look, I still felt like an outsider at Cornell. It being Rush Week, all the inanities of the fraternity system were in full swing. Everyone was obsessed with which house they'd be invited to pledge, or which freshmen they could sign up as pledges for their house. I'd just come from a place where people were struggling to survive from day to day, and to gain their freedom. Their social structure was based on community and cooperation, not on separating into competitive cliques. I felt more alienated than ever from campus social life.

Still, I decided to participate in a traditional Cornell ritual, a mixer in the student union, Willard Straight Hall. Freshman girls went to get eyeballed by the upperclassmen they hoped to meet. Cornell maintained a 3:1 ratio of undergraduate men to women. As a typical freshman or sophomore guy, you had almost no chance of getting a date with a coed, when they could have their pick from the juniors and seniors. Younger guys were bused off on Saturday nights to women-only Wells College, a half hour away, or to Syracuse University, an hour away. Cornell men were in demand there.

The new crop of girls milling around in the student union of course knew nothing about my mohaired past. I looked like what they'd expect a well-dressed Cornell senior to look like, casually clad in a cable-knit tennis sweater. Ivory, not white. I found myself standing next to the prettiest girl there. Normally I wouldn't have had the nerve to strike up a conversation with her, but jammed next to her in the crowd it was too awkward not to talk. She introduced herself, hi, I'm Susie. Hi, I'm Steve, and trying to make small talk, asked her, where are you from? To my surprise, she said Great Neck. So am I, although my parents only moved there over the summer while I was in Peru. Peru?, she asked. That got us to talking the night away.

As we did, I noticed three guys standing around together and glancing over at us, as if saying to each other, "What's *she* doing with *him*?" I recognized them as Zeta Beta Taus, and they recognized me, despite my new look. I had crashed a few parties at ZBT, usually stag, because on Saturday nights I sometimes cruised past fraternity houses listening for a live band to dance to. One of them which played at ZBT from time to time was a black R&B group

Susie

called The Upsetters. They did great versions of "What'd I Say" by Ray Charles, "Money (That's What I Want)" by Barrett Strong (in 1960 it was the first hit for the new Motown label), and their signature finale which always brought down the house, "Shout" by The Isley Brothers.

I guess they let me into their parties because I provided entertainment. I danced occasionally with a girl named Angel, one of the very few black students at Cornell, perhaps the only black coed in her class of 1500 students. One of the dances we did was the shimmy, originally popular with flappers in the 1920s when it was banned in some places as too suggestive. Basically, you held your body still and swiveled your shoulders, first one forward and the other back, then vice versa, fast. For a woman it meant throwing one breast forward and then the other, along with the shoulders, which was why it became a move adopted by strippers. I'm sure it was easier to do if you had breasts, because they'd help create the momentum to keep the shoulders going back and forth. Maybe that's why I never saw any guys doing it, it was a girl thing.

But I did it, locked in to the heavy beat of The Upsetters. In a way the shimmy was sort of like the 1960 dance craze the Twist, but with the upper body instead of the hips. Angel and I would lean back and forth shimmying in unison with each other, then add a little hip movement and gradually swivel down to the floor. We were laughing and digging it, because it wasn't easy to do, requiring a lot of agility and coordination. The fraternity boys were titillated by our floor show; their sorority dates probably thought it was obscene. A ZBTer had put out the fire of his cigarette on my dorm room floor. Now I lit a fire on the floor of his fraternity house.

So yes, *she* was with *him*, Susie was with me, and we fell in love. I'd had a few girlfriends before, most memorably Naomi from the Bronx. I met her while working as a camp counselor during high school summer vacation. She was my "first time," in my little French car with front seats which folded all the way down flat. But I'd never really been in love the way I was with Susie. I was crazy about her. She was smart and she was beautiful. Mostly I loved her because she was loving and warm, which radiated from her smile. And she was talented. Even though just a freshman, she landed the lead role of Polly Peachum in a Cornell student production of "The Threepenny Opera." I watched her performance in awe, as though I couldn't quite connect the poised girl singing and dancing on stage with the sweet girl I knew.

From The New York Times, Sunday, September 17: After going for a week without a home run, Maris hit his 57th of the season in game #150. Mantle was not far behind with 53. • The U.S. resumed testing nuclear weapons with two underground blasts. The Soviets responded with their eleventh test, all in the atmosphere. Meanwhile, Western foreign ministers agreed to see if there was any "reasonable basis" to negotiate with the Soviets over Berlin and Germany.

4. OFF AND ON CAMPUS

BY MY SENIOR YEAR, Bill and I still shared an off-campus apartment, but Michael had graduated, and Dave had passed away from leukemia. He had been an engineering student with a love for harness racing. He explained to me his system for betting, which involved tracking which horses won races from which post positions. If no horse had won over so many races from a particular favorable post position, then under his system it was "due". As a math guy, I was more than a little skeptical of his scheme, but as his friend and a fan of harness racing myself, I kept an open mind.

In the summer of 1960, after our sophomore year, Dave became convinced that the #2 post was due to produce a winner after a long drought of also-rans. But he couldn't get to Yonkers Raceway that night because his sister was getting married. This was before off-track betting, so he asked me to go and handed me an envelope with $1,000 in it to play his system. This basically involved increasing the bet on the #2 horse after the previous #2 horse lost until, so his theory went, #2 would come home a winner, and pay off the previous losses, plus more.

When I had been to the track before, I was strictly a small time player, placing my bets at the two-dollar window. As that night wore on and the #2 post continued to lose, I had to move to a window where you could make bigger bets. Racetrack regulars hung around hoping to glean some winning wisdom from the "smart money" playing at that window. So the touts kept an eye on this young guy putting down increasingly large wagers. By the last race my bet was up to $500, almost half the annual tuition at Cornell. Dave told me to call him with the results no matter how late it was. When I got home around midnight I did, and told him he'd lost his grand. His money had run out, and so had his time. More seriously ill than he'd let on, Dave didn't return to school.

From The New York Times, Sunday, September 24: Maris had 59 homers through 156 games, missing the Babe's mark of 60 in a 154-game season. But Maris still had six more games to play. After several days out with injuries, Mantle returned to hit #54. • Both sides were indicating that they were open to "honorable negotiations" over the Berlin crisis. But in a statement reflecting the position of the Kennedy Administration, a leading Senator said that the U.S. was prepared to use nuclear weapons against aggression, and as a show of strength a Titan missile was test fired and delivered a mock warhead on a target 4,500 miles away. The Soviets set off their 15th atomic blast since September 1.

Susie and I were together whenever we could be. But as a freshman required to live in a dorm, she had a strict curfew. Many a night after a date or at my apartment, I'd race her back there just in time, urging the low-powered Herald with body language faster faster as it struggled up the steep climb to the campus. Susie never spent the night with me, and made it clear that, curfew or not, she wasn't giving up her virginity at any hour. Once I accepted that, I never pressed the issue, and still loved her and wanted to be with her.

The iconic feature of the Cornell campus was a clock tower with a carillon which rang every quarter hour – at a quarter of, as classes were about to end, and then on the hour, as the next classes began. During that interval students poured out onto the quad and rushed back and forth. I often studied in the library, finding a desk by a window. The chimes were my signal to look outside, hoping to catch a glimpse of Susie in the crowd. She carried herself like a dancer. I loved the way she walked.

I was plodding through school. Not fully readjusted to academic life, I often found my mind wandering from a cramped classroom to the vast spaces of Peru. I took a computer programming class taught by a visiting professor from Poland. He spoke with such a thick accent I couldn't understand half of what he said, which might as well have been in Quechua. After learning some programming basics, students were required to write out a short program in longhand on paper and turn it in. Then it was sent to the computer lab, where they punched cards and ran them on the mainframe overnight. You might find out two days later in the next meeting of the class that you had one character wrong, and the program failed.

It wasn't just this cumbersome process which made me question my future in math. While I was good at it, I didn't feel that I was good enough to become outstanding in the field. As for jobs, I basically had three options: to teach, to be an actuary at an insurance company (developing models which enabled the company to make a profit on the policies it issued), or to go to work for the International Business Machines Corporation. I had no interest in teaching, and thought the actuarial business would be boring. As for IBM, they required employees to wear white (and only white) shirts with ties, and to keep sideburns trimmed just below the tops of the ears. I didn't see myself fitting into such a regimented environment. There had to be something else out there.

5. PASSING THE TEST

From The New York Times, Sunday, October 1: After hitting his 60th home run in game #158, Roger Maris was now down to the last day of the season in his quest for #61. Due to injuries Mantle had been hospitalized, finishing his season with 54. • The U.S. Secretary of State and Soviet Foreign Minister held their third in a series of talks about resolving the Berlin crisis. 75,000 U.S. reservists were reporting for duty, with another 82,000 to be mobilized in two weeks. Some major businesses in the U.S. were planning how they would operate in the event of a nuclear war.

Being from Boston, Bill and Michael were Red Sox fans. But everyone was talking about Maris when on October 1st he became the first man in baseball history to hit 61 home runs in a season. For his effort he earned an asterisk in the record books from Baseball Commissioner Ford Frick, differentiating his 162-game record from Babe Ruth's 60 in 154 games. Baseball fans hotly debated whether this was fair. You didn't have to be a math major to know that 61 was more than 60. Prolific home run hitters over the years, the Yankees were known as the Bronx Bombers. Due to his intimidating demeanor, a Times columnist dubbed Maris the Mad Bomber.

October 1st was also a day when the Soviets tested another atomic bomb, and did so almost daily for the rest of the month. Cornell students usually went about their lives on campus with little concern for current events, domestic or foreign. But by the 26th you could feel the tension around the campus. Everyone was aware that American and Soviet tanks were faced off in Berlin, 100 yards apart at Checkpoint Charlie, with live ammunition loaded. When Susie and I met that day, we hugged tightly, hardly knowing what to say, scared. One shot from either side, deliberately or in panic, and the other would retaliate, triggering war.

After about 18 hours of this confrontation, Kennedy and Khrushchev agreed to withdraw the tanks. First one side backed up a few yards, then the other did, then it was the turn of the first to continue their slow dance alternately moving away from confrontation step-by-step, until they finally stood down. The Berlin Wall remained in place, while Khrushchev dropped his plan to sign a treaty with East Germany, which had precipitated the crisis. A de facto peace prevailed. As JFK said, "It's not a very nice solution, but a wall is a hell of a lot better than a war."

I normally drove home for Thanksgiving break but Susie and I flew together on Allegheny Airlines, a.k.a. Agony Air. Still, it was like flying first-class compared to those DC-3 flights in Peru. I met her parents and her two sisters, the older an aspiring classical musician. I'm sure she'd told them some nice things about me, her first serious boyfriend, because they all were warm and welcoming when we met. Her father ran a seafood distribution business at the Fulton Fish Market in Manhattan, where his workday began at 3 am. When Susie and I came back from a late date and were making out in the living room, his moving around upstairs told us it was time to fix our clothes and say goodnight.

After returning to school, I finally finished my paper for the Summer Field Studies Program, entitled "Secondary Education for Students of Vicos." That immersed me in thoughts of Vicos, and reminded me of my promise to write a letter to the Sanchez family. I felt bad that I hadn't, too preoccupied with my life at Cornell, and Susie. I had also decided by then that I didn't want to become an anthropologist, which would certainly involve teaching, as every anthropologist did. Still, to keep my options open about going to grad school, I took the Graduate Record Exam. With nothing to lose, I went into it in a very relaxed frame of mind. That was always the key for me in doing well on an exam. I aced it.

One day I was chatting at the library with a friend, Peter Schuck, about our plans for the future. He was going into the law, and suggested that I take the Law School Aptitude Test. I had no lawyers in the family who might have inspired me to become one. Nor had I taken the usual pre-law undergrad courses in government, history and economics. But Pete thought I'd do well on the LSAT, given my logical thinking as a math major and my aptitude for test-taking. It was thoughtful advice, and as I thought about it, it made sense. Law is a system by which a society governs itself, so it appealed to the anthropologist in me too. I had nothing to lose taking the LSAT, and was challenged to see how I would do. So I signed up for the next exam in February.

6. TWIST OF FATE

IN DECEMBER 1961, "The Twist" by Chubby Checker started climbing the charts, quickly reaching #1 by mid-January. The record had already been #1 in September 1960, a monster hit which stayed in the Top Ten for three months and created a national dance craze. Now it was back for another three-month stay, the first time a #1 record fell completely off the charts and then topped them again later. After two weeks at #1, it was followed in the top slot for three weeks by "The Peppermint Twist – Part 1" by Joey Dee & the Starliters.

The Twist was back, bigger than ever. Even Jackie Kennedy was doing it. But former President Dwight Eisenhower bemoaned that it represented "some kind of change in our standards. What has happened to our concepts of beauty and decency and morality?" '50s rock 'n' roll dancing could be a little suggestive. But The Twist changed our standards of "decency," at least on the dance floor. Millions of women shed their girdles, gyrated their hips and wiggled their rear ends. Sorry, Ike, that looked beautiful to me. Besides, everyone was having fun.

The Starliters home club, the Peppermint Lounge, became the epicenter of the revived craze. It was an unlikely place, a hole in the wall just off Times Square which held less than 200 people, originally a mostly gay crowd. Some say that "go-go girls" originated there, when some women got up on tables to do the Twist. After the club was featured in the movie "Hey, Let's Twist" the "Peppermint" theme song shot up the charts. Then the limos began to pull up and celebrities piled into the club: Marilyn Monroe,

Chubby Checker

Movie poster for "Hey, Let's Twist!" with Joey Dee & The Starliters

Frank Sinatra, Truman Capote, Liberace, Judy Garland, Norman Mailer, even Annette Funicello, "America's Sweetheart" from "The Mickey Mouse Club."

I went there with my sweetheart Susie during Christmas vacation. The Starliters were on the small stage, the joint was jumping. There was a small dance area up front, surrounded by a wrought iron railing which kept the dancers packed in. People not dancing were enjoying the impromptu floor show from their tables. Susie and I twisted the night away, hardly taking a break. As we were leaving, someone from club management came up to me and asked me if I'd like a job dancing there every night. Thanks, I said, flattered, but we're college students heading back to school. With the noise in the club, Susie couldn't hear what he said. When we got outside, I told her, and we walked down 45th Street chuckling. I'd missed my big chance to be a go-go boy.

A few weeks later, I woke up early for a Saturday. It was the day of the LSAT, and I looked out the window in the dim winter light. It was snowing. I got dressed and went downstairs from my second-floor apartment to get a better look at weather conditions outside and check out my car. Bill and I lived on the far side of Ithaca, on flat land near the lake. With the snow coming down, I might make it across town but doubted I could get up the long hill to the campus, where the test was given. I thought, well, I guess I wasn't fated to go to law school after all, and went back upstairs. But then I thought, I paid for the test, I'm ready to go, and I've got nothing planed for the day. Besides, I didn't like quitting so easily. So I took fate in my hands and headed off in the Herald. State Street, the main road through town, had been plowed but still had a light snow cover. I did make it up the hill, barely. Going into the exam, I was about as relaxed as I could be about the whole thing. Okay, let me spend a few hours doing brain puzzles. I had nothing to lose.

7. LOSING AND WINNING

As THE LONG ITHACA WINTER turned to spring, I found out I did have something to lose: Susie. When we were alone together, we were still tender and loving. But we weren't alone. The boys from Zeta Beta Tau never got over *her* being with *him*. When Susie and I were not together, they were whispering things in her ear about me. That I was a lothario, a seducer of coeds. When word of this got back to me (not from her), I was rather amused. Other than Lucy, my girlfriend for a few months during my junior year, I'd hardly had a date in my first three years at Cornell. Now I was supposed to be the campus Casanova. My dancing got exaggerated into a wild tale of my having sex on the floor at a ZBT party, for which they gave me the epithet The Mad Humper. I guess they didn't care what that said about Angel, or whoever I was supposed to have been down on the floor with.

I could take the bad-mouthing and name-calling. I'd been living outside the fraternity system and even flaunting my apartness with my dress. But Susie was being subjected to enormous social pressure. She came to Cornell a young girl just out of high school, and merely because she fell in love, found herself caught in a crossfire she was totally unprepared for. How could she be? Some of her friends in her dorm were also saying, you're just a freshman, you should be dating. And so she did. Dion's recent #1 hit "Runaround Sue" kept going through my head: "She took my love then ran around / With every single guy in town." That was not fair to her. She wasn't running around, just trying to cope with an intolerable situation. But the song expressed my fear of losing her. And the more I tried to hold onto her, the more I drove her away.

But I got some good news. I did really well on the LSAT. Wondering how this would affect my chances of going to law school, I met with the Cornell Law School admissions office. They told me I could get into any law school in the country, even Harvard. When I graduated from high school, I was admitted to Cornell but was waitlisted for Harvard College, the top candidate from

Wheatley. After I withdrew from the wait list to take the financial aid for Cornell, my best friend Julien Hennefeld, second on the list from Wheatley, was admitted.

Maybe it was my competitiveness, maybe I was exaggerating the importance of Harvard, but it really mattered to me to go there, to reach the summit of achievement Harvard represented to me. Law School looked like another chance to make it, so I applied there, but as a backup also applied to Columbia and Yale. On April 30, the Director of Admissions at Harvard sent me a letter. When I opened it, the very first words were, "I am pleased to...." I'd made it to the top.

The letter went on to say that my application for a scholarship was pending. I also got into Columbia, but a letter from Yale said that they'd lost my paperwork and would I please resubmit it. I wrote back and told them to get lost. A letter from Harvard dated May 29, 1962, my 21st birthday, congratulated me on getting the scholarship. That ended any doubt. I was going to Harvard Law School in the fall.

John Glenn was going to an even higher place. One of the first group of astronauts chosen for the manned space flight program, known as the Mercury 7, he became the first American to orbit the earth, circling it three times in defiance of gravity. Adolf Eichmann was going nowhere. Convicted of crimes against humanity and war crimes, he was executed by the force of gravity, hung in an Israeli prison.

8. SUMMERTIME BLUES

WHEN SPRING TERM ENDED, Susie went home while I stayed on campus for graduation. We'd been drifting apart, but I didn't feel that it was over between us. We saw each other before she went off to work in a summer camp in Canada, and kept in touch with a few letters. I needed a summer job, and exaggerating my experience as a waiter at Mickey Schwerner's fraternity during my junior year, landed one at Johnnie's Steak House in Queens. The place was popular and the food pricey, so I'd be able to make good money on tips. The chef could see that I was a hard worker and took me under his wing, showing me how to make a Caesar salad and cut the aged prime steaks.

Johnnie's had a jukebox by the bar; the favorite song by far was Tony Bennett's "I Left My Heart in San Francisco," originally released as the B-side of an obscure single. Standing in the bar was another kind of jukebox called a Scopitone, made in France and one of the very first imported into the States. You put in a quarter and pushed a button to select one of 36 three-minute films stored inside on reels. What you saw were primitive music videos, projected on a 24" screen, really huge compared to most home TVs. They typically featured lip-synched singing with scantily clad women dancing, often doing Le Twist, a sensation in France.

The manager asked me if I'd work late to serve a private party which came in regularly after normal hours. They ate in a private room on the second floor, which meant I had to schlep the food, drinks and dirty dishes up and down a narrow set of stairs. Still, it was a chance to earn more tips, and with Susie away, I didn't have any other plans for the evening. Plus, I got a steak dinner every night before the party arrived, along with a mug of real draft Lowenbrau from Germany, not the imitation version brewed in the U.S. and sold in bottles to lovers of "imported" beer. Then the late-night guests showed up, 8 or 10 guys dressed in dark suits. I didn't think much about who they were, just hustled to give them good service. But an investigation by the Justice Department revealed that to promote its musical talent, the William Morris agency cut a deal in 1961 with the notorious Genovese crime family to import Scopitones. I was serving dinner to the mob.

The job kept me busy at night, but I was at loose ends during the day. Sometimes I went to the beach, always a haven for me. But I missed Susie, all the more so hearing the new dance crazes on the

French promotion piece for Scopitone

Matchbook from Johnnie's Steak House

radio but without her to dance with. "The Wah-Wahtusi" by The Orlons reached #2 on the pop singles charts. Dee Dee Sharp had a Top Ten hit with "Gravy (For My Mashed Potatoes)," a follow-up to her smash "Mashed Potato Time," which was #1 on the R&B and #2 on the pop charts (with The Orlons doing backup vocals on both). Little Eva topped the charts with "The Loco-Motion," written by husband-and-wife Gerry Goffin and Carole King.

Before Susie left for summer camp in Canada, we'd talked about my coming up to visit her at the end of the summer, maybe to drive her home. Yet now she was hesitant about seeing me. Still, when I persisted, she gave in and said okay. It was a long drive to the camp, a couple of hours north of Toronto. I was somewhere near Rochester on the New York Thruway, late at night, when it started raining hard. I should have stopped, but I kept telling myself, soon but not yet. Before long I was near Buffalo and then crossed the border into Canada. I pulled into a motel and got maybe four hours sleep.

Back on the road in the morning, I drove to the place where I was staying, near her camp. After checking in, I headed off to see her. "Near" was actually about 20 miles away, down a rolling two-lane back road. It was sparsely populated, I don't think there were 20 houses along it. When I got to the camp, she seemed happy to see me, and introduced me around. We hung out and swam in the lake, the camp a little scandalized by my skimpy swimming briefs I bought in a store Times Square. I drove her back to my motel and found us something to eat. Then we spent a couple of hours making out, still according to her ground rules. Far from Ithaca and Great Neck, from Cornell students and family, it was bliss. But on the drive back to camp in the dark, we hardly spoke. We had such a beautiful day together, but the fire briefly rekindled died down, leaving awkwardness in its ashes.

After dropping her off, saying goodnight and I'll see you tomorrow, I went back down that road yet again. It got pretty cool at night that far north, so I turned on the car heater. The next thing I knew I was being bounced around as the car was heading through the woods. After so little sleep and so much sex, I was exhausted, and the blast of hot air in my face had knocked me out. The car didn't get very far and wasn't going very fast when it came to an abrupt stop against a boulder. I wasn't hurt, other than a bloody nose from my head hitting the steering wheel. The car hardly looked damaged, although I couldn't restart it. Amazingly, on that desolate road I had crashed right next to a house whose owner had just gotten home from a late shift at work. He heard the crash and came right over to help. After seeing that I was okay, he called the police, who had the car towed and drove me back to my motel.

In the morning I walked over to the garage where the tow truck had left the car. While it looked okay on the outside, it had run over some large rocks which ripped the guts out of the engine and drive train. The Herald was history. I was able to call Susie at camp and tell her what had happened and that I wouldn't be driving her back to Great Neck. Then with great trepidation I called home. My mother had not been happy about my road trip, because of course she was going to worry, which was always her way. She was relieved when I was able to convince her that I wasn't hurt, but my father was not pleased. He ran a small import-export business, and quickly determined that because the car was never leaving Canada again, it was considered to have been imported. So it was subject to a stiff duty, 35% of its value when it had crossed the border, even though it was worthless now.

He flew up to Toronto and I took a bus there, so we could deal with the customs paperwork and payment. Then he rented a car to drive home. It was not a pleasant trip, with very little talking. When I was 15, before I could drive, he was taking me somewhere and, classical music lover that he was, listening to WQXR on the car radio. I asked if I could put on a station I liked. He reluctantly agreed, and I tuned to WINS. On came Chuck Berry: "Roll over Beethoven and tell Tchaikovsky the news." My father was outraged. Now, I didn't dare suggest listening to the radio. We rolled along the New York Thruway in silence.

Back in Great Neck, I had no car and wasn't able to get together with Susie before she went back to Cornell and I left for Cambridge. I never saw her again.

9. INDOCTRINATION INTO THE LAW

BY THE WEEKEND BEFORE CLASSES were to begin on Monday, the incoming Harvard Law School Class of 1965 had assembled in Cambridge. Everyone was abuzz with excitement, eager to meet their classmates -- high achievers like them -- and to size them up. These were people with a lot of self-confidence. By now I was becoming more confident, just by virtue of being there among the chosen (and dressing very much the part), after experiencing Vicos and having a beautiful girlfriend in Susie. I felt ready for this new challenge and for the competition. Still, most of us harbored some inner doubt about how we would do in the coming year. Not only competing with our classmates, but finding our place within the intimidating institution that was Harvard Law School. The faculty was the high priesthood, we were mere novitiates.

Most of the dorms were built in the 1950s as part of a complex designed by Walter Gropius, founder of the Bauhaus, the famed school of art and design which flourished in Weimar, Germany until Hitler came to power and Gropius fled to America. But I was glad to have been assigned to the old red-brick residence building Hastings Hall, right on Mass. Ave. opposite the Cambridge Common. It had multiple entries, and at each landing of the four-story building there was a small cluster of suites, each with a shared bedroom and a living room. In a class of 536 students, this made it easy to make friends with my immediate neighbors.

My roomie was Ron Johnson, a quiet and serious Yale grad from New York City. Among my neighbors were roommates Cary Clark and Frank Lena, both Dartmouth alums. Cary was from a small town in northern New Hampshire, a moderate New

England-style Republican. "Freddy" Lena's Italian family owned a very successful chain of submarine sandwich shops around the Boston area. In another room were Rick Sharfman and Ron Alenstein, both from Maryland and both Jewish. Rick came across like a fast-talking brash New Yorker, while blond Ron was a charming soft-spoken Southerner. Also on our landing was Tony Hope, the adopted son of the famed comedian. He never made anything of that, and worked just as hard as any other Harvard Law student.

The women in our class had separate living arrangements. There were just 21 of them. It had only been nine years since the first dozen women graduated from the law school. It was tough to get admitted as a man, so I could only imagine the hurdles these women had to overcome, even to have the chutzpah to apply. They were not fully welcome there. A few old-time faculty members still had not reconciled themselves to having women around. There was not a single woman in any teaching position. Dean Erwin Griswold invited the new group of women to a dinner every year. He went around the table and asked each of them to justify having taken a place in the student body which otherwise would have been filled by a man.

The main event of that weekend was the welcoming address by the Dean. He told us to look to our right, then look to our left. Some of the people sitting on either side would go on to be leaders in law, government and business. We were the crème de la crème, destined for greatness. At least, in his mind, the men were. But he also had a warning in an old legal adage: "He who has himself as a lawyer has a fool for a client." I suppose the idea was to spread the money around in legal fees to your fellow attorneys.

We also had a homework assignment. Yes, homework even before school began, and before most of us had any idea what it was all about. The law school taught by the Socratic method, which meant analyzing and arguing cases in a dialogue with the professor. This was a very different method of learning than in college, where you might get an A in an English history course if you memorized the names and dates of all the kings. So we were assigned to read a case and to be ready for 9 a.m. Monday.

Most of the classes were held in the large lecture rooms in Langdell Hall. Oddly enough for me, it was only yards from the Harvard College physics building, so it seemed as if I hadn't come that far, from physics to law, since my freshman year at Cornell. Inside Langdell, the seats and desks rose in tiers of semicircular arcs from the lectern in a center well. The windows above provided light but were too high to look out, lest you be distracted. The walls were covered with paintings of great (and perhaps not so great) men of the law (no women, of course). Some were hundreds of years old, their subjects in white wigs and bedecked in robes. It was like being in a museum; Harvard Law was said to have the largest collection in the world of such portraits of jurists. Their collective presence looking down on us was intimidating. My taste in art ran more toward Vincent Van Gogh and Pablo Picasso.

As though he had stepped out of a painting, one of the legends of Harvard Law could still be seen shuffling around the halls of the school with a cane. Roscoe Pound served as Dean from 1916 (when Woodrow Wilson was President) to 1936 (when FDR was). He wore an eye shade and a celluloid shirt collar, looking very much like a man from the past. Before his legal career, he was an eminent botanist. Now, at 92, he was working on a big project he could not possibly finish in his remaining years. But he came into his office just about every day, a living example of dedication to work and to the law.

Our class was divided into four sections with about 135 students in each, and you went to all of the same courses with everyone in your section. This made the class size more manageable, and easier to get to know your classmates in your section. For our section, the first class was property law, taught by A. James Casner, the author of the leading casebook on property, used in many law schools. A Harvard Law institution in his own right, he was the very embodiment of the imperious law school professor. The assigned case, a legal education classic, was *Pierson v. Post*, about a hunter on horseback (Post) in pursuit of a fox, which is captured and killed by Pierson. The issue was: who had the right to the fox?

I thought to myself, fox hunting? What century was this? Actually, property law was based on rules, often arcane and convoluted, that went back centuries in England.

The issue uppermost on the minds of me and my classmates was not so much who got the dead fox, but which of us would be ensnared by Prof. Casner as the first victim of an intense grilling on the case. It would not be one of the women in the class. Casner had an infamous policy of not calling on female law students except one day a year, which he called "Ladies' Day." When he emerged from a small door behind the lectern, the nervous whispering in the room stopped immediately. We all sat in assigned seats in every class, and the professor had a large chart with headshots of everyone and their seat number. While Casner scanned the chart, we held our breath. This was the moment we'd been dreading all weekend.

"Mr. Black," he said. Poor Jerry froze in his seat while everyone else quietly breathed a sigh of relief. But our turn would come, including the "ladies," because none of our other professors treated the women any differently than the men. We all quickly learned that you'd better have read the assigned cases before class, or face public humiliation, easy prey for the prof. Law school was boot camp for the mind. They tore you down, along with what you thought you knew, only to build you up stronger mentally, able to defend your position in a legal argument.

Brilliant as they all were, not all the faculty were autocratic like Casner. My favorite professor as a "One-L" (first-year student) was Paul Bator. He was born in Budapest, Hungary, as was my maternal grandfather, but had no accent, unlike my former Polish computer professor at Cornell. He graduated first in his class at Harvard Law and was president of the Law Review. They didn't come any smarter. Just 33 years old, he was as lively and engaging in class as Casner was reserved and aloof. He taught civil procedure, which was about the "rules of the game" in civil trials (criminal trials have their own set of rules). Math also had its own rules and procedures, so Bator's course was a natural for me.

10. A Taste of Harvard Square

OUR PROFESSORS GAVE US plenty of food for thought, as did our casebooks and the small study groups we formed to help each other cope. For real food, we usually went to the cafeteria in Harkness Commons, part of the Gropius complex. My first time there, we were moving in front of the steam tables while the elderly ladies behind the counter spooned our food choices onto our plates. I was puzzled when one of them asked me, "Buh-day-diz?" Turning to my friends for help, they pointed to the container she was hovering over. Potatoes! Yes, please. She wasn't speaking in tongues, just a heavy Boston Irish dialect.

The law school was just north of Harvard Square, and sometimes I liked to get away for a little while and wander down there, looking in the windows of the small shops and bookstores. It was as low-key and casual as the law school was high-pressure and buttoned-up. During the day you might see Harvard College professors and MTA bus drivers, Radcliffe girls and elderly ladies, and always students with their green book bags slung over their shoulders. By mid-afternoon local high school students came there to hang out.

There were plenty of cheap places to eat: Elsie's roast beef sandwiches, Bartley's Burger Cottage, and the Tasty, a hole-in-the-wall diner in the middle of the Square which stayed open late. There were also four cafeterias to choose from. At one of them, Albiani's, I noticed a traditional New England dish on the menu: whale steak. If I could eat goat meat and guinea pig, I could eat whale. It was a heavy piece of meat. By this time the commercial whaling industry, once a major economic driver in New England, was essentially over. I don't know where Albiani's got the whale meat from, but it wasn't the only place in the Square serving it. The high-end restaurant Chez Dreyfus advertised "Venison and Bear Meat when in Season," but also boasted of "Whale Meat at all times."

A group of us formed an informal dining club, and went to a different restaurant every Sunday evening. Since a couple of us had cars, we ventured into Boston to sample the food there. We

Postcard for Elsie's, with Elsie and her husband

went to Durgin Park, down in the rough-edged commercial market district, where the slab of roast beef just about hung over the edges of the plate, truly a whale-sized portion. And of course we had to eat at Locke-Ober's, one of the oldest restaurants in Boston, where everyone who was anyone in Boston ate, including John F. Kennedy. But not if you were a woman, because you would not be admitted to its all-male dining rooms.

Among the places we tried, my favorite was the fish store in Inman Square, only a mile or so from Hastings Hall. It had sawdust on the floor and a mouthwatering array of fresh seafood for sale, sitting on ice in display cases. You could also have them broil or fry a piece of fish and eat it at a picnic table, clam shack style with cole slaw and french fries on the side. I was fascinated by the piercing light gray Irish eyes of my waitress, as silvery as the fish. The place had an appropriate name for hosting our group of law students: Legal Seafood.

Aside from food breaks and brief forays into the Square, almost all my time was spent in class, at the law library or studying back in the dorm. Law school was all-consuming, no time for thinking about past girlfriends or getting a date, precious little chance to listen to the radio. I did manage to catch Arnie "Woo Woo" Ginsburg's show, which was as loopy and chaotic as my Cornell roommates Bill and Mike had said. But popular music was at a low ebb. Peter, Paul & Mary had a #10 hit with, of all things, a remake of a lefty folk song, "If I Had a Hammer." Arnie broke a novelty record by a guy from Somerville, a small city next door to Cambridge. It rose to #1 on the national charts, "Monster Mash" by Bobby "Boris" Pickett and The Crypt-Kickers.

11. LEARNING FROM THE MASTERS

ONE AFTERNOON I TOOK TIME to attend the Model Trial held every fall, in which Cambridge residents (not students) sat on a jury hearing a mock case argued by two professors. One of them was Robert E. Keeton, whose field of expertise was insurance law and torts (wrongful but noncriminal acts). A Texan, Keeton spoke to the jurors slowly in plain and straightforward language, as though he were just a country boy. It was a masterful performance, a vivid demonstration of persuasive communication.

Goings-on in the outside world scarcely penetrated our law school cocoon, but one event was inescapable, the Cuban missile crisis, which began in mid-October. Unknown to the American public, the U.S. had put ballistic missiles in Turkey and Italy, capable of reaching the Soviet Union. And in April 1961, the Central Intelligence Agency sponsored a failed attempt by Cuban exiles to invade the island at the Bay of Pigs and spark a counter-revolution against the Castro regime. At the request of the Cuban government, and for their own military purposes, the Soviet Union secretly began installing nuclear missiles there in the late summer of 1962.

Proof of their presence by an American U-2 spy plane flight that fall led to a blockade of the island by the U.S. Navy, coupled with a demand to remove the missiles already in place. The stand-off between the two superpowers lasted for 13 days and was the closest we'd ever come to nuclear war. It was a terrifying situation, if anything even more so than the Berlin Crisis. Like my fellow students, I tried to keep focused on my studies, an escape from what was happening out in the world. Once again Kennedy and Khrushchev negotiated their way out of a dangerous confrontation. The Soviets pulled their missiles from Cuba, while the U.S. removed our ballistic missiles from Turkey.

In the middle of the crisis a true man of peace came to the school as one of the distinguished speakers presented by the Harvard Law School Forum: the Rev. Dr. Martin Luther King Jr. I had seen Dr. King address the crowd at the "Youth March for Integrated Schools" in 1959. But here was an opportunity to see him in a different light, speaking to a few hundred Harvard professors and students. He was eloquent, with his familiar mellifluous voice and preacherly delivery. He was erudite, citing legal cases, philosophers and writers. He was engaging, speaking to this scholarly audience about the three words for love in ancient Greek. And he was ennobling, with an impassioned argument for nonviolence. His main policy point was that the full force of the federal government, not just that of the judicial branch, had to be brought to bear against segregation, and that the key was removing legal barriers to "Negroes" registering and voting.

Mid-term exams gave us our first chance to learn how well we were doing, and to compare ourselves to our classmates. Your standing in class based on the final exams would determine who made Law Review, the ultimate goal we were all supposedly shooting for. But I was already feeling some uncertainty about what I was doing at law school. I proved that I could get into Harvard, and proved that I could compete against the best when I scored very high on the mid-terms. But did I really want to become a lawyer, if the law school grind was what it took to get there? There were times in class or in the library when my mind wandered back to Peru, a mental escape to a place removed from law school in every way imaginable.

In a sense it was unfortunate that I did well on the mid-terms, because it made me overconfident I could ace the finals in the spring. So I eased off the gas, a big mistake. It's not that I didn't keep studying, because you'd quickly fall hopelessly behind if you didn't. But I was no longer driven by the fear of not cutting it against the competition, or even failing. I knew I'd do well on the final exams, but I wasn't giving it absolutely everything to get there.

The big event at the law school in the spring was the finals of the Ames Moot Court Competition, the oldest such competition at American law schools. Through a series of elimination rounds, two teams emerged to face off in the final round, which typically took place before a three-judge panel which included a Justice of the U.S. Supreme Court. Each eight-person team included two oral presenters arguing the case, with the others doing supporting research.

The argument was announced by posters hung throughout the school. I noticed that one of the oralists that spring was one Pierre S. DuPont IV. Yes, those DuPonts. Although I was a good student on paper, I was not one who would voluntarily speak up in class to display his legal acumen, or perhaps to look like a fool. So I could not imagine myself in DuPont's position. He came from a WASPy world of wealth I'd never know, and as a finals oralist had attained a level of accomplishment and confidence I felt I could never achieve.

On a Sunday night in late April 1963, I witnessed a very different kind of oral presentation. I should have been studying, with final exams just around the corner, but instead I was on a long line waiting to get into a folk music club at 47 Mount Auburn Street. I wasn't much of a folk music fan, and I wasn't even sure what I was doing there, but I'd picked up on the buzz around the Square about someone who was going to play there that night. I'd never heard of him, yet somehow I was drawn there. It was hootenanny night at Club 47, when a succession of performers each did two or three songs. I didn't know who they were, but the stars of the Cambridge / Boston folk scene were all out that night at the hoot.

At one point Joan Baez came out and sang. I did know who she was. Then she introduced a scrawny little guy to do his turn. His last song, an antiwar anthem with searing lyrics, rang true after the Cuban missile crisis. But it was the power of his delivery that floored me. He was a folkie with an acoustic guitar, but his music hit me in the gut, like hearing Elvis sing "Heartbreak Hotel" for the first time. I'd never heard anything like it, half-sung half-spoken in a nasal voice while he pounded out a repetitive rhythm on the guitar. The song was called "Masters of War," his name was Bob Dylan.

12. ROUTE 66

WE WERE ALL UNDER PRESSURE as final exams approached. But for me, it was heightened by my not studying hard enough, which conflicted with my ingrained compulsion to do well in school. Subconsciously, it was gnawing away at me. I developed abdominal pain which was diagnosed at the student infirmary as an incipient ulcer. I was put on Maalox and told to lay off spicy food. I wasn't surprised that I scored reasonably well on the finals, but not good enough to make Law Review, which required finishing in the top 25.

Many of my classmates were off to summer jobs at law firms, long hours for low pay. But I needed a break from all that, and wasn't sure if I had a future at law school. Through Peter Schuck I met a good friend of his, Richard Zeckhauser, also from Great Neck, who was studying economics at Harvard, not law. He was going to California to work for the summer at the RAND Corporation, a leading think tank in Santa Monica. Was I interested in driving there with him and sharing an apartment? I wanted to get away from Cambridge and the law. The Pacific Ocean beckoned; I could get a job waiting tables at night and have days free to go to the beach. So I said to Dick: when are we leaving? After a short visit home to see my family and to pack, it was early June when we two young men headed west in his Ford Falcon.

Until then, the furthest west I'd been was Buffalo, New York, when Dave Scudellari and I drove from Cornell to go to the harness racing track there. As far south as it was, Peru was not even as far west as Ithaca. The scenery got more interesting when we motored west out of St. Louie on Route 66, "the highway that's the best," in the words of the classic song. "Route 66" was originally a hit for Nat King Cole in 1946, then was recorded by Bing Crosby with The Andrews Sisters, by Perry Como, and by Chuck Berry. The road was in its glory days as a tourist route, and we got our kicks seeing roadside attractions like the teepee-shaped Wigwam Motel. We stopped off along the way at the Grand Canyon, then took 66 all the way into Santa Monica, where it ended at the Pacific Ocean.

We found a furnished apartment near the beach, a typical mid-century California two-story building surrounding a courtyard with tables and chairs, palm trees and a swimming pool. We were joined there by my law school buddy Rick Sharfman, who drove out from Maryland in his Corvette convertible, like the car featured on the hit TV show *Route 66*. I think Rick would have made the trip just to be cruising that road in that car, but in fact he had a summer job with a law firm in L.A.

13. SANTA MONICA

To GET AROUND I BOUGHT myself a little 50cc Honda motorcycle, and went looking for a job at a restaurant. I checked out a place in Santa Monica called the San Francisco, an early theme restaurant. Inside it was elaborately done up like a Victorian bordello on the Barbary Coast of Frisco, with velvet flocked red wallpaper and ornate brass lighting fixtures. You'd think they'd want appropriately-dressed (or semi-dressed) beautiful young women to complete the illusion. Instead, it had a wait staff of handsome young men. They liked how I looked and my Ivy League pedigree, so I was hired. The menu of American and Frenchified food was pricey, and the tips were good. Five nights a week I rode there on my Honda wearing the tux that was required on the job.

That left me free to hit the beach every day. It was always sunny, and just two blocks away. An area at the land end of the Santa Monica pier was known as Muscle Beach, the birthplace of the bodybuilding culture. The guys there spent their days working out on the weight-lifting and exercise equipment, or just hanging out and flexing their muscles for all to admire. Several cheap restaurants and bars just beyond the sand provided a convenient place for me to sit and watch the spectacle for a while. But I was more interested in the beach and watching the California girls.

Someone at work told me that the place to go was Will Rogers State Park, a few miles up the coast. So every day, after Dick and Rick went to work, I'd toodle up there on my little Honda. It was a popular surfing beach, where I'd watch the surfers sit out in the water waiting for a good wave, then jump up on their boards and ride to shore. Lacking the budget to buy a board, I became an avid bodysurfer, spending hours every day in the water when I wasn't just lying around sunning.

The waves were a lot higher and rougher than I was used to at the beaches on Long Island. Once I got caught in a big one which churned over me – wipeout! -- and left me tumbling under water and disoriented. With the sand stirred up and diffusing the light, for a few seconds I was totally disoriented, and couldn't tell up from down. But after finding my way back to the surface, I went ashore to catch my breath. Then I swam back out to wait for the next wave to come rolling in.

The Southern California surfing culture began to penetrate the national awareness in 1962 when surf music made it onto the Billboard charts. The Beach Boys first single, the doo-wopish "Surfin'", only made it to #75 in early '62. Their second, "Surfin' Safari", was their break-out hit, rising to #14 that summer, with its B-side car song "409" riding along to #76. By the time I was getting ready to go to California in 1963, their "Surfin' USA" reached #3, and Jan & Dean's #1 hit "Surf City" (written by Brian Wilson of The Beach Boys) declared "Surf City, here we come!"

There I was, in surf city. The Southern California surfing crowd was proud to be the hottest thing going. Then The Beach Boys released a song that went beyond the usual fun of surfing and cars to touch the emotions. The ballad "Surfer Girl" only made it to #7 nationally, but it was an instant sensation on L.A. radio. Everyone had a transistor radio on their beach blanket. As I walked along the water's edge, it seemed to be playing everywhere all the time. It spoke to me too: "I have watched you on the shore / Standing by the ocean's roar." I was really aching, seeing all those beautiful tanned bodies in their bikinis, but so unapproachable. To them I was all wrong, a hodad, a dark-haired outsider in swim briefs, not a blond California surfer in baggies. As I strolled on the boardwalk not long after arriving in Santa Monica, a group of teenage girls giggled and pointed at my preppy madras shorts.

When I came home from the beach every day, I'd shower off the sand before putting on my tux to go to work. To get that surfer look, I began combing hydrogen peroxide through my wet hair, which gradually turned dirty blond. One afternoon, when I was off work that night, I was lounging in the pool when I noticed someone I hadn't seen around before. An ash blonde, maybe a little older than me, with a beautiful body barely covered by a skimpy bikini, three small pieces of white cloth held on by strings tied in bows. She wasn't shy, and seeing this tanned and fit young guy, struck up a conversation with me. She'd come to L.A. recently from Hungary, where I also had roots. Her name was Zsuzsa, the equivalent in Hungarian of Susan.

She wasn't put off by my brief swimwear, which was normal in Europe. Before long we were up in her apartment and I was pulling on her strings. That began an intense sexual relationship over several weeks. We fucked all over her apartment, in the living room, in the bedroom, in the kitchen, in the stall shower, in the bathtub, and back again. Compared to Zsuzsa, I was a sexual neophyte when we met, but not for long. Forget the surfer girls, she was all woman. Dick and Rick teased me about my prolonged absences from our apartment -- a little jealous perhaps? -- but I hungered for my lady from Hungary, as did she for me.

As the days passed, I was trying to decide what to do when summer ended. Should I go back to Cambridge and take Zsuzsa with me? Or should I stay with her in California? I even thought about taking her with me to Long Island and opening the first surf shop there. Then I heard from my mom that I got an unexpected invitation to a wedding in late August. It was from my roommate at Cornell, Bill Pagell, so I felt that I had to go, and then I'd figure out what to do next. I sold the Honda and flew home. And once I was back east, faced with the new semester at Harvard, my California dream faded away.

Martin Luther King, Jr. spoke of his dream on August 28 at the March on Washington for Jobs and Freedom: "One day this nation will rise up and live up to its creed, 'We hold these truth to be self evident: that all men are created equal.' I have a dream." It was followed by a nightmare less than three weeks later, when a black Baptist church in Birmingham, Alabama was bombed by Ku Klux Klanners and four girls were killed.

14. BACK IN CAMBRIDGE

I WAS AMBIVALENT ABOUT GOING back to law school, but my father put a lot of pressure on me. As a young child he'd emigrated from Belarus to the U.S., and graduated Phi Beta Kappa from the City College of New York. He was a strong adherent of the Jewish belief in education as the foundation for social and economic advancement. I knew he was right, don't quit now. He even offered to buy me a car. I took the bribe, and left for Cambridge in a 1955 XK-140MC Jaguar roadster, which I bought used for only $900. On the radio, Bob Dylan was no longer the obscure folkie I'd seen in the spring; Peter Paul and Mary's version of his "Blowin' in the Wind" was #2 on the charts. It was the heyday of the "girl groups": Martha and the Vandellas ("Heat Wave"), The Crystals ("Then He Kissed Me"), The Ronettes ("Be My Baby").

The Jag was supposedly once owned by the musical stars Marge and Gower Champion. It had a brilliant red custom paint job set off by a black leather interior. Driving around town the dual mufflers rumbled loudly, but accelerate on the highway and they roared. I was curious how fast it could go. Early one Sunday morning I took it out on the Mass Pike. There was only one other car on the road when the Jag screamed past it at 125 mph. It was designed to perform at high speed. Some things work better going all out.

Because my plans had been uncertain at the end of first year, I hadn't made housing arrangements. Rick Sharfman and Ron Alenstein let me sleep on the sofa in their dorm suite for a couple of days, while I went apartment hunting. I found a place in a large house just across the Cambridge line in Somerville, near Porter

Ready to return to law school, with bleached surfer hair

Jaguar XK-140MC roadster

Square. There were eight of us in the house, each with our own bedroom, a mixed group from law school, architecture school and grad school. By the time I settled in I'd already missed a lot of classes, which made it that much harder to get back in the law school routine.

The weather didn't help me focus on school. It was an unusually warm and sunny fall, perfect for driving around with the top down, cruising through the Square like I was back in L.A. and enjoying the attention as people checked out the Jag. One October afternoon I parked my car on Mass. Ave. and walked into Harvard Yard. Sitting on the ground under a large tree facing Widener Library, enjoying the sun, I lazily watched people going to and fro, especially the girls. I suddenly became aware of someone standing over me. Looking up, I could see hazily against the backlight of a brilliant blue sky that she was tall, statuesque and beautiful. She said, "Do you mind if I sit down?"

15. BETH

OF COURSE I DIDN'T MIND. Her name was Beth. She confessed that she'd been watching me for a while, and after hesitating, got up her nerve and came over. We had the usual get-to-know-you conversation. I could see she was impressed that I was at Harvard Law. She was a freshman at Radcliffe who'd just graduated from Miss Porter's School in Farmington, Connecticut. I'd never heard of it, but she explained that it was a prep school for the sheltered daughters of the very rich. Her roommate there, Janet Auchincloss, was a younger half-sister of Jackie Kennedy, who also had gone to Miss Porter's. Beth grew up in a posh suburb of Pittsburgh, where her father was a corporate executive. Through her mother she was a direct descendant of Civil War General William Tecumseh Sherman.

I was a little overwhelmed by all this, since she was from a social class that was way out of my league. She could tell, given

Beth

my ignorance about Miss Porter's. Yet she wasn't being boastful, and spoke of her background almost sardonically, as if it was something she had to get out of the way in our introductions. For someone so young she was very self-confident, more so than I. She came across as brash and tough, spunky, with an offbeat sense of humor, a bemused way of seeing things and expressing herself. She was really fun to talk with, and we lolled away the afternoon together under the tree, our mutual sexual attraction obvious but unspoken. The heat intensified when I gave her a ride back to her dorm in my red sex machine.

We began seeing each other, our feelings for each other growing. She confided that one of her goals coming to Cambridge was to lose her virginity. So she did, on the mattress on the floor of my bedroom. Afterwards, she was all smiles -- she'd done it! I was smiling too, never having deflowered a young woman, and seeing how happy about it she was. In a sense I was a convenient and only-too-willing co-conspirator in her effort to break free of her background. And for her it was all the sweeter that I was Jewish, not something her parents would approve of (not that they'd approve of her having sex either). Maybe her plan had been to consummate her rebellion by fucking some Harvard guy and then moving on. But she fell in love with that guy, and I fell in love with her.

Beth asked me to visit Miss Porter's with her, so I could see it for myself. She wanted to show me off to the girls there – look what I got! – signaling that she was no longer a virgin. So we drove down to Farmington one sunny afternoon. I would have dressed for the occasion, to look like a Harvard Law student. But no, she wanted us to go in jeans. We pulled into the parking lot, top down. Some faces appeared at school windows when they heard the car growling. Beth greeted a school official and introduced me, then led me through the library. It was dead silent, as the rules required. It was rare for the girls to even see a young male during the middle of the week, much less in the library. I could feel their eyes on me as we walked, their repressed sexuality permeating the room. No wonder Beth wanted to get laid after leaving Miss Porter's.

16. Dropping Out and Dropping In

Back in Cambridge, time had run out for law school and me. On a Friday afternoon I went to the office of Louis Toepfer, Vice Dean and Director of Admissions, whose name was on that letter "pleased to report" I'd been admitted. I told him that I needed a break, and signed the required paperwork to formally withdraw from the school. It was embarrassing to acknowledge in writing that I'd failed. Dean Toepfer informed me that I was entitled to return if I chose to, but that if I didn't before September, I'd lose my place in the class and would have to reapply to get back in. I didn't know if I'd be back, but for now it was over.

As I drove to the Square, I was relieved that the weight of Harvard Law School was no longer hanging over me. I wanted to keep seeing Beth, but planned to take off for the weekend and drive somewhere, just to get away. Needing a bite to eat and a cup of coffee before hitting the road, I noticed a little café downstairs on Boylston Street, the Patisserie Francaise. I ate and relaxed at an outdoor table, enjoying the fall sunshine and watching the people passing by.

When I got back in the car and started it, the engine was misfiring. With twelve cylinders and dual overhead camshafts for each cylinder, there was a lot that could go wrong. Jaguars were notorious for their unreliability. The joke was that if you owned one, you needed to drive at all times with a mechanic in the passenger seat. I got the car up to the garage a block away at the corner of Mt. Auburn Street, and was told I'd have to leave it there, they couldn't get to it until next week. So much for my getaway.

Beth knew of my plans, so she was surprised and happy to see me when I showed up at her dorm. Over the weekend I realized how much I wanted to continue being with her. But what was I going to do, hang around the Square as a dropout while she went to Radcliffe? I decided that if I was going to stay in Cambridge, I might as well be going to school too. So on Monday morning I returned to the admissions office. They were hardly expecting to see me so soon, if ever again, but made no comment about my reappearance. With the appropriate decorum they prepared the paperwork, and I signed myself back into law school.

The qualifying round of the Ames Moot Court Competition was about to get underway. Students joined one of the many Ames clubs, typically named for a professor or some legal legend. Since I was unaffiliated, my friend Cary Clark got me into the Keeton Equity club, which was under the guidance of the Professor Keeton I'd watched with admiration at the Model Trial. Like Cary, most of the club members were Dartmouth grads. That made me, from archrival Cornell, the odd man out in "Indian" country. In the competition itself, each of four two-man teams argued a case against a team from another club. Lawyers and upperclassmen judged our performance. Teamed with Cary and being poorly prepared, I brought us down to defeat. But the other three Keeton pairs won. With a 3-1 record, that qualified us for the quarterfinal round in the spring.

17. TRAGEDY

EARLY ONE FRIDAY AFTERNOON in late November I went to meet Rick and Ron at their dorm to walk together to our 2:00 class. When I entered the room, it was dark, except for the light from a small black and white TV set. Strange for them to be watching TV in the middle of the day. Walter Cronkite was talking about the assassination of President Kennedy. We were all profoundly shocked. It was a blow to our rationality as law students. This was not how we expected our Constitution and government to work, presidential succession by reason of murder. We felt that JFK was one of us, a Harvard man. Some law school professors were on leave serving in his Administration.

Classes were cancelled, of course. I drove over to Beth's dorm around 4:00, when she was expecting me to pick her up. After I'd waited a few minutes, she came out, chatty and high-spirited as usual. This surprised me; I was almost angry about her seeming to be indifferent to the day's events. Don't you know what happened?, I asked. No, what?, I was taking a nap. It pained me to have to tell her that President Kennedy had been assassinated. She looked at me in utter disbelief, maybe the only person in Cambridge at that moment who was unaware of his murder. No wonder, she remarked, everyone in the dorm seemed so gloomy when she came down to meet me. We all felt an intangible connection to JFK. Having roomed at Miss Porter's with Jackie's half-sister, for Beth it was more personal.

America was in mourning, nowhere more deeply than in Cambridge. On Saturday I walked alone down to the Yard. A service was being held in Memorial Church. The place was full, but I didn't really want to go in anyhow. I just sat on the steps, sharing the grief of the mourners emanating from inside the building. On Sunday morning I met up with a group of law school friends at the House of Pancakes. We often had brunch together before hitting the books. We were astounded when the news broke that Lee Harvey Oswald had been shot and killed at the Dallas jailhouse. There was no way we could study that day. But getting back to the routine of classes and schoolwork gradually helped life return to normal. Beth and I had each other, and we needed each other. Grief brought us closer together.

At Christmas vacation I drove Beth home to meet her family in Pennsylvania. The Jag may have been hot, but its heating system was not. It was a long cold ride, made worse by the wind coming through the leaky ragtop. When we arrived at her house, large but not ostentatious, her parents greeted me politely but coolly. They knew I was a Harvard Law student, and Jewish, but I didn't know what else she'd told them. I was not comfortable being there, but at least her two sisters and three brothers were friendly toward me.

We arrived in time to see the local Hunt Club conduct one of its regular fox hunts. Shades of *Pierson v. Post*, fox hunting! But not really, because there was no fox involved. Rather, a bag of meat or animal droppings was dragged around the countryside to create a scent which the foxhounds tried to follow, with riders and horses in close pursuit. Beth's father was the leader of the hunt as Master of Foxhounds, which entitled him to wear a bright red blazer called a "Pink coat."

The participants in the hunt gathered in front of her house. The dogs were barking and straining at their leashes. They knew what was up, and were eager to have at it. The horses were also excited and ready to run. At the blast of a hunting horn they all took off, the dogs eagerly leading the way in pursuit of the fox that wasn't. Beth drove us out to a place where we could get a good view of the hunt racing across the countryside. I had to admit, it was quite a spectacle, and a demanding athletic endeavor for the riders, the horses and the dogs. Afterwards, there was a big reception back at the house, with drinks, food, and a blazing fire to warm the hunters and guests. She whispered to me that such-and-such a person was so-and-so, Mellons and such, the cream of Pittsburgh society.

I went with Beth to her coming out as a debutante at the Cinderella Ball, a major annual social event in Pittsburgh. Not being used to formalwear, I needed help from one of her brothers to tie my bow tie. He told me I looked like Arthur Schlesinger Jr., who had left his professorship at Harvard to serve as a Special Assistant in the Kennedy White House. I suppose I should have been flattered by the comparison to this brilliant man. But I didn't think I looked at all like Schlesinger, not a particularly good-looking guy.

Beth came back to New York with me, where she met my parents. Even though she was a *shiksa* (not Jewish), they were far more welcoming to her than her parents had been to me. The main purpose of the trip for her was to participate in another coming-out event, at the Waldorf-Astoria. This time I tied my own bow tie.

Beth and me at my parents' house, dressed for a debutante ball

18. YEAH! YEAH! YEAH!

AFTER THE HOLIDAYS, I managed to get through mid-year exams. Even so, I still wasn't fully readjusted to being a law student. My class attendance was erratic, but I was putting in some study time at the library. Sometimes Beth would come to meet me there, causing a stir as she strode through and heads looked up from their law books. On a Sunday night, February 9, I took a break from working in the library and walked over to the Harkness Commons. It had a large lounge with tables and chairs, some sofas, and a TV set. The room could easily hold 100 or more, but there were only half a dozen guys watching TV. At 8:00, it was time for "The Ed Sullivan Show," which I hadn't seen in quite a while. In my high school days I rarely missed it, catching performances by Elvis Presley, Buddy Holly, Fats Domino, Bo Diddley and more of my favorite rock 'n' rollers.

I was at Harkness that night to see a band I'd read about in *The New York Times*, a sensation in England. Ed Sullivan opened his show and went right to them. "Ladies and Gentlemen...The Beatles!" The audience for the show was mostly young girls, who began screaming even before the band began to sing, "Close your eyes and I'll kiss you, tomorrow I'll miss you." Wow, what's going on here? I could hear the influence of American rock 'n roll in their music, but these Beatles had created a completely new sound, as well as a new look with their long shaggy hair. "She loves you yeah yeah yeah!" And we loved them, joyous relief from the gloom hanging over the country since the Kennedy assassination 79 days ago. After the Sullivan show The Beatles went to The Peppermint Lounge, where Ringo twisted to The Starliters playing my old favorite, Barrett Strong's "Money," which The Beatles themselves had recorded.

I walked back to the law library, amazed at what I'd just witnessed, a tectonic shift in popular music. "I Want to Hold Your Hand" was #1 on the charts. But the inner sanctum of the Harvard Law School library was impervious to such trivial matters.

From the raucous sound of The Beatles and the shrieks of the girls, I returned to the stillness of people quietly turning the pages of law books, scratching notes on yellow legal pads, and speaking in a whisper, when they spoke at all.

19. Ames Games

I WAS AT THE LIBRARY that night preparing for the Ames Competition. The quarterfinal round was little more than a month away, on March 12. The Keeton club members were now working together as one eight-member team. Two of us – Norm Slonaker and Gary Spiess – were chosen as oralists to present our case before the panel of judges, the other six (including me) doing research and helping to write the legal briefs detailing our legal position. Andy Bartlett was team captain. His wife Stephanie was also on the team, the first married couple competing together in Ames. I was glad to be part of the team and contributing. When I put my mind to it, I was a more than capable researcher and writer. Andy made a good captain, keeping everyone involved and focused on their tasks. We all spent long hours in the library, in pursuit of our goal of winning our quarterfinal matchup and making it to the semis. That sometimes meant neglecting our normal classwork, which made some people uneasy, but I had plenty of experience at doing that.

The fictional case was about someone injured in a car accident while failing to wear a seat belt. The issue was whether by not using the belt the injured party had been negligent and therefore not entitled to recover damages. A jury had awarded her $300,000. The Keeton team was assigned the role of appealing the award and asking that it be thrown out. [Professor Keeton was soon to become the co-inventor of no-fault insurance. It replaced the system, especially corrupt in Massachusetts at the time, in which people in car accidents faked injuries with the connivance of doctors -- "Oh my neck, it's killing me!" -- and sued insurance companies for outlandish sums.]

The opposing team was Casner Equity. Having seen several of them in class confidently displaying their legal acumen, we definitely felt like we were the underdogs. One of their two oralists, Henry Weiss, was a Jewish kid from Brooklyn who went to Oxford for his B.A. and came back with an English accent. He sounded like a distinguished barrister. The three-judge panel included a federal district court judge and two lawyers. They were to rule on which team did the better job, not necessarily which side of the case would have prevailed in court. Their verdict was for Keeton. That put us in the semifinals next fall. Sorry, Henry old chap.

I'd been so caught up in Ames that I hardly knew what was happening in the outside world. There hadn't been much earth-shaking news, other than the Great Alaskan Earthquake, which at 9.2 was the most powerful ever recorded in North America, killing 139 people. But The Beatles were still shaking up popular music. By early April "Can't Buy Me Love" was #1, with "Twist and Shout" #2 and three other Beatles singles completing the top five. It was an unprecedented feat, having all top five records, plus they had seven more songs in the top 100. Of course I bought the *Meet the Beatles!* LP, but my favorite new album when it came out later in the spring was *England's Newest Hit Makers, The Rolling Stones.* On it they took a rockin' ride on "Route 66."

At the time of JFK's assassination, we were still living in a 1950's Cold War world. It was all about the USA versus the USSR. The #1 single in America that November was "Dominique" by The Singing Nun. Now JFK was gone, more American soldiers were being sent to a place called Vietnam, and the Stones were singing "I Just Want to Make Love to You." At Saturday night house parties, we all danced enthusiastically to our new records. Beth and I loudly and laughingly sang along with The Beatles, "I want to hold your gland!" The '60s was happening.

20. ME AND MY GAL

BETH AND I WERE still happening too. I especially loved her sense of humor. It was her idea to sing "gland" instead of "hand," and it was her idea to make a pair of earrings from two objects I had. We went to a custom jeweler in Harvard Square called The Cockeyed Dove. I put the objects on the counter for the proprietor to examine. He looked at them kind of suspiciously and with a heavy French accent asked what they were. Teeth, I said. What kind of teeth, he wondered. Human teeth. At that he reacted with horror and threw us out of his shop. The teeth were two extra canines -- my dentist called them supernumerary lateral incisors -- which grew in behind the canines I already had. He pulled them cleanly, with the long root intact, and I'd saved them. We did find a willing jeweler, who made them into a pair of dangle earrings she proudly wore.

Still, it was not all fun and sex with me and Beth. While I sometimes made light of skipping my law classes, the "A" student inside me was not happy about it. I didn't realize how angry I was at myself for pissing away two years at one of the leading educational institutions in the world. This sometimes came out as anger at Beth. She had her own issues, dealing with her relationship with her parents and the pressure they put on her to live up to their expectations while disapproving of her Jewish boyfriend. And that really ticked me off, so I pushed back at her, making matters worse. She may have lost her virginity and rebelled against her past. But in some ways she was still the rich girl she'd been when we met, which I resented, and still wanting her parents approval. We came from different worlds, which at times became a barrier to understanding and accepting one another.

21. ANOTHER YEAR GONE BY

ONCE AGAIN I MANAGED to get through another year at law school. I showed up at my Tax Law course in the spring after being absent all year – taxes was not my cup of tea. When I took an unassigned seat in the back of the room, the professor noticed and made a point of welcoming me to the class, to laughter from my classmates. What saved me in final exams was my ability to cram by reading on my own. There was a certain way we'd been taught to open our large case books when they were new, so as not to crack their bindings. You carefully folded back a cluster of pages on the right, then a cluster of pages on the left, and so on and so on, until the book was flexible. When I did that with an unopened case book at the library a few weeks before finals, I could see a guy who was studying at the same table watch me in disbelief.

For students aiming to further their legal career, the summer after second year you worked for a law firm or had some other law-related job. But spending the summer in an office was not what I had in mind. After surfing in the Pacific last year, this time I was hoping to head out into the Atlantic on a cruise ship by working as a waiter. You got a job on a ship through the union hiring hall in New York. But there was a Catch-22: you had to belong to the union to get a job, but to get your union card required having previously had a job at sea, to get which you would have needed a union card.

A business colleague of my father in the shipping business provided me a letter which got me around the Catch-22 and into the union. I also had a "Z" card, a required form of I.D. issued by the Coast Guard, which I got in Santa Monica when I first thought about going to sea instead of back to school. So there I was, with my seaman's papers in hand, ready to ship out.

Beth and I had moved from my apartment in Somerville to a small house in Cambridge we rented for the summer, along with one of my former roommates, Jeff, an architecture student. She wasn't happy about my going to sea, even though it was just for a couple of months. But after Peru and California, I felt that urge

Dinner party at my parents' house in Roslyn Heights, 1961:
(L-R) Nikka Cottin, Nat Schwerner, Annie Schwerner and my father

again to go somewhere far away, and by shipping out I could bring back some money.

So I left for New York to spend my nights at my parents' house and my days hanging around the hiring hall. When your name was called, you could sign on for a job opening on a ship, usually departing in a day or two. I was the lowest man on the totem pole, so the jobs were taken before my name ever got called. Finally, after several boring days waiting, I got the call. Problem was, it was to fill a slot which unexpectedly opened up on a ship due to sail in two hours. I wasn't packed and ready to leave on such short notice, and missed my chance.

Frustrated by the hiring process and living with my parents, I went back to Cambridge to decide what to do, and to see Beth. She seemed ambivalent about my sudden return: gone yesterday, here today, where tomorrow? The next night, June 21, the phone rang. I answered it. My mother said, "Mickey's missing."

22. Mississippi

I KNEW IMMEDIATELY WHAT she meant. Mickey Schwerner had gone missing in Mississippi. He was the son of Nat and Annie Schwerner, best friends of my parents since before I was born. Another couple, Lou and Nikka Cottin, also long-time close friends of theirs, traditionally hosted a big party on New Year's Day. On January 1, 1964, Mickey was there with his parents, as was I. He and I talked about his plans to go live in Mississippi with his wife Rita and work for the civil rights group CORE, the Congress of Racial Equality. I knew Mickey as a very sociable guy, but now I saw that he was also a very dedicated one. I admired him for it, knowing that I wasn't prepared to make such a commitment. That day, a happy one with friends and family, was the last time I'd seen him.

According to the sketchy information on TV, Mickey had driven from Meridian to Philadelphia, Mississippi to investigate the burning of a black church which housed a CORE Freedom School. He was accompanied by James Chaney and Andrew Goodman. For James, a young black man born in Meridian and a Freedom Rider, working with Mickey on voter registration was at great risk to himself. For Andy, a student from New York, it was his first day in Mississippi working for CORE's Freedom Summer voter registration project. When they hadn't returned to Meridian by evening, people became alarmed. Merely driving around rural Mississippi at night in mixed racial company was dangerous.

I left for Long Island immediately. My mother was distraught, and on the phone back and forth with Annie to support her and to learn if she had any news. We all feared the worst, but didn't speak of it. Family and friends had always called him Mickey, but the TV and newspaper reports referred to him as Michael, his given name. That added to the sense of unreality about what was happening, as though it was a story about someone else.

I went into the city to join demonstrators demanding that the federal government look for them. We chained ourselves to the federal courthouse in lower Manhattan. I stayed there a couple of days, sitting on the stone steps and sleeping on them one night. I kept to myself and didn't tell anyone of my relationship with Mickey. I didn't want to talk about it. I just wanted to feel that I was doing something by being there.

On June 24 we were horrified when we saw on TV that their station wagon had been found, a burned-out shell. President Johnson called Annie and Andy's father Robert to tell them that FBI Director J. Edgar Hoover had informed him that there were no human remains in the car. That raised a glimmer of hope, which faded as several more days passed with still no sign of them. The local police in Mississippi claimed that they were in hiding, a stunt to get publicity and bring the feds to town. The same story line was parroted in Washington by Mississippi's two U.S. Senators, staunch segregationists, one of whom, James Eastland, was chairman of the Judiciary Committee. It was painful enough that our families knew that of course he was not in hiding, but likely murdered. What made matters worse was watching the story play out in the news. That was especially so for Mickey's wife Rita. She was part of the story, and a TV reporter approached her, stuck out his microphone and asked, "Did you love your husband?"

The lack of news and the denials by Mississippi authorities led to a bizarre turn of events: my father consulted with a psychic. Normally he would have dismissed psychics as phony purveyors of mumbo-jumbo. He was a man of logic, rational perhaps to an extreme, a Phi Beta Kappa chemistry major in college, a businessman, and a part-time math teacher at City College of New York. For him to do something so totally out of character showed just how much stress everyone was under.

He had a friend in the New York City police department who told him about a psychic in Holland, Gerard Croiset. Apparently he had been helpful to the police there in solving a number of cases. So on June 27 my father contacted a man in Connecticut, Jack Harrison Pollack, who had written a book called *Croiset The Clairvoyant*. He also contacted Congressman Ogden Reid, who represented the district where Nat and Annie lived. Reid agreed to transmit to the U.S. Justice Department any information Croiset provided.

Pollack immediately set up a call with my father to Croiset, whose first words were, "The three boys are dead." That was reluctantly becoming obvious to all of us, but this was the first time anyone actually said it. Croiset also provided some vague information about where their bodies were, "about fifteen to twenty miles from their car in a deep, swampy place near some kind of construction." That information was relayed to the FBI, who were interested in learning more. Three weeks after his call with Croiset, my father flew to Holland, bringing along a piece of Mickey's clothing as what Pollack called an "inductor" to help Croiset focus his thoughts. He spent several hours with Croiset, tape-recording their conversation, a transcript of which was sent on to the FBI. Still, there was nothing new to report out of Mississippi.

23. HOT TIMES

AT THIS POINT I LEFT for Cambridge. I hadn't been expecting to stay for so long at my parents' house, and with the fruitless search dragging on, there was nothing I could do there. The initial shock had subsided, and my mom was settled into her grief. It felt good to be driving the Jag top down on a hot summer day, catching some rays and listening to the radio again. "Don't Let the Sun Catch You Crying," sang Gerry and the Pacemakers on their #4 record. Johnny Rivers reached #2 with a cover of Chuck Berry's "Memphis, Tennessee." I loved the original in the Fifties, kind of a tearjerker, but now the song took on added poignancy with the singer's lament about trying to find a loved one missing down South. The Beach Boys had their first #1 hit with "I Get Around." It brought back the feeling of riding my Honda up the Pacific Coast Highway to the beach. It was only last summer yet so long ago, before some big waves rolled into my life: Beth, JFK's assassination, The Beatles, Mickey's disappearance.

I was happy to be back in Cambridge with Beth. Unlike when I returned from the union hiring hall, this time she welcomed me with open arms, there for me when I needed her so badly after the painful vigil in New York. Sex put that pain out of my mind, if only for a while. And it did with Beth that summer, especially one hot night.

In my senior year at Cornell, a pre-med friend Lenny Lebow loaned me a book about multiple female orgasms, which people were just becoming aware of. I was fascinated, because men usually just got one shot. That night Beth had orgasm after orgasm. After a while it was almost beyond sex, two minds and bodies in perfect synch, like ice dancing without ice. I came with her three times. The sweet smell of sex filled the air. In high school I was constantly buzzing with sexual energy. Kissing a girl sent me in a fever. If I got a hand inside her bra I was overwhelmed. With Zsuzsa I learned to use that energy to satisfy a woman's sexual desires. From a premature ejaculator as a teenager, I'd become a proficient partner in pleasure. And with Beth it was all the better, because it wasn't just sex. We were still very much in love.

24. An End, and a Beginning

On August 4, the FBI dug up an earthen dam near Philadelphia, and found the bodies of Mickey, James and Andy. After being shot near their car, they were brought there and buried by a large bulldozer. The FBI was acting on a tip from an informant about the dam. Croiset hadn't helped solve the case, but his mental image evoked the burial scene.

The FBI unearthing the bodies of the three civil rights workers

I went back to New York to attend a memorial service on August 9. Mickey and Andy's parents and James's mother were there, as were my parents, nearly 2,000 other mourners and of course the media. After the service I waited outside for Annie. She had been

a vivacious woman but now was withdrawn and subdued, looking older and shorter than she had at the party on New Year's Day.
When she saw me she stopped, said "Hi sweetie" in a weary voice,
and put her hand on my cheek. She'd known me since I was born,
as my mom had known Mickey. It was as though Annie touched me
to assure herself that I was still there. Her son was gone.

On the same day the bodies were found, President Johnson went
on national TV to announce that the U.S. was conducting air strikes
against military facilities in North Vietnam. This was supposedly
in retaliation for attacks by gunboats on U.S. aircraft carriers in the
Gulf of Tonkin, off the North Vietnam coast. At Johnson's request,
the so-called Gulf of Tonkin Resolution was introduced in Congress
the following day and passed two days later, by a unanimous vote in
the House and with only two Senators voting no. It authorized the
President "to take all necessary steps, including the use of armed
force, to assist [South Vietnam] in defense of its freedom." He could
do so without a formal declaration of war. It was the legal justifica-
tion for U.S. military operations already underway in Vietnam.

25. BACK TO SCHOOL

IN AUGUST I SPENT several days at Beth's family's waterfront
compound in Blue Hill, Maine. My presence was barely tolerated
by her parents, and of course we didn't sleep together. But compared to what had been going on in my life and the world, it was
a welcome escape. A highlight of my stay was a big lobster and
clam bake on the beach, cooked over hot rocks under a layer of
seaweed, just like a *pachamanca*.

I looked forward to getting back to law school in September.
Having made it this far, to my third and final year, I was committed to finishing and getting my degree. A lot of the coursework
in second year had been required subjects relating to corporate
law, but I had no intention of becoming a corporate lawyer.

With Beth in Blue Hill, Maine

Courses in third year were all electives, which let me pursue my interest in areas like constitutional law. I also signed up for a course on "Psychiatry and the Law" taught by a new young professor, Alan Dershowitz.

My Ames team met to start preparing for our semifinal argument in November. But we had some bad news. One of our teammates had taken a leave of absence for the year. But even worse, one of our oralists, Gary Spiess, had to withdraw. He had fallen ill during second year final exams and as a result didn't complete those courses. The school administration ruled that he had to repeat them and could not participate in Ames that semester. That left only six of us to go up against a full eight-member team. And most critically, someone had to take Gary's place as an oralist. That would require a tremendous amount of preparation, made all the more daunting by stepping in to the semifinals with no prior experience in such a pressure-packed situation. We all looked around nervously at each other, as if to silently say, "No, not me."

But I thought, maybe this is what I need to become involved with law school and make up for my two years of sliding by. I'd always been argumentative by nature, perhaps too much so, trying to win my point with the force of logic, or loudness. And after going to Peru I certainly wasn't afraid of doing something new. This could be a lot more interesting than the usual routine of going to class and studying. My self-confidence had grown in my relationship with Beth, and I didn't want to tell her that I had the chance to be an Ames oralist and turned it down. Most of all, I didn't want to face myself, backing down from the challenge.

There was no time to ponder about what to do; we had to get busy preparing our case. So I said OK, I'll do it. Everyone smiled and congratulated me, relieved to be off the hook. Andy Bartlett, our team captain, was especially pleased. He had in mind all along that it was going to be me, but didn't push me to volunteer. I guess he saw the raw material of an oralist in me, and believed he and the team could shape it.

In preparing for our quarterfinal round, Gary and Norm practiced by presenting their oral arguments to the rest of us, sitting as their judges, and we did our best to tear them apart. Norm had proven himself as an oralist in winning the quarters. So while he still had to go through the practice drills for the semis, the focus was on me, the unknown quantity. Day after day I had to stand up in front of my teammates and try to put across my argument. They were relentless in questioning everything I said and forcing me to keep rethinking and refining my position. On one occasion Andy even mocked my appearance and gestures. At times I was ready to explode in frustration. But I knew I had to keep calm and proceed with my presentation. While I struggled with my self-control, I never resented their tough questioning. They were my teammates and friends, and we all wanted to do whatever it took to win. By November 18, our day in court, I'd been honed into a weapon ready to do battle.

26. May It Please The Court

THE JAMES BARR AMES COURTROOM, where the case was to be heard, was named for the first dean of Harvard Law. It was on the second floor of Austin Hall, the original law school building, in fact, the first building in America devoted solely to the teaching of the law. The architect, H.H. Richardson, worked in the second half of the 19th century and was considered one of the giants of American architecture. His signature style, known as Richardsonian Romanesque, was best exemplified by his masterpiece, Trinity Church in Boston. His buildings used varied colored stone, and were highly and imaginatively detailed. Fortresslike, they projected power.

It was in that same courtroom where I'd seen Dr. King speak. I was awed by the building's history and the courtroom's visual grandeur. A spectacular space, it had a high domed ceiling, a massive stone fireplace at the back, and exposed wood beams carved with the heads of dragons and wild boars. Were they waiting to tear into me like the judges?

Austin Hall at Harvard Law School

When we convened there for the oral arguments, I was well-prepared, not really nervous but definitely keyed up by the pressure, yet with a lingering shadow of a doubt in my mind about my being there. I'd dressed for the occasion, in a three-piece gray suit and the only white shirt I owned. For the ultimate conservative but stylish touch, my tie was held neatly in place with a gold collar pin.

There was a full house in the courtroom, 300 students and professors. Given my checkered history in class, I wondered if they were asking themselves what I was doing up front with Norm at counsels' table? Then the clerk intoned: "Oyez, oyez, oyez, the Supreme Court of the Commonwealth of Ames is now in session." We all rose as the three judges filed in. One of them was wearing a gold collar pin just like mine. Seeing that was just what I needed, not because the judge would look favorably on me, but because it symbolized for me that yes, I really did belong there. When my turn came, I confidently stepped up to the lectern and addressing the judges uttered the ritual opening to the argument: "May it please the Court."

The fictional case involved the appeal by two men of their convictions on drug and weapons charges. Two undercover cops were on patrol late at night in a "Negro" neighborhood when the men pulled up in a Volkswagen, got out and walked up to a bar at the corner, looked in, walked away, and then walked back and looked in the bar again. Then one of them said something to the other, apparently having spotted the cops, and they began walking quickly back to their car. At that point the two cops stopped and frisked them on account of their "suspicious behavior." The driver of the car was found to have a straight razor in his back pocket, and after being placed under arrest for carrying a concealed weapon, a further search turned up a packet of heroin in his coat pocket. That prompted one of the cops to stick his head through the open window of the VW, where he spotted a paper bag, in the driver's side door pocket, which turned out to contain more heroin.

The driver was convicted on the weapons charge and on possession of the packet and bag of heroin. The passenger was convicted of possession of the bag of heroin, under a state statute which presumed anyone guilty of drug possession if they were in a passenger car where narcotics were found. On appeal in the fictional "Supreme Court of the Commonwealth of Ames," the defendants were represented by the Jaffe Club, under the guidance of Professor Louis Jaffe, a leading member of the faculty. The Jaffe team argued that the evidence against the men was obtained illegally and could not be used against them, in accordance with *Mapp v. Ohio*, the decision rendered by the Supreme Court on the day I was en route to Peru.

Keeton Equity was assigned to represent the government and argue that the convictions should stand. Personally I did not believe that. But lawyers are supposed to represent their clients without regard to their personal opinion, so for me this was a good test of that assumption. As a team we worked hard together to develop our position in support of the convictions. We didn't spend any time discussing what we really thought about the case, because we had to immerse ourselves completely in our role of representing the prosecution. Since we were shorthanded, and I'd shown ability during the quarterfinals in legal research and writing, I threw myself into that aspect as well as preparing my oral argument. It meant long long hours in the law library, but I did try to at least attend my classes even if I couldn't spend any time on homework.

The three-judge panel hearing our case was headed by the Chief Justice of the Supreme Court of New Jersey, who was no doubt well-versed in how *Mapp v. Ohio* applied to state courts. Norm and I handled our oral arguments well. I never had any doubt that he would, but over the many weeks of my daily inquisition, I'd become increasingly confident that I would too. As in the quarterfinals, the judges' decision was not based on the facts of the case, but on the quality of the arguments and briefs of the two teams. They ruled for Keeton Equity. It was an exhilarating moment, to have won despite being shorthanded and having a rookie oralist. But it was a daunting one too, as it sank in that we made the finals. We had a lot more work ahead of us.

27. HOLIDAYS

WITH A WEEK TO GO before Thanksgiving break, Beth and I got to spend a few days together. She had been totally supportive of my preparation for Ames, despite keeping us apart more than we liked, and was proud of my success. For the first time since the fall of my first year, I felt like I truly belonged at Harvard Law. No more ambivalence, no more uncertainty, no more thoughts of hopping in the Jag and taking off, leaving Beth and Harvard behind. Over the holiday I drove down to Long Island to see my family, who of course were thrilled about my Ames victory. On the ride I heard The Shangri-Las #1 single, "Leader of the Pack." Vroom, vroom, yes I am. The Rolling Stones were in the Top 10 with "Time Is on My Side." Yes it is. And so were The Kinks with "You Really Got Me." Oh yeah, you really got me now, Harvard.

The only thing that briefly disrupted my post-Ames idyll was the first anniversary of JFK's assassination, two days before Thanksgiving. The occasion was inescapable in the Boston area, all over the papers and TV. Everyone was asking each other, where were you when you heard the news? It was something you never forgot. Two months earlier the Warren Commission had issued its report concluding that Lee Harvey Oswald acted alone. There was plenty of fodder for late-night law student debates about the evidence the Commission made public (although most of its material was sealed in a government archive). Despite the Commission's conclusion, it was still hard for many of us to accept that a lone weirdo with a cheap rifle could change the course of history, and our lives. The anniversary brought back a lot of painful feelings, because the assassination was not the only political murder I'd experienced in the past year.

Back in Cambridge after Thanksgiving, I settled into the grind of catching up on the coursework I'd missed while preparing for Ames. It was nice for a change not to have a deadline looming, and to quietly go about my reading and note-taking without having to defend myself every day from the questioning of my teammates. I could just enjoy what I'd accomplished, which was reinforced by the recognition of my friends and classmates. The prestige of the competition, its high awareness around the school and the drama of the faceoff in the theatrical Ames Courtroom gave it a special aura.

I planned to spend most of the Christmas holiday in Cambridge, still working to catch up, but I was going to be alone. Beth was heading off to join her family at a posh resort on Sea Island, Georgia. I was not invited. And I didn't have the money to go on my own. Not that it would have done me any good. They didn't allow Jews there. Our separation just brought home the fact that there was still a world which she was part of and I was not. I suppose I couldn't blame her if she didn't want to stay in Cambridge freezing her ass off instead of basking in the southern sun, and she felt no hesitation about going.

Maybe I just should have sent her off with cheery wishes for the holidays. But I was not happy about her leaving and being left behind. I was never a fan of Christmas music, even the pop songs on the radio. But hearing Elvis sing about a "blue blue blue Christmas" got to me. I was alone without her, while she was having fun in the sun. Over the holidays my unhappiness at our separation turned to smoldering anger. When I picked her up at the airport, we had a cool January reunion. I couldn't hide my feelings, and she was put off by them, coming back from a wonderful holiday with her family. The divide between us – which we'd bridged with love and respect and laughter and grief and sex – was still there.

28. MURDER AND MAYHEM

WHEN CLASSES RESUMED, the countdown began toward the Ames Final on April 14. But going into it we no longer considered ourselves underdogs, as we had in the quarters and semis. Not that we thought we were better than our opponents, the Kaplan Club, under the guidance of Professor Benjamin Kaplan, a giant of the faculty. But we knew what it would take to win: discipline, teamwork, commitment and work work work. Gary Spiess was allowed to rejoin our team, but in reality more in honorary recognition of his past contribution as an oralist than as an active participant. It was still basically the six of us versus Kaplan's eight, with our Stephie Bartlett as the only woman on either team. At least this time we didn't have the challenge of breaking in a novice and undisciplined oralist.

Outside the cloistered confines of Harvard Law School, explosive events were happening in rapid succession. On February 21, there was another assassination, this one of Malcolm X, the controversial Muslim African-American rights advocate. On March 2, the U.S. launched an intensive campaign of bombing North Vietnam. This was followed six days later by the landing of 3,500 U.S. Marines in Da Nang, South Vietnam, the first American ground combat troops of the war. On Sunday March 7, Alabama state troopers attacked civil rights demonstrators attempting to cross the Pettus Bridge in Selma and march to the state capitol, Montgomery, in support of the right to vote.

A second march two days later, led by Martin Luther King Jr., stopped at the bridge and held a prayer vigil in commemoration of "Bloody Sunday." That evening a white minister, who had come from Boston to Selma for the march, was fatally beaten by white supremacists. On March 15, in a televised address, President Johnson called for equal voting rights, saying "We shall overcome," and sent his proposed Voting Rights Act of 1965 to Congress. Then on March 21, under the protection of the federal government, 3,200 marchers led by King and leaders of several religions crossed the bridge and reached Montgomery four days later. That night a white mother of five, who came from Detroit to march, was shot dead by Ku Klux Klansmen as she drove other marchers back to Selma.

Inside the law school, we were all well aware of these events. How could anyone not be, no matter how deeply you were buried in your books? It was not only the shocking violence in Selma which got our attention, but its intended purpose in denying African-Americans their constitutional rights. That too was the main motive for the murder of the three civil rights workers, working to register voters in Mississippi. At least in the area of civil rights, the U.S. government was on the side of right. But there was a growing sense, especially on university campuses, that in Vietnam it was on the side of wrong. I shared that feeling. The seeds of our antipathy toward that war and any war had taken root in the radioactive ashes of Hiroshima and Nagasaki.

AMES FINAL ARGUMENT

Wednesday, April 14

AT EIGHT O'CLOCK
IN THE SUPREME COURT OF THE UNITED STATES

LOWELL LAMBERT

v.

THE POSTMASTER-GENERAL OF THE UNITED STATES

On Appeal from the United States District Court for the Southern District of New York

QUESTIONS PRESENTED:

A federal statute requires the Postmaster-General to detain unsealed mail matter originating in specified countries and found to be "communist political propaganda" until the addressee indicates a desire to receive such mail. Where the addressee, upon receipt of notice that his mail is being held, immediately files suit to enjoin enforcement of the statute:

1. Does the suit become moot when the government interprets the complaint as an expression of a desire to receive such mail?

2. Does the plaintiff have standing to challenge the constitutionality of the statute on behalf of others who may be fearful of responding affirmatively to similar Post Office notices?

3. Does plaintiff have standing to challenge the inclusion of his name upon a Post Office list of persons desiring to receive "communist political propaganda," which list is used to facilitate prompt mail delivery, when the government has indicated by affidavit that the list has not been, and will not be except upon proper application, disclosed to other governmental persons or agencies?

4. Is the statute unconstitutional?

BEFORE

Hon. Potter Stewart
United States Supreme Court

Hon. Robert P. Anderson
United States Court of Appeals for the Second Circuit

Hon. George Edwards
United States Court of Appeals for the Sixth Circuit

APPELLANT KAPLAN CLUB	APPELLEE KEETON EQUITY CLUB
Edgar Howbert	Steven R. Nelson
A. James Robertson	Norman D. Slonaker
Richard Campbell	Anderson G. Bartlett, III
Harry Miller	Stephanie K. Bartlett
Philip Reynolds	Cary P. Clark
Reade Ryan	Gary Spiess
Peter Tredick	Robert G. Tunnell, Jr.
W. Harvey Webster, III	

JAMES BARR AMES
COURTROOM - AUSTIN HALL

*Law School poster for the final round
of the Ames Competition*

29. Tell it to The Judge

The Ames Final was unique compared to the earlier rounds. The case, although fictional, was typically based on a real one pending before the U.S. Supreme Court, and the three-judge panel was traditionally led by a Supreme Court Justice, in our case Potter Stewart. Our other two judges were from Courts of Appeals, the next highest level of federal courts, so we'd be facing three of the most senior jurists in the U.S. legal system. Stewart was a centrist who was often the swing vote on a divided Court. He became noted the year before for his decision in a case which turned on whether French director Louis Malle's film *The Lovers* (starring Jeanne Moreau) was obscene. Stewart wrote that he was not going to try to define exactly what would constitute hard-core pornography, which would not be protected by the First Amendment. Instead, he simply said that "I know it when I see it." He concluded that the film was not obscene. This left some legal scholars unsatisfied with the vagueness of his declaration, but it had a common-sense wisdom to it. Law was not math, and often must rely on human judgment rather than formulaic certainty.

Our Ames case also involved the First Amendment. At issue was the constitutionality of a federal statute intended to prevent people from receiving unsolicited newsletters and magazines from Red-bloc countries (it did not apply to subscriptions or to sealed mail). The statute required the Treasury Department to determine whether such a publication was "Communist political propaganda." If Treasury decided it was, then the Post Office held it and sent the addressee a notice that he was the intended recipient of propaganda. He could then either return a form saying that he wished to have it delivered, or if he did not, the Post Office would destroy it. To allow him to continue receiving such mail, the Post Office put his name on a list that it kept on file.

For the purpose of the Ames case the plaintiff's name was changed to "Lowell Lambert." But in reality he was Corliss Lamont, a leftist activist, professor and author who used such publications as source material in his writings and lectures. He sued the Postmaster-General, claiming that by requiring him to request delivery of such mail, and by keeping his name on a list, his First Amendment rights of free press and free speech were being infringed. He lost in the U.S. District Court, but appealed to the Supreme Court.

In the Ames final, our Keeton Equity team was assigned to represent the federal government, the defendant in that appeal. Once again, as in our stop-and-frisk case in the semifinals, I found myself on the opposite side of what I believed, representing the government. Although we never discussed where we stood personally, it was obvious that most if not all of the team shared my point of view, that the First Amendment protected Lambert/Lamont. But like the good lawyers we were supposed to be, we carried on.

Once again, Andy kept us working together and working hard. Norm and I still went through the role-playing drill, facing our teammates as questioning and skeptical judges. But having proven myself as a capable oralist, I didn't have to face the level of aggression from the "bench" as I had before. Still, their questioning was tough, to force us to hone our arguments so they would stand up on our day in court. I also contributed again to the research and writing, putting in long days and nights in the library. Legal briefs had to follow very exact rules of format. Math required a similar exactitude. I seemed to have an eye for picking up errors and typos, so in addition to everything else I had to do, I was designated proofreader of last resort before our briefs were sent off to the printer. My only relief from the grind was looking up from the books and the briefs to see Beth coming down the aisle to meet me for dinner, when I could take the time.

There were two parts to the case. Norm handled the "substantive" aspects involving the constitutionality of the statute. I addressed the "procedural" requirements the plaintiff had to meet in order to be eligible to bring the case. That involved two issues. First, when the plaintiff sued the Postmaster-General, he was in effect saying that he wanted to receive the kind of mail in question, and in fact

Keeton Equity team in Ames Courtroom before final argument: (L-R rear) Cary Clark, Bob Tunnell, Gary Spiess, Stephanie Bartlett and Andy Bartlett; (L-R front) me and Norm Slonaker

The judges ready to enter the court: (L-R) Judge Robert Anderson, Justice Potter Stewart, Judge George Edwards

did continue to get it without further disruption. So we argued that the question of whether his First Amendment rights were being abridged was "moot," that is, no longer at issue. He was getting the mail and therefore had no further claim against the Post Office.

Second, the plaintiff maintained that even so, he should be able to continue with his suit on behalf of others whose mail might be held if the statute remained in force. The legal term for whether he was eligible to represent them was "standing." To have standing, he had to be directly and adversely affected himself, not merely be concerned about how others might be affected. Our position was that he was not eligible, because he was not personally affected if their mail was held. Plaintiff maintained that he was affected due to his continuing presence on the Post Office list. Should it be released to a Congressional committee or the public, he would be cast in a negative light as someone wishing to receive "Communist political propaganda."

Our opposing Ames team, Kaplan Club, represented "Lowell Lambert." Because their client had lost in the lower court and was appealing, they were first to file a brief on his behalf, then we filed our brief on behalf of the Postmaster General, and then they filed a shorter reply brief. Of course we analyzed their briefs in great detail, and they'd done an excellent job. I could hardly spot a typo. Likewise, when it came to the oral arguments, they would go first, then we would follow, after which they would deliver a short reply. Their oralists Edgar Howbert and A. James Robertson set a high standard, but we expected nothing less of a team in the finals. Like us, they'd been through the crucible of the lower rounds and won.

When they finished their presentation, it was our turn. Norm likewise rose to the challenge, so it was now on me whether we won or lost. I could see Dean Griswold sitting up front next to the bench, my parents and brother Peter were in the audience. The packed courtroom was hushed, knowing the outcome was in the balance. I rose from my seat and stepped up to the lectern. "May it please the Court."

In preparing for the argument, I'd made notes on some index cards, not with a speech I'd have no chance to deliver with interruptions by the judges' questions, but with the main points of my argument and the cases I had to cite to support it. I was doing well in my presentation and the initial back-and-forth with the bench when Justice Stewart asked me a tough question. But it was one we had anticipated and practiced for. I was looking for it. And when it came, all I had to do was slide over one index card and my response, a complex piece of legal reasoning, was laid out on several cards that followed.

I had to hold back a smile when I slid that card over. I was ready for the hard one Stewart threw at me, and connected. I knew it was going out of the park, like Roger Maris when he hit #61. I delivered my argument, rounding the rhetorical bases and heading home with not a single interruption by the judges. I sat down and Kaplan gave their reply. The judges adjourned to confer. They came back in a few minutes and announced their decision. Best briefs: Keeton Equity. Best oral arguments: Keeton Equity. The winner: Keeton Equity.

It was a moment of sheer joy -- we won! -- and of immense relief – the ever-present pressure of the looming competition, since qualifying for the quarterfinals, was gone. There were many words of congratulations and handshakes, which continued with a reception which followed at Harkness Commons. I soaked it up, made that much sweeter by the presence of my parents. At last, to their way of thinking, they could again recognize the straight-A student they'd raised. So could I.

When the evening and the excitement ended, and I headed back to my apartment with Beth, it really began to sink in. I felt triumphant, yet almost in disbelief at what I'd achieved. In a year and a half I'd gone from a dropout, unsure of myself and what I was doing, to the pinnacle of Harvard Law School. As our team worked in the library preparing our case, we were well aware of the bronze plaques on the walls listing the members of the winning Ames teams. Now our names would be added. Usually you had to die in a war to have your name memorialized in bronze.

Despite my erratic history at Harvard, I never doubted that I'd earned the honor. I knew how hard I'd worked to get there, after taking the risk of volunteering to be an oralist. But beyond personal pride was knowing that we had accomplished it as a team, and my immense gratitude for being part of it. A winning athlete often talks about how he couldn't have done it without his teammates. It was never truer than for me.

There was actually some prize money for the winning oralists, $300. We used it to help pay for a trip to Washington for the team, to see the actual case argued in the Supreme Court on April 26. The government was represented by former Harvard Law professor Archibald Cox, the Solicitor General of the United States, who was named to that post by JFK. We all felt that we did a better job than Cox, but recognized that he probably took very little time to prepare for the case. It was not a high priority for the Justice Department, and they no doubt saw it as a loser anyway.

The Supreme Court issued its ruling just four weeks later, a lightning-fast turnaround, when decisions normally lag oral arguments by many months. The Court held unanimously that the statute was unconstitutional, the first time in U.S history that a federal law was invalidated for violating the First Amendment. With Ames over, having performed our lawyerly duty but no longer having to take the government's side, we all concurred with the decision. Under the law, passed in response to the "Red Scare," the USA was acting like the USSR, taking names and controlling what people could read.

30. AFTER AMES

RESISTANCE TO THE WAR in Vietnam had been growing, intensified by the launch in March of "Operation Rolling Thunder," a massive U.S. campaign of bombing North Vietnam. The first large antiwar protest in Washington, with 25,000 marchers, took place on April 17, organized by Students for a Democratic Society. I was a little leery of leftist groups like SDS, but my own opposition to the war was growing too. When I would graduate from law school in June, I might well be drafted. So I decided to seek another student deferment by applying to the Littauer School of Public Administration at Harvard [it later became part of the Kennedy School of Government]. It also made sense from a career standpoint, since I was focused on working in the public sector and not corporate law. I would fill in gaps in my education with courses in government and economics I never took at Cornell as a math and anthropology student. And I could stay in Cambridge with Beth.

Ordinarily the Masters in Public Administration degree required two years of study, which would get me past the age of draft eligibility. But when the school accepted me, they said that with my legal background, I would earn my MPA in one year. That would leave me out of school and out of deferments having just turned 25, but eligible for the draft until my 26th birthday. I decided to go ahead and buy the year, then take it from there. When I appeared before my draft board in Great Neck to request my student deferment, they had no choice but to okay it. But they weren't happy about it. As I was getting up to leave, the chairman of the board said, "We're going to get you, Mr. Nelson, we're going to get you."

There was also still the little matter of having to graduate from the law school. That required my writing what was called the Third-Year Paper. And here I was in mid-April, not having started on it because of working on Ames. I went to see my advisor, who understood my situation and agreed that it was okay to miss the normal deadline, so long as I turned it in before graduation. So other than the short trip to the Supreme Court, I went from one nonstop grind to another.

My paper was on the Voting Rights Act pending before Congress. In his lecture in the Ames Courtroom, Martin Luther King Jr. stressed the importance of voter registration in the drive for equality. Mickey, James and Andy had died working for voter registration in Mississippi. And the marches in Selma, the deaths and beatings, were all about the fight for the right to vote. It was trivial by comparison, but the least I could do was write a good paper about how segregationists used legalistic means to prevent blacks from registering and voting, and how the proposed federal law would overturn those barriers and prevent new ones from being erected. As I wrote in my introduction, it must respond "not merely to tried-and-true methods" of disenfranchisement, but as well "to those devious means which ingenuity may devise for severing, time and again, the first strand from which the net of full suffrage is to be woven."

I barely got the paper done, having to study for my course finals at the same time. It would have been nice to attend the Harvard commencement and savor earning my law degree after what it took for me to get it. But I had to leave immediately for D.C., where I'd committed to work for the summer as a volunteer with the Washington Human Rights Project. It was founded by William L. Higgs, a graduate of Ole Miss and Harvard Law, who formerly was the only white civil rights lawyer in Mississippi. He had to flee the state in fear of his life.

I still found time to listen to music, but I was more interested in my growing LP collection than Top 40 AM radio. Still, there was some great music on the air. The Beatles had #1 singles with "Eight Days a Week" and "Ticket to Ride," as did The Beach Boys with "Help Me, Rhonda." The Rolling Stones had their first #1 with "(I Can't Get No) Satisfaction," and although Bob Dylan didn't make the singles chart, The Byrds' version of his "Mr. Tambourine Man" went to #1. Elvis was still selling records too, with his version of "Crying in the Chapel" going to #3. But increasingly, singles were just the tip of the iceberg of what was on the albums, a way to promote LP sales. Artists were writing and recording music that went far beyond the limits of AM radio's format, both in the length of songs and with content – politics, sex, drugs -- that radio station programmers and owners would not allow to be played on air.

31. Judging the Judge

BILL HIGGS KNEW WELL that critical civil rights decisions were being handed down by the U.S. Appeals Court for the Fifth Circuit, which covered Mississippi and the other Deep South segregationist states. But when seats opened on that court, due to retirement or death, nominations to the bench followed the time-honored tradition of Senatorial courtesy. The President would nominate a judge either at the direct suggestion of the Senators from the nominee's home state, or at the very least with their approval. There was little consideration of the nominee's background or suitability for the position.

When Lyndon Johnson nominated James P. Coleman for a seat on the Fifth Circuit, Bill decided that the time had come to object. Coleman was the former Attorney General of Mississippi and was elected Governor in 1956 with a promise to uphold segregation. In 1958 he went to the University of Mississippi to personally block the attempt of a black man to enter. He helped establish the Mississippi Sovereignty Commission, a state agency which he chaired as Governor and whose mission was to protect the state from "encroachment" by the federal government, especially with regard to segregation. The commission accumulated the names of almost 90,000 people it deemed to be associated with the civil rights movement. They took a special interest in "outside agitators" like Mickey, and in effect targeted him for murder. In a 1963 primary Coleman lost to the son of a former Mississippi Governor who accused him of being too moderate on race. Needing a job, Coleman had friends in politically high places, and there happened to be an opening on the Fifth Circuit.

Bill gathered a group of volunteers in Washington to challenge the Coleman nomination, researching his past and writing a brief and supporting documents in opposition. On July 12 and 13, a subcommittee of the Senate Judiciary Committee held hearings on his nomination. The full Committee was chaired by Senator James Eastland of Mississippi, who had dismissed the disappearance of the three civil rights workers as "a publicity stunt." The subcommittee hearing was chaired by Senator Sam Ervin of North Carolina. After Coleman and a few supporters spoke on his behalf, Ervin was about to gavel the hearing closed when I spoke up from where I was standing, against a wall toward the back of the hearing room. He looked at me with surprise and suspicion. I had been designated to speak on behalf of the Project, and succeeded in getting our materials entered into the record, detailing Coleman's segregationist history. We were disappointed but not surprised when Coleman was approved unanimously. But we had made the point that judicial nominees should be scrutinized, not rubberstamped.

32. IN TROUBLE

BETH CAME TO VISIT me in D.C. I was stunned when she told me she was pregnant. She used a diaphragm for birth control. It was highly effective, but there was always that slim chance of failure. Having a baby was out of the question for both of us. We agreed that we had no choice, she'd get an abortion. The money would have been no big deal for her parents, but there was no way she could tell them she was pregnant, much less ask them to pay for it. So it came down to getting it from my liberal and supportive parents, for whom the money at that time was a big deal. But they came through.

Getting a safe abortion was not easy. We found out about a clinic in Puerto Rico that did walk-in abortions and flew down there, adding airfare to the tab my parents were picking up. We took a cab from the airport to the clinic, where we checked in. They didn't ask for much information, because they really didn't want it. We waited for an hour or so, although it seemed far longer. During that time a couple of women ahead of us were taken inside. After they left, the doctor came out into the waiting room, and began yelling at us. Get out of here, get out of my office. We were stunned, having no idea why. But we left, humiliated. We wandered around until our flight was due to leave, tourists to nowhere, the sights of Puerto Rico blurred by our state of dismay.

We got home wondering what to do next. I got in touch with my friend Lenny from Cornell, the guy with the female orgasms book, now a medical student. He came from the Washington area and knew a doctor there who did abortions. With his "referral," we were able to get an appointment, after normal office hours. This time, Beth wanted to go in alone, so I waited and fretted in the car. She came back about an hour later, walking awkwardly, her face ashen, her voice strained. Yes, she had the abortion, but the procedure was more painful than she'd expected. The anguish which followed, and lingered, was even more so. It was one thing to have chosen to have the abortion; it was another to live with the remorse of having made that decision. What might have brought us closer together, her pregnancy, only pushed us apart.

33. A STROKE OF FATE

I WAS BACK WORKING with the Human Rights Project when I got a call from my mom on August 1. My dad had suffered a stroke that day and was hospitalized. I was shocked, he was just 52. After a hurried goodby to the people at the Project, I left in the morning for Long Island. When I arrived at the hospital I learned that he would survive, but had suffered extensive loss of motor skills on his left side.

This happened at a particularly bad time, because my mom was on the verge of filing for divorce. He had been carrying on an affair with his assistant at the small import-export business he ran in Manhattan. This ugly relationship, not spoken of but an open secret, was particularly awkward. She lived with her husband just a few blocks from us in Roslyn Heights, and one of her sons was a school friend of my brother Peter. My parent's marriage had been bad for years, but my mom tried to stay together "for the sake of the kids." But by this point only my youngest brother Rich was still living at home, finishing high school. Fed up, my mom told me she was finally ready to make the break. I supported her decision, but after he had the stroke, she was unable to go through with it. It was just not in her to abandon him in his condition.

His business had been doing poorly, and with the open threat of divorce, he was under a lot of stress. Maybe this triggered the stroke. For the rest of the summer I spent hours every day with him at the hospital. It was painful to see him incapacitated. The medical staff tried to encourage him to do physical therapy for his left arm and leg, but he had never been much for physical activity and was not very cooperative about the therapy. He didn't respond to my encouragement either. This bothered and even embarrassed me. I thought that if I were in his position, horizontal in bed, I'd be working hard to regain as much use of my body as I could. He did recover some movement, and his slurred speech returned to normal. We were all relieved that at least his mental faculties seemingly had not been affected, because he was a man who valued intelligence above all else.

My dad was an avid chess player, and asked me to bring his chess set to the hospital. He and I had played a lot before I became a teenager obsessed with other things. But a good part of the reason I lost interest in chess was because I never could beat him, which was really frustrating. He could have made a bad move once in a while, to let me win and encourage me, but that was not him. The 10-year old would have to defeat the experienced player with no help, and I wasn't good enough to do it. It seemed like chess would be a good way for us to relate during his hospital stay, although I hadn't played in years. I was surprised to win our very first game. At that point I knew, and he knew, that the stroke had affected him mentally. He didn't ask me to play again.

By the end of the month he was sent home. He had recovered enough to be able to hobble around with a cane, but the doctor said he wouldn't make any further progress. My mother was trapped there as his caregiver. With him unable to continue running his business, which was failing anyhow, she became the breadwinner, through her job as a child day care administrator. She was depressed about her situation, he was depressed about his condition, and Rich was depressed about being in the middle of the two of them. At least he'd been able to get away for a night on August 15 to see The Beatles at Shea Stadium. By the beginning of September "Help!" was the #1 single. Help, indeed!

At #2, Bob Dylan had his first hit single, "Like A Rolling Stone," from his new LP *Highway 61 Revisited*. He created a controversy at the Newport Folk Festival that summer when he first played the song live, with an electric guitar and band, before the LP was released. I don't know why people were so shocked. His previous LP, *Bringing It All Back Home*, released back in March, featured one side of electric music. I remembered his performance of "Masters of War" at Club 47 -- solo on acoustic guitar, but with the soul of rock 'n' roll. To me, it was only a matter of time until he plugged in. The purists would just have to get over it. I loved his early work, but these two LPs put him up there with The Beatles and the Stones, spinning a musical and cultural revolution on my turntable.

34. BACK IN CLASS AGAIN

JAMES BROWN, ALREADY A MAJOR R&B star, had his first Top Ten single in the Billboard Hot 100, "Papa's Got a Brand New Bag." I got a new bag too, as a graduate student. With school about to resume, I felt guilty about leaving my family behind, especially my mom, but relieved to get away from that emotional morass. I was sure I'd made the right decision to stay in school to avoid the draft. During the summer LBJ increased U.S. forces in South Vietnam from 75,000 to 125,000, and doubled the number of draftees a month to 35,000, to support future needs for more troops. The war was escalating, and so were protests against it, with 100,000 people taking to the streets in the U.S. and around the world on October 16.

I no longer had the Jaguar, it got too expensive to keep on the road. I rented an apartment only a few blocks from the Littauer School, where my classes would be held. The building was just across a parking lot from Austin Hall, where the Ames Courtroom was. It was strange being around there, my friends and acquaintances in my law school class all having moved on. I had been a recognizable figure around the law school. Now, at Littauer, I was a complete unknown. That was fine with me. I'd been under a lot of pressure in the past year, arguing two rounds of Ames, writing my third-year paper, fighting the Coleman nomination, going through the abortion with Beth, and coping with my father's stroke. I was content for now to lead a quiet life as an anonymous Harvard grad student.

While I was in Washington and on Long Island over the summer, Beth was at her family compound on the coast of Maine. We didn't see each other until we got back to Cambridge, but we soon realized we still wanted to be together. We even got engaged, and I got her a ring. In certain social strata, the diamond would have been considered puny, but it was all I could afford and she understood that. She showed the ring to some friends at school, but not to her parents. Just how we would get married was a question for another day.

For the most part I didn't find grad school very interesting. It was the usual academic rigmarole of going to lectures, taking notes, maybe asking a question occasionally, writing papers and taking exams. Law school was far more challenging, with its Socratic method of teaching, involving dialogue and debate between professor and students. Even when you weren't called on, you stayed mentally involved with the discussion, like playing along while watching a TV quiz show. You had to be ready in case the professor suddenly turned to you next.

I did encounter a bit of Socratic teaching one day in a class on federalism, about the relative roles of the federal versus state governments. The professor referred to a 1956 Supreme Court case,

Pennsylvania v. Nelson, which invalidated state laws against sedition (insurrection or treason), ruling that this was the sole and proper realm of the national government. The defendant was a man named Steve Nelson, at the time a prominent member of the Communist Party of the United States. The prof was amused to inform the class that among them, in that very room, was Steve Nelson. He made me role-play Nelson's argument against Pennsylvania, which he correctly maintained had no authority to prosecute him. I was annoyed about being singled out because of my name. He had no way of knowing that I could be a tough person to debate with, and might have given him a hard time in front of the class if I'd chosen to. But that would probably not be how to get a good grade in the course. So I played nice and went along with his little joke.

He also had no way of knowing that it was more than a coincidence that I shared my name with the defendant, and that this was a sore point for me. During the 1930s American volunteers went to Spain to join the Abraham Lincoln Brigade in the fight on behalf of the Spanish Republic against the fascist forces of Generalissimo Francisco Franco. This was a popular cause among the American left. Steve Nelson became a leading figure in the Brigade and was wounded in action, a worthy role model for my leftist parents to name a baby boy after when I was born in 1941. Back in the states Nelson went on to become a leading American Communist, and was convicted under federal and state sedition laws for conspiring with a Soviet agent.

My parents were liberals but certainly not Communists, and in the days of McCarthyism and the "Red Scare," didn't want to risk any association with my namesake. Being accused as "Commie sympathizers" could hurt my father's business, maybe get my mother fired from her teaching position. So they claimed that I'd actually been named for a distant relative I'd never heard of, whose name also began with an "S". Not a very likely story.

They did admit that my middle name Reed was that of another American Soviet sympathizer, the journalist (and Harvard graduate) John Reed. His claim to fame was a book he wrote in the

John Reed

midst of the 1917 Russian revolution, *Ten Days That Shook The World*. Reed died in Moscow in 1920, and after a hero's funeral became the first of only three Americans ever to be buried in the Kremlin. I was never comfortable with the Red tinge to my names, and by the mid-1960s wasn't comfortable either with the increasingly radicalism of some people in the antiwar movement. I was against the Vietnam War because it was morally wrong, wrong for America, not because I had any sympathy for the Communists of North Vietnam or anywhere else.

One course I took at Littauer which did engage me was called "Presidential Power." The professor, Richard Neustadt, was an adviser to Presidents Truman and Kennedy. He brought real-world experience and a practical perspective to his teaching, stressing that everything a President did and said was based on how he used his power in accumulating and spending political capital. Some students found it hard to accept this realpolitik perspective versus the more idealistic view of the Presidency they'd learned from government classes in college. To me, trained at law school to question everything, it made perfect sense.

Neustadt pointed out that the presidency was a unique job that no one was fully prepared for when he entered the White House. This often led to Presidents making mistakes early in their term. He cited the Bay of Pigs fiasco as a prime example. Kennedy admitted later that he was wrong in unquestioningly accepting the conclusion of his military and intelligence advisors that the invasion would trigger a counter-revolution against Castro. He vowed not to make that mistake again. Some people have speculated that as a result of American involvement in the assassination of South Vietnam President Ngo Dinh Diem on November 2, 1963, Kennedy was rethinking the growing U.S. role in Vietnam championed by his generals. But if he was, his own assassination twenty days later ended that.

35. LITERARY WORLDS

DURING THE WINTER I attended a seminar with Beth one evening a week in her dorm. The teacher was P. L. Travers, an "artist-in-residence" at Radcliffe and a poet, author, actress, and journalist. The world knew her best for her beloved books about Mary Poppins, recently adopted by Walt Disney into a musical. The subject of the seminar was not likely to become a Disney movie, Truman Capote's new book *In Cold Blood*, about two ex-cons who invade a farm house in Kansas and murder the four members of the family. Ms. Travers cited an episode in which one of the killers puts a pillow under the head of the father, before cutting his throat. This showed, she said, that "sentimentality and cruelty were two sides of the same coin."

That spring the literary magazine *The Paris Review* threw itself a benefit at the famed New York music club The Village Gate. A Harvard friend of Beth had two spare tickets and offered them to us. We couldn't pass them up, and went down to New York for the night. The event attracted the literati and glitterati of New York society, over 1000 people including Senator Robert Kennedy and his wife Ethel, according to *The New York Times*. Guests were greeted at the door by the *Review's* editor George Plimpton. Aside from the magazine, he was popularly known for writing about his athletic stunts, like pitching to some major league baseball players prior to an exhibition all-star game at Yankee Stadium, or quarterbacking a few plays in an intrasquad game with the Detroit Lions [soon to be the basis of best-selling book and feature film *Paper Lion*].

Late in the evening Frank Sinatra showed up at the Gate. The club had three floors. At the entrance level people mixed and mingled. One floor up featured jazz, one floor down rock bands. That's where Beth and I were, in a seething swarm of dancing bodies. Under my lawyerly suit I was wearing a vest Beth had custom-made for me out of snakeskin, with Boston Police brass buttons. She was wearing my teeth.

I saw Sinatra coming down the stairs, pausing before he reached the bottom. The band had their amps cranked way up. Flashing strobe lights added to the chaos, creating a stop-action effect like jumpy frames in an old movie. Sinatra took in the scene, blasted by the sound and the light. With a shocked look on his face, he quickly turned around and fled back upstairs. Definitely not his scene. I didn't know who the band was, maybe I'd missed the introduction if there was one. I'd never heard anything like it, so powerful, so pulsating, so hypnotic. Beth and I kept on dancing into the wee wee hours. The sound echoed in my head for months.

With finals coming up, we spent a lot of time studying at Agassiz Library in Radcliffe Yard. One beautiful spring day, we took a break and sat outside. We talked about my vulnerability to the draft. She told me her father had pulled strings to protect one of her brothers from being drafted by getting him into the reserves. Why couldn't I do the same? She was just assuming, from her position of privilege, that I could. I snapped back at her, because I didn't have a daddy with connections. Never did I feel the class gap between us was greater, that she couldn't really understand the tough spot I was in.

36. MOVING ON

MY TWENTY-ONE YEARS of school days ended in June. I got my degree, pleased and surprised to get an "A" in "Presidential Power." Having just turned 25, I still had a year of draft eligibility remaining. During the spring I'd landed a job with NASA, in the Office of the General Counsel at Washington headquarters. The Apollo Program to send a man to the moon was in full swing. The job seemed like the perfect fit for me, a lawyer with a science and math background. Plus, and critically important, I was unofficially assured that I wouldn't get drafted out of NASA, because of the military applications of its work on long-range rocketry. It had no connection to fighting in the jungles and rice paddies of

Vietnam, or to bombing Hanoi, so I didn't feel conflicted about being against the war while working for the space agency. In June I wrote my draft board in Great Neck requesting an occupational deferment. They brushed that aside, replying that my employer would have to make such a request.

My job didn't begin until September. Before then I took the bar exam in D.C., which I'd put off for a year after finishing law school to work with Bill Higgs. Then I spent some time around Cambridge. One weekend I went to down to Woods Hole, on Cape Cod, to visit my brother Peter, who was working for the summer at the Oceanographic Institute. He was really eager to play me Dylan's new album, *Blonde on Blonde*. We listened in his room on his KLH Model 11 portable stereo. Made in Cambridge, the system had a turntable and two speakers which clipped together into a molded-plastic suitcase. It was a trailblazing product which made stereo equipment available at a reasonable price, about two hundred bucks, ideal for younger people who moved a lot and just had to hear the latest stereo LPs. It provided the technology for rock groups to have their records played, while those recordings in turn drove the market for stereo equipment like KLH.

With *Blonde on Blonde*, Dylan achieved a new mastery. It was the kind of record you loved to turn someone on to. The opening cut "Rainy Day Women #12 and 35" was released as a single and had by then reached #2 on the charts. From there it was one great song after another, including homages to The Beatles with "4th Time Around" (in the vein of "Norwegian Wood") and The Stones with "Obviously 5 Believers" (a shuffling blues with harmonica). But the song that really hit me was "Just Like A Woman:"

"She makes love just like a woman, yes, she does
And she aches just like a woman
But she breaks just like a little girl."

Beth was a self-assured young woman, but she could hurt, and I'd hurt her, with things I'd said thoughtlessly or in anger. Once I told her that I didn't love her, that I'd never loved her. It wasn't true, it was cruel, and she was stunned. I regretted saying it, trying to get back at her in my frustration over our relationship.

"I just can't fit
Yes, I believe it's time for us to quit
But when we meet again
Introduced as friends
Please don't let on that you knew me when
I was hungry and it was your world."

I never did fit in Beth's world, nor did she fit in the world as I wished it would be, one in which she didn't have anti-Semitic parents. Our relationship had been deteriorating for months. When school ended, it ended too. But later that summer I persuaded her to let me visit, maybe the last time. So I hitchhiked up to her family's place in Maine. The roots in which we were entangled ran deep and were not easily severed. We still hungered for each other. The cabin we were in was separated from the rest of the compound, so no one would know I was there. I agreed to be gone by dawn. After making love all night I was ready to roll over and go to sleep. But at 5 a.m. she pushed me out of bed. You have to leave, that was our deal. She meant it. As I was getting ready, she opened a dresser drawer and said here, you might as well take this. It was the engagement ring.

37. LIVIN' ON MY OWN

IN MID-AUGUST I APPEARED before the draft board in Great Neck for a hearing on a request by NASA that I be classified as 2-A, deferred because of the nature of my job. As a lawyer, I expected a certain amount of decorum in the proceeding. But waiting outside the meeting room, it was unnerving to hear raucous laughter inside. When I was called in, it seemed like a social gathering, not a hearing. The board members (all men) had taken off their jackets and loosened their ties. The table was littered with coffee cups and pastries. In the course of the discussion, one of the members asked me, with a smirk, if NASA was going to send me to the moon. That got a big laugh from the board. My fate was in the hands of a bunch of clowns. NASA's request for my deferment was brushed aside and I was ordered to report for a Selective Service physical later that month, which I did. Afterwards I received in the mail a small slip of paper called a "Statement of Acceptability." On it the box was checked saying "found fully acceptable for induction into the armed forces." That made me 1-A, prime draft material.

By then I'd moved to Washington and was working for NASA. I rented an apartment on the seventh floor of a building in Southwest Washington, an area being newly redeveloped after years of languishing. It was in walking distance to NASA headquarters, where I worked on the seventh floor. In Cambridge I'd lived and studied in old buildings. Now I was now living and working in new ones, a daily reminder that I'd moved on.

My apartment was not far from the Potomac, so on weekends I took long walks along the river, as I often had along the Charles in Cambridge. I also liked to roam around Georgetown, with its brick row houses, shops and restaurants. Clyde's was a Georgetown institution with a long wooden bar, dark paneling and antique fixtures. It quickly became my favorite watering hole. I would walk in feeling quite splendid in my new Burberry's trenchcoat, an expensive reward to myself for achieving my new station in life and earning a regular paycheck, after years in school living on parental support. Wearing it made me feel like Humphrey Bogart in Casablanca, which I'd seen several times at the Brattle Theatre in Harvard Square. We'll always have Cambridge.

Movies became another regular fixture of my life in Washington, or I should say, films. I reconnected with an old Cornell friend,

Humphrey Bogart

Joel Siegel, who was teaching at Georgetown University. On Sunday mornings we went to screenings of foreign films at the Janus Film Society, and then to lunch. When I arrived as a freshman at Cornell, a raw rock 'n' roller, Joel was two doors down in the dorm. He gave me an informal and ongoing one-on-one seminar on jazz, listening to his large record collection: Bird, Miles, Coltrane, Monk, the MJQ, Ella, Lambert Hendricks & Ross, and so many more. His lessons stuck and I became a jazz lover as well as a rocker. But at Janus I was no introductory student. It wasn't only Bogey flicks I saw at the Brattle, but films by Bergman, Fellini, Antonioni and many other great directors of the '60s.

At NASA, I was assigned work in two areas: developing the agency's position for an international treaty being drafted to cover personal injury and property damage caused by space junk falling from the sky, and drafting rules to implement the newly-enacted Freedom of Information Act. I became friends with another new lawyer there, Helen Slotnick. She was a Smith grad who went on to study at the Royal Academy of Dramatic Arts in London and to perform in the theatre. But after a few years, she decided that she needed more stability in her life and went to Boston College Law School. She was about ten years older than me, like a big sister. It was good to have a friend in the sterile world of Washington bureaucracy. She too was Jewish, liberal and against the war, but we only talked about Vietnam and politics away from the office. Everyone at NASA appeared to support the war, or perhaps like us some other people there kept their opposition to themselves.

Back in my place, alone at night, I was haunted by the end of my relationship with Beth. I just couldn't seem to fully accept that it was over. I spent hours listening over and over to the Stones latest LP, *Aftermath*, sometimes lying on the floor with my head between the speakers and the volume turned up. In the opening cut, the #1 hit single "Paint it Black," Mick sang "I see the girls walk by dressed in their summer clothes / I have to turn my head until my darkness goes." It was the pain of seeing a woman, of wanting a woman, of being alone, just as I'd felt seeing the surfer girls "standing by the ocean's roar." But this was no vague longing, it was about missing Beth. "It's not easy livin' on your own."

The last cut, "Goin' Home," was the longest one the Stones had ever recorded, an 11+ minute bluesy riff on goin' home "to see my baby." That's what I wanted to do, go back to Cambridge to see her. I wrote a long letter, eight typewritten pages, about our love and what went wrong. It was written to her, but it was also for me, to try to understand what had happened by putting my feelings on paper, a cathartic brief for my grief.

Through an intro from my Cornell friend Lenny, I became friends with an aspiring young actress from Washington, Marilyn Sokol. I was not looking for a relationship, but happy to have someone to talk to. She and I would meet in the spectacular gardens at Dumbarton Oaks, and walk and talk. I kept a copy of the letter I'd sent Beth, and one day let Marilyn read it, sitting on a bench in the gardens. She was touched by my sharing it with her, and by the deep emotions it expressed. But she knew better than to say to me, don't go back to Cambridge. It would have been good advice, but I wouldn't have listened.

Beth agreed, extremely reluctantly, to see me. I don't know what I was expecting to come of it, but it didn't matter, I just had to see her. On Saturday, October 15, three years to the day from when she asked if she could sit down next to me in Harvard Yard, we met there again. It was awkward and uncomfortable for both of us. She was sympathetic but unwavering, it was over between us. Maybe that's why I went, to hear her say it to my face. She told me she had a new boyfriend now, my old roommate Jeff. My heart turned black.

The next day I trained it back to D.C., leaving Cambridge for good. I took a cab from Union Station to my apartment building and stopped in the lobby to get the mail. An official-looking envelope caught my attention. I opened it in the elevator. Inside was a single-page document. It read:

The President of the United States,

To Steven R. Nelson

GREETING:

You are hereby ordered for induction into the Armed Forces of the United States.

PART THREE

Greetings

"To live outside the law you must be honest."
Bob Dylan, "Absolutely Sweet Marie"

SELECTIVE SERVICE SYSTEM

ORDER TO REPORT FOR INDUCTION

Approval Not Required.

The President of the United States,

To   STEVEN R. NELSON
      800 4th ST. S.W.
      WASHINGTON, D.C.
      APT. S 723

LOCAL BOARD NO. 3
161 GREAT NECK ROAD
GREAT NECK
NEW YORK 11021

(LOCAL BOARD STAMP)

OCT. 14, 1966
(Date of mailing)

SELECTIVE SERVICE NO.			
30	3	41	863

GREETING:

You are hereby ordered for induction into the Armed Forces of the United States, and to report
CIVIL DEFENSE HQTRS. (ELKS CLUB) 47 GRACE AVE.
at .... GREAT NECK, N.Y. (PARK AT GRACE AVE. PARKING LOT)
                   (Place of reporting)

on .... NOV 7 1966 .... at .... 7:15 A.M.
      (Date)   (Hour)

for forwarding to an Armed Forces Induction Station.

L. S. Pfaff
(Member or clerk of Local Board)

IMPORTANT NOTICE
(Read Each Paragraph Carefully)

IF YOU HAVE HAD PREVIOUS MILITARY SERVICE, OR ARE NOW A MEMBER OF THE NATIONAL GUARD OR A RESERVE COMPONENT OF THE ARMED FORCES, BRING EVIDENCE WITH YOU. IF YOU WEAR GLASSES, BRING THEM. IF MARRIED, BRING PROOF OF YOUR MARRIAGE. IF YOU HAVE ANY PHYSICAL OR MENTAL CONDITION WHICH, IN YOUR OPINION, MAY DISQUALIFY YOU FOR SERVICE IN THE ARMED FORCES, BRING A PHYSICIAN'S CERTIFICATE DESCRIBING THAT CONDITION, IF NOT ALREADY FURNISHED TO YOUR LOCAL BOARD.

Valid documents are required to substantiate dependency claims in order to receive basic allowance for quarters. Be sure to take the following with you when reporting to the induction station. The documents will be returned to you. (a) FOR LAWFUL WIFE OR LEGITIMATE CHILD UNDER 21 YEARS OF AGE—original, certified copy or photostat of a certified copy of marriage certificate, child's birth certificate, or a public or church record of marriage issued over the signature and seal of the custodian of the church or public records; (b) FOR LEGALLY ADOPTED CHILD—certified court order of adoption; (c) FOR CHILD OF DIVORCED SERVICE MEMBER (Child in custody of person other than claimant)—(1) Certified or photostatic copies of receipts from custodian of child evidencing serviceman's contributions for support, and (2) Divorce decree, court support order or separation order; (d) FOR DEPENDENT PARENT—affidavits establishing that dependency.

Bring your Social Security Account Number Card. If you do not have one, apply at nearest Social Security Administration Office. If you have life insurance, bring a record of the insurance company's address and your policy number. Bring enough clean clothes for 3 days. Bring enough money to last 1 month for personal purchases.

This Local Board will furnish transportation, and meals and lodging when necessary, from the place of reporting to the induction station where you will be examined. If found qualified, you will be inducted into the Armed Forces. If found not qualified, return transportation and meals and lodging when necessary, will be furnished to the place of reporting.

You may be found not qualified for induction. Keep this in mind in arranging your affairs, to prevent any undue hardship if you are not inducted. If employed, inform your employer of this possibility. Your employer can then be prepared to continue your employment if you are not inducted. To protect your right to return to your job if you are not inducted, you must report for work as soon as possible after the completion of your induction examination. You may jeopardize your reemployment rights if you do not report for work at the beginning of your next regularly scheduled working period after you have returned to your place of employment.

Willful failure to report at the place and hour of the day named in this Order subjects the violator to fine and imprisonment. Bring this Order with you when you report.

If you are so far from your own local board that reporting in compliance with this Order will be a serious hardship, go immediately to any local board and make written request for transfer of your delivery for induction, taking this Order with you.

SSS Form 252 (Revised 1-57 AD)   (Previous printings may be used until exhausted.)   U.S. GOVERNMENT PRINTING OFFICE : 1965 O—785-198

Draft Notice

1. DRAFTED

W HEN I GOT INTO MY apartment, I put my bag down and took another look at the draft notice. Odd, I thought, it said "Greeting," singular. I'd always heard they sent you "Greetings," plural. It said I was to report for induction on November 7 at Civil Defense Headquarters in Great Neck, at the Elks Club. The "Benevolent and Protective Order of Elks." I didn't think Uncle Sam was especially benevolent or protective by sending draftees to Vietnam. But I wasn't all that upset about being drafted, because I expected NASA to get me out of it.

The next day a senior NASA administrator, William Rieke, sent a letter to my draft board, requesting reconsideration of my induction. On October 25 the board replied that "after careful consideration" I was to report as ordered. However, because I was living and working in Washington, they recommended that I have my case transferred to a board in D.C.

Rieke immediately wrote to Colonel William Boughton in Albany, the director of Selective Service operations in the state of New York, requesting my deferment. He noted that through its aeronautical activities, NASA works with the Department of Defense. He made the point that with my degrees in math, law and public administration, "such qualifications are seldom combined in one person," which made me "most desirable" to NASA. He added that "it would not be possible to replace him." That was literally true, because LBJ had imposed a freeze on hiring federal employees. Rieke concluded by requesting that if I could not be reclassified, then my induction be postponed.

On November 1, Selective Service in Albany replied to Rieke in a one-sentence letter that I did not qualify for a deferment or a postponement. But that same day the draft board in D.C. sent me a notice that my request for a transfer of my induction from New York to Washington was approved and my November 7 induction was postponed. Two weeks later they sent me an order to report for induction in Washington on December 5. So now I had received two "Greeting"s, plural.

I was glad to learn earlier in the fall that I passed the bar exam, and was notified that I was to have a character interview in December, which was required before I could be admitted to the federal bar. I requested the Great Neck draft board to delay my induction so that I could do the interview. No dice, they replied, report as ordered on December 5.

At this point I was running out of options, and starting to become concerned. I went to see my boss, the Deputy General Counsel, about my status. He told me that recently he had been part of a NASA contingent which flew the Deputy Director of the Selective Service, Colonel Daniel O. Omer, to Cleveland for a tour of the NASA Lewis Research Center there. He was going to call him about my situation. I recalled the argument I'd had with Beth about her father using his connections to get her brother out of the draft. Now here I was, using my own connections.

When he called, Omer came right to the phone. After some Deputy-to-Deputy chit chat about their trip, he got around to the reason for his call. There's this young lawyer in my office, he said, looking at me and smiling, and went into my qualifications, that I couldn't be replaced, why they needed me, etc. Getting to the point, he asked, How can we get him deferred? I couldn't hear what Omer was saying, but I watched my boss nodding his head and saying oh, I see, yes I understand. After thanking Omer and concluding the call with some social niceties, he hung up the phone. I knew what he was going to say, that there was nothing Omer could do. Because the deployment of troops to Vietnam was accelerating, Selective Service needed every man they could get their hands on. They were even drafting lawyers out of the Defense Department. He apologized for not being able to help. I thanked him and left his office.

2. Trapped

In a state of shock, I went back to my office and closed the door. It was a small windowless airless room which always gave me a slight feeling of claustrophobia, but now it seemed oppressive. There was a knock on the door. It was Helen Slotnick, who'd seen me coming back down the hall. She'd been following my jousting with Selective Service, and wanted to know how my meeting went with the Deputy General Counsel. She too was stunned at the outcome. "Oh Steve, I'm so sorry." She insisted that I come over to her place for dinner that night. I was grateful for her company and support. She and I talked about what I was going to do, but I really didn't know, and was facing induction in 10 days.

Later that night, back in my apartment, I thought about my situation. My gambit had failed, hoping to ride out the draft with student and job deferments until I was 26. With hindsight, when I got out of law school, I probably could have gotten into JAG, the Judge Advocate General's Corps. But that was just a cushier way of serving in the military. And what if I'd been assigned to prosecute a soldier who refused orders to Vietnam? If I refused, then I could face a court-martial and prison time. Anyway, JAG was no longer an option. As draft calls mounted, law school grads flocked to get in, and by now there were no openings.

So I considered my options. Be inducted and likely be shipped to Vietnam. No, that was definitely not acceptable. Refuse induction and likely go to jail. No, that was definitely not acceptable. Seek asylum in Canada and leave my family and friends behind, likely for many years. No, that was definitely not acceptable. Which brought me back to the first option. Over the next few days, these three options kept going around in my head, from one to the next to the next and back again. Vietnam, prison, Canada, Vietnam, prison, Canada. I was trapped, with no way out. After a few days of this mental agony, my head spinning, I was walking in a long windowless corridor at NASA. It began to spin. I had to lean against a wall for support, to keep from falling over. As though I'd been hit by an enormous wave, I could barely tell up from down.

I got a brief reprieve thanks to NASA reaching out to the Director of Selective Service for the District of Columbia, Colonel John Martin Jr. He agreed to postpone my December 5 induction so that I could do my character interview and then appear on January 20 in federal court for a ceremony when new admittees to the bar were to be sworn in. From NASA's point of view, I'd be more valuable as a member of the bar when I returned there after my military service. I was grateful for the postponement and for the opportunity to be admitted to the bar. But I wasn't thinking much about my future career. I had far more immediate concerns.

3. ROLLIN' ON

WITH THE HOLIDAYS COMING up, I took some time to visit my family on Long Island. They were aware of my draft dilemma and totally supportive, opposed to the war themselves. But I didn't let on just how dire matters were and how much I was suffering. As far as they knew, I was using my legal skills and channels at NASA to resolve the situation. While I was in New York I went to see a well-known civil liberties lawyer I was referred to by Mickey Schwerner's dad Nat. He was willing to take on my case to fight my induction, but for a fee, of course. In the Civil War, it was legal to pay a bounty to someone to take your place in the draft. Now you paid a "bounty" to a lawyer, but the result was the same. If you had the dough, you wouldn't have to serve. I didn't. So all I could do was keep fighting the draft as my own lawyer.

Reading the December 18 Sunday *Times* over breakfast of bagels and lox, I saw a full-page ad for Antonioni's first English language film, *Blow-Up*, which was having its world premiere that evening at the Coronet Theatre in New York. I was a big Antonioni fan and had seen his classic trilogy at the Brattle in Cambridge:

The Yardbirds: Jeff Beck on far left, Jimmy Page second from right

L'Avventura, *La Notte* and *L'Eclisse*. The next day, when the regular run of *Blow-Up* began, I was there for the first show at noon.

When the film ended and the house lights came on, I didn't move from my seat, transfixed by Antonioni's evocation of swinging London and the photographic mystery at the heart of the story. Then the lights went back down as the 2:00 show was about to begin. I'd never before sat through back-to-back showings of a film, but I couldn't leave. And if I didn't have to catch the Long Island Railroad to get home for dinner, I might have stayed for the 4:00, if only to rewatch The Yardbirds, with Jeff Beck and Jimmy Page, doing "The Train Kept A-Rollin'."

At my parents' house I passed some time listening to the radio. Donovan had the #2 single with "Mellow Yellow," which was not how I was feeling. The Beach Boys were at #1 with "Good Vibrations," but I wasn't pickin' up any. The Supremes were still in the Top Ten with their recent #1 single, "You Keep Me Hangin' On," and Selective Service was doing just that. They sent me another "Greeting" from the President, my third draft notice, ordering me to report for induction in Washington on January 24. My draft board in Great Neck was furious that I hadn't been inducted as previously scheduled on December 5, due to the postponement for my character interview and swearing in. Unlike their typical brief communications, they wrote a lengthy letter to the D.C. board demanding an explanation.

4. IN GOOD CONSCIENCE

THE LETTER FROM THE Great Neck board also noted that I had requested Form 150, to apply for conscientious objector status. This was part of my strategy to keep pushing paper at them so as to delay my induction. But I was not going to lie on the form, so the question was, could I in good conscience claim to be a conscientious objector? This was something I'd been considering all fall, as I faced the reality of going to war. I believed in non-violence, as preached by Dr. King. But I had been wrestling with myself for weeks over whether I was opposed to all wars – in a nuclear age any war might lead to Armageddon -- and to the use of force against violence. These were the sort of questions I had to answer on the form. What were my beliefs, how had they been formed, how had I demonstrated and expressed them? The toughest issue for me was the Nazis. I had grown up highly sensitized to the murder of Jews in the Holocaust. Could I, a Jew, say that I would not have fought in World War II? After much soul-searching and some tough questioning from my lawyer -- me -- I concluded that I would not have.

On January 5 the board in Great Neck sent me an order to appear five days later at noon with Form 150 in hand, along with any other documentation, to present my case for exemption from the draft as an objector. According to the Form, I was supposed to have ten days to submit it. But the board was in no mood to be bothered with such details, or to read what I'd written in the form about my belief in "the supreme value of human life." They'd made up their minds that I was not eligible for exemption, since I was not brought up in a religious tradition of nonviolence nor was I a practicing member of any religion. Yet in fact religious affiliation was not a legal requirement for C.O. status.

Along with Form 150, I also submitted several letters as character references. One was from my Ames advisor Professor Robert E. Keeton. He wrote: "There is not the slightest doubt in my mind about the sincerity of Mr. Nelson's position as a conscientious objector," and called me "a person deeply concerned about moral and social issues." I was humbled and grateful for his support. If the Board even read the letter, they could have cared less.

I also submitted a letter from Nat Schwerner. He noted that as a friend of my family for some 30 years, he was convinced that my objection to military service was from "deep conviction that such involvement is ethically and morally wrong." Since Mickey's murder I'd questioned how I could ever measure up to his dedication. He'd made the supreme sacrifice, not in battle but in pursuit of justice. For Nat to say in his letter that he would "unhesitatingly subscribe to every superlative" about my character moved me deeply. But it didn't move the Board.

5. Making a Move

The fact was, the Board had no interest in anything that I might have to say. They told me that I could submit my documentation and then leave. I tried to initiate a discussion about my beliefs, but that went nowhere. They said that I'd submitted my claim to C.O. status only after being drafted, which in their view disqualified me. But I knew from legal research I'd done that this was not true.

In the case of *United States v. Gearey*, just decided in October, the U.S. Court of Appeals in New York ruled that a draft board was required to determine when a C.O. applicant's beliefs against war had crystallized. The Great Neck Board made no such determination. The very day of my appearance they sent me a letter stating its foregone conclusion, that my draft status remained unchanged, and that I was to report for induction on January 24. When I received it, I immediately called the Board about the procedure for appealing their decision. I was told that I had no right of appeal, and that the Board did not even consider the meeting to have been a hearing, just a courtesy "interview."

Their dismissive response gave me an opening. On January 17, I wrote to the Director of Selective Service for New York State, Colonel William H. Boughton, to whom William Rieke at NASA had written back in October requesting my deferment. In my letter I cited the *Gearey* decision, stated that the board had failed to comply with it, and argued that I was entitled to a good faith consideration of my claim to C.O. status.

The next day I called the Board and when I raised the issue of *Gearey*, was told that they had no information about it.

Boughton must have been persuaded by my letter that the board was in violation of *Gearey*. And maybe he remembered that people in high places in Washington were concerned about my draft status. So on January 23, the day before I was to be inducted, his office issued a Postponement of Induction until "further review by the State Director." That was followed the next day by a letter to me saying that the Board was told to review my case in light of the *Gearey* decision.

With all this going on, I realized I couldn't do my job and took a leave of absence from NASA. Having no income, I had to give up my apartment. Fortunately, my good buddy from law school, Joe Gibson, a Texan who was working for a Congressional committee, let me move into a spare room in his apartment. I felt restless, agitated and disconnected. I'd stay at Joe's place for a few days, then take a bus to New York and stay with my family, especially when I had business before the draft board, as I had for my January 10 "interview." Then I went back to Washington for the ceremony on January 20 admitting me to the Bar, along with Joe and a group of other young attorneys setting out on their careers. I celebrated completing the process of becoming a lawyer, which began for me that first day in Professor Casner's property class. But I felt like the fox in that famous case, on the run and trying to survive.

While staying with Joe, I met a young woman who lived across the back alley from his place. Her name was Marie, and she'd come from Maine to find a job in D.C. Blond, slender, quiet and gentle, she was nothing like Beth, which suited me fine. I needed to be with a woman, but was too messed up to satisfy Marie emotionally or sexually. Not that she was overly demanding, it was just that I couldn't be the lover she needed and deserved. I'd disappear for days, then show up unexpectedly at her place for a while before disappearing again.

I went back to New York when the Great Neck draft board summoned me to appear on February 7 for what they continued to call an "Interview" (which they now spelled with a capital "I"), despite

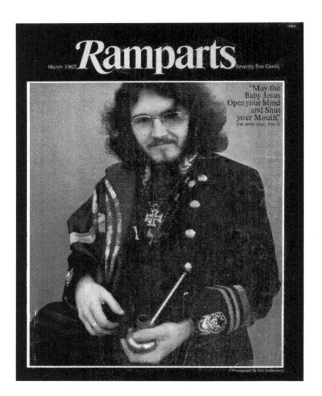

Cover of Ramparts Magazine with Stanley Mouse

the direction from Colonel Boughton about making a finding under the *Gearey* case. But Mother Nature intervened on my behalf with a snowstorm that forced the cancellation of the meeting. The Board ordered me to return in two weeks, on the 21st.

With some time on my hands, I went back to Washington. For something to read on the bus, I picked up a copy of *Ramparts*, a leftist political and literary magazine. I didn't usually read it, but was intrigued by the cover. It was a photo of a young man with long hair and a beard, wearing a military-looking jacket with big brass buttons, an iron cross hanging around his neck and some sort of metal pipe in his hand. His name was Mouse, a poster artist mentioned in the cover story, "The Social History of the Hippies."

I didn't know much about hippies, a social movement in San Francisco involving the likes of author Ken Kesey, poet Allen Ginsburg and ex-Harvard professor Timothy Leary, whom I vaguely remembered reading about in *The Harvard Crimson* when he was fired for something to do with drugs. Hippies had more than something to do with drugs. Their lifestyle rejected social convention and embraced drugs, free love and rock 'n' roll, dancing to bands with strange names like The Grateful Dead and Quicksilver Messenger Service at ballrooms called the Fillmore and the Avalon. The hippies offered a vision of personal freedom and expanded consciousness far removed from the physical and mental trap I was in.

6. Back to the Board

On February 21st I went to Long Island again for my "Interview" with the draft board. I provided two more letters for my file. One was from Joe Gibson, who made the point key to *Gearey*, that "his beliefs in conscientious opposition to war matured and crystallized only after he received his induction notice and was faced with the real prospect" of being trained "in the techniques of killing and war."

In the course of my yo-yoing between DC and NY after leaving NASA, I was able to get together occasionally with Helen Slotnick, who was deeply concerned about me. She also wrote a letter to my draft board. In it she said that after I was drafted, she saw me "go through an agony of self-appraisal," that I was on "the verge of complete despair" and "close to the point of breaking apart." She concluded a la *Gearey* that the "imminence of induction into the military service served as the catalyst to crystallize the beliefs he now holds."

Again, the Board refused to be drawn into any discussion. Other than the presiding member, the others remained stone silent. He never asked me anything that would lead to the determination under *Gearey* for which the "Interview" was intended. I was not surprised when a few days later, on February 27, they sent me a brief letter saying that "the information submitted at your interview...was not sufficient to warrant the reopening of your classification." Not a word about *Gearey* or when my beliefs had crystallized, not that they ever gave that issue any serious attention.

They also sent me a form cancelling the postponement of my induction and rescheduling it for March 22nd in Great Neck. It was not another "Greeting" from the President to add to my collection, but amounted to the same thing, my fourth order to report for induction.

When I got the Board's letter and order to report, I immediately wrote back to the chairman about their failure once again to follow the requirements of the *Gearey* case, and their "arbitrary disregard" of the material I'd submitted. That went nowhere, as I might have expected. When informed that I would be returning to Washington, where I resided and where my prior inductions were all to have taken place, the Board delayed my induction briefly. This was to allow the transfer board in D.C. to issue me yet another form, my fifth induction notice, rescheduling the date for March 28th at 6:45 am in D.C.

I knew I was dead right and the Great Neck board dead wrong about *Gearey*. The Board had said they were going to get me, and now it seemed like they were making good on that promise. I was running into a stone wall, adding to the severe stress I was under. By now there was nothing more I could do but report on the 28th, so it would not appear that I was just ignoring the induction order, but then refuse to be sworn in. Then somehow I'd need to find a lawyer to fight my case, on the grounds that the board had denied my rights under *Gearey*. It was a case I could win, but I didn't have the strength to fight on by myself any longer. Dean Griswold was right when he'd warned us that "he who has himself as a lawyer has a fool for a client." As Elvis put it, "Now and then there's a fool such as I."

7. SPIRITS

BEFORE RETURNING TO D.C., I was sitting alone at my parents' house late one night when I felt a strange sensation. Something inside me was stirring, like an alien creature in sci-fi movie struggling to get out. I wasn't experiencing any physical pain, and the feeling wasn't in my body but in my head, unlike anything I'd ever felt before, a powerful compulsion to create something, to somehow express myself. But how? I remembered my father's camera, the one I'd taken to Peru. It was still in their house, and there was some black and white film for taking family snapshots. But what was I going to shoot? There was nothing I could see of interest around the house.

Then it occurred to me, take a photo of myself. Needing more light, I found a candle and lit it. Pointing the camera at myself, I looked at the lens and clicked. In that moment something clicked inside me. It was as though my left brain, the rational brain of science and math and law which so defined me, was too exhausted from my ordeal to go on, and my right brain, the brain of an undiscovered creativity, emerged at that moment to help me see the way forward. That's exactly what the photo showed. The candle cast a deep shadow over the left side of my head, making it invisible. The right side

Self-portrait

of my head was emerging from the shadow, my face aglow, with a pinpoint of light from the flame reflected in my eye, like some spirit shining from within. I was not nearly a skilled enough photographer to have consciously set up that lighting scheme and captured that revealing image in a single shot.

Back in Washington, I was marking time until the 28th. I could scarcely relate to Marie, Joe or anyone else except in the most superficial way. One early spring afternoon I took a bus out to Alexandria, Virginia and went to the old Christ Church burying ground, which dated back to colonial times. It was a beautiful and peaceful place, there among the dead. I did some rubbings of old gravestones, with their archaic images and epitaphs, a spirit speaking from the stone: "All you who come my grave to see / As I am now you soon will be."

On March 20th I sent my final document to Selective Service, another letter to Colonel Boughton at New York State Headquarters. It detailed the "blatant disregard of my rights" by the Great Neck Board. I asked him to intervene again "to finally put to a halt the long course of illegal behavior in which the Board has indulged." With my induction date so near, I had little expectation that anything would come of it. But I wanted the letter to be on record after I refused induction.

As Tuesday the 28th drew near, I grew even more agitated and had trouble sleeping. I took a bus back to New York to visit my family on the weekend before my big date. I didn't talk a lot about the details of my draft situation, so they didn't fully realize how desperate I was. When I went back into the city on Easter Sunday the 26th to take the bus to D.C., I saw a poster for a be-in in Central Park, so I wandered up there. Thousands of people were gathered on a sunny day, like hippies in San Francisco, laughing and dancing and sharing flowers. I was too stressed to share their joyous spirit, but it felt good to be among so many happy people, no doubt all opposed to the war.

8. INDUCTION DAY

When I got back to Joe's place, I stayed awake all that night and the following one, too tense to sleep. Unshaven and unshowered, I looked and felt like a nervous wreck by the time I left for the induction center early Tuesday morning. But I was not going to a job interview, and was not wearing my best suit to impress a future employer, the U.S. Army. I didn't want the job. But I intended to show up as ordered, go through the induction process until asked to raise my right hand and be sworn in, and then refuse to do so.

My walk that morning to the place where I was to report took me along Pennsylvania Avenue, past the front of the White House. At a little after 6:00 a.m., I stopped at the iron fence surrounding the grounds, and shouted loudly, "Fuck you, Lyndon Johnson, fuck you!" I don't know if anyone heard my "Greeting" to the President, but I felt better and walked on.

A bus was waiting to take the draftees to the induction center at Fort Holabird in Baltimore. A long-haired guy was standing on the sidewalk next to the bus, holding a stack of newspapers and handing out a copy to everyone boarding. It was a local leftist weekly, and on the front page was a familiar image from old recruiting posters of a man with a top hat and a wispy white chin beard. In large bold letters it said, "Uncle Sam wants you, nigger!" The cover story was about how black men were being sent as cannon fodder to Vietnam in disproportionate numbers to whites. The week before there had been a big protest against the draft at all-black Howard University in D.C. The crowd shouted down the speaker, General Lewis Hershey, the head of Selective Service.

I stopped to talk to the paper guy. When he learned I was getting on the bus, he asked me if I'd be willing to hand out the papers. Sure, why not, so he gave them to me and left. I took the seat right by the door and gave a paper to everyone entering. They were all black. As ordered they were all carrying a small overnight bag with a change of clothes and toiletries. I didn't bring one.

At Fort Holabird we stripped to our underwear to go through the physical, as I had before in the summer of 1966, when I got classified 1-A. We were poked, prodded and told to drop our drawers, bend over and spread our cheeks. Whatever they were looking for up there, none of us had it. We were then told to sit down on some benches and wait. I saw a couple of soldiers talking to each other and looking my way. Then one of them came over and asked whether I was the one who'd been handing out the papers in the bus. I didn't hesitate to say yes. Then he asked if I wanted to become part of the "glorious history" of the U.S. Army. I didn't hesitate to say no. That took him aback, and he walked off.

My next stop was upstairs to see a doctor for an evaluation of any disqualifying physical conditions I might have, none that I knew of. He asked whether I had this or that disease or condition, checking boxes on a form. Did I ever have an ulcer? I mentioned being treated for a possible ulcer in the spring of my first year at law school, which I'd forgotten all about until now. I'd been under a lot of stress then, but a summer on the beach in Santa Monica proved to be the cure. The doctor then told me that information about the ulcer was insufficient to make a final determination of my physical acceptability for military service. So he was issuing what he called a 3-T deferment, to allow me three months to submit any further information.

I could hardly believe what I was hearing. The deferment cancelled my pending induction. In two months, after my 26th birthday on May 29th, I would automatically be reclassified as 1-Y and no longer subject to being called up. The doctor saw that I was in a state of physical and mental exhaustion, and used the ulcer to give me an out with the deferment. It was an act of mercy.

For months I'd been in a three-dimensional trap of Vietnam, prison and Canada. Now suddenly a door opened into a fourth dimension. I saw the light and walked through it, into the sunshine outside Fort Holabird. The bus was waiting for the return trip to D.C. I was the only passenger. All the black guys who'd ridden out that morning were in the army now, many of them to return from Vietnam damaged, or in a box.

I was damaged, a casualty of the war I fought against. But I was alive, and I was free. I was free. I was free.

9. Escape from D.C.

When I got back to Joe's apartment, everyone was excited to see me and find out what happened. They congratulated me on beating the draft. I suppose I had, by pushing paper, and experiencing the agony of victory. But I knew well what being a winner was really like. This was more like being rescued from the clutches of the draft dragon by a knight in a white doctor's coat. My new draft status was made official in a letter from the Great Neck Board, requesting that my "physician submit a statement regarding your claimed ailment," described as an "ulcer condition." I knew I didn't have to bother submitting anything else. Enclosed with the letter was a form on which a box was checked that read: "Found not acceptable for induction under current standards."

Now I wanted to get the hell out of Washington. Most people there lived and breathed war and politics, and I wanted nothing to do with either. "I gotta get out of this place / If it's the last thing I ever do," to paraphrase The Animals' big hit. The song had become an anthem for U.S. troops in Vietnam, so we had that much in common, a desire to escape from our present circumstances.

I needed to go somewhere to heal from my ordeal. I thought about those sunny beaches in southern California, but didn't want to be so far away from family and friends. So the obvious place was Cambridge, where I would be comfortable in a hotbed of opposition to the war. And that opposition was on the rise everywhere. On April 4 Dr. King denounced the war in a sermon from the pulpit of Riverside Church in New York. On April 15 there were big antiwar demonstrations in New York and San Francisco. On April

28 Muhammad Ali refused induction into the armed forces. It was great to have the champ on my side, but I knew well that he'd pay a big price for refusing to serve.

10. An Exile in Harvard Square

I FOUND A CHEAP ONE-room apartment at the end of Mount Auburn Street, near Putnam Circle. It was spring, and from my place it was an easy walk to the Charles River or into Harvard Square, where I could wander around for hours among the shops and through the Yard. I didn't have a lot of money for food, but there were plenty of cheap eats to be had around the Square, and I'd survived on a far more meager diet in Peru. Occasionally I'd stop for coffee and a croissant at the Patisserie Francaise, the place where I had lunch after dropping out of law school, when my Jag broke down. It was an arty-looking crowd hanging out there, with lots of long hair. Mine was growing out too. There were always people to watch at the Patisserie and around the Square. I saw the girls go by, but I was just looking. I was still feeling too withdrawn and sexually insecure to even think about a relationship.

I was content being by myself and savoring my freedom, an exile from the war. I had a record player and plenty of time to listen to music. And there was so much to listen to. The Beatles, The Stones, Dylan, The Byrds, The Doors, I couldn't afford to keep up with the flood of new LPs. The Harvard Coop had a huge record department, mostly classical with a good selection of jazz. As a token nod to what was happening in popular music, they had a couple of bins of rock LPs. I would stop by from time to time and flip through them, to see what was new.

One day I came across a white album with a yellow banana on front, above Andy Warhol's name. I was a fan of Warhol's pop art, so I pulled the album out from the bin. Turning it over, I saw in bold lettering at the top, "The Velvet Underground & Nico." Under that there was a picture of a band playing, and at the bottom individual headshots of band members with light patterns projected on them.

There was something familiar looking about them. Could this be that unforgettable but unknown band I'd heard a year ago at the *Paris Review* party? I bought the record and went back to my apartment. When I played it, I immediately recognized that yes, it was them, The Velvet Underground. I listened to the album over and over. On the front cover in small type next to the banana it said "Peel Slowly and See." So I did, revealing a pink phallic banana beneath. I stuck the yellow banana peel on my refrigerator, a visual reminder of my serendipitous discovery.

I spent many late nights at the Hayes-Bickford cafeteria in the Square. With a cup of coffee and an order of English muffins, I could pass hours at a table in the corner, watching the cast of characters who wandered in and out of the place. But mostly the Bick was my reading room. I devoured Ken Kesey's *One Flew Over the Cuckoo's Nest* and *Sometimes a Great Notion,* Tom Wolfe's *The Kandy-Kolored Tangerine-Flake Streamline Baby,* Jack Kerouac's *On The Road,* Henry Miller's *Tropic of Cancer* and *Tropic of Capricorn,* Jean-Paul Sartre's *Nausea* and *No Exit,* Louis-Ferdinand Celine's *Journey to the End of the Night,* and Fyodor Dostoyevsky's *The Idiot* and *Notes from the Underground.* I'd never been a big reader of fiction, so this was like taking a course in cutting-edge literature, not at Harvard but right across the street from the Yard. These books were the perfect complements to my favorite literary work, The *Velvet Underground & Nico.* I couldn't get enough of those notes from the Underground.

But at the same time, my musical tastes were expanding, thanks to Club 47. It had moved from its original location at 47 Mt. Auburn Street, where I'd seen Dylan, to a space behind the Harvard Coop, 47 Palmer Street. Admission was cheap, and I could go by myself and nurse a cup of tea and maybe a light snack while listening to the music. I was drawn there by the electric blues of Muddy

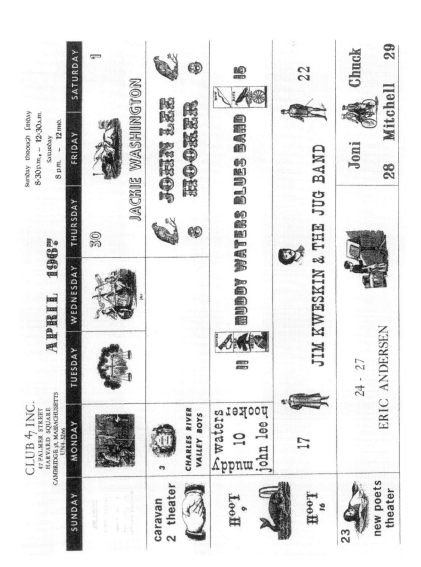

Club 47 calender for April 1967

Waters and John Lee Hooker, but got turned on to the bluegrass picking of The Charles River Valley Boys and the good-time music of The Jim Kweskin Jug Band. It put a smile on my face to watch Fritz Richmond plucking a single-string washtub bass or huffing and puffing into a jug.

11. FRIENDS

AT DESIGN RESEARCH ON Brattle Street, I bought some little colored transparent plastic boxes. I had my father's camera and took a lot of slides of the colorful shadows they cast. Inspired by the images of The Velvet Underground on their album cover, I projected the slides onto a model and photographed her. It was Marie, who'd moved to Cambridge. She wasn't following me there, but decided that she too had had enough of Washington. Alone in my exile, not knowing a soul in Cambridge and still too withdrawn to relate to strangers, it was good to see someone I knew. We were friends but no longer lovers.

Wandering around the Square, I went into a place called Leather Design to check out the sandals and belts. Aside from Marie, I'd hardly had a conversation with anyone in weeks. But a guy working there started talking with me as soon as I walked in. He was short, slim, bearded and friendly. In my withdrawn state of mind, for a moment I thought he might be gay and coming on to me, why else would he take an interest in me? But as we talked I quickly relaxed. He asked what I was up to and I briefly explained my situation. He was sympathetic. This was Harvard Square, after all, and being a draft resister meant you were a good guy, not a law breaker. His name was Bob Driscoll, and I could see from other people coming into the shop that he had an aura about him which drew people to him and made them feel comfortable.

I really needed a friend at that point, and Bob soon became one. He involved me with his circle of hippie friends: Rodney

Bob Driscoll

Hippie family: Alison Deming and Scott Williams with daughter Cindy

*Laura Grosch painting Hillary Rodham's face
at Charles River be-in*

Deming, his sister Alison, her husband Scott Williams and many others around the Square. I began smoking marijuana with them. I'd never smoked cigarettes, so I had a hard time inhaling. At first I was just high on the idea that I was high, without really being stoned. But I got the hang of it, and smoking pot became part of my everyday life, sharing a joint with hippie friends and listening to music together. More than anything getting high was letting go, being comfortable with myself and open with other people. I was feeling better than I had in a long time, emerging from my shell.

Bob and I did a photo shoot together, for which he styled his friend Ellie as our model. Then on Sunday, April 30, to get ready for a be-in, Bob painted the faces of our group of hippies in a unique minimalist style, just a swirl of paint or a dab of color. Then we all strolled down to the river. With Memorial Drive closed to traffic for the afternoon, the road and riverbanks were swarming with young people. I met up with a friend of my brother Peter, Laura Grosch, a student at Wellesley and an artist in the making. She was from North Carolina, but he knew her from Woods Hole, where her father was a scientist. She was exuberant and engaging, and I was happy to befriend her. A crowd gathered to watch Laura paint the face of her college roommate, Hillary Rodham.

12. GOT MY MOJO WORKING

WHEN I DECIDED TO MOVE back to Cambridge, it was not because I was hoping to see Beth, who by then would be finishing her senior year at Radcliffe. That was over for me and I hadn't given her a thought for months, too overwhelmed to be thinking about old girlfriends, even her. But it was inevitable that I would run into her around the Square sooner or later. Still, it was a shock when I did. At first, our conversation was awkward, without much eye contact. She quickly let me know that she was still in a serious relationship with Jeff. That got that out of the way.

I told her about my confrontation with the draft, and how it had left me mentally and physically exhausted. Then, maybe because I'd become more comfortable talking to her, I said that it had also left me feeling sexually insecure. It was a peculiar subject to bring up with her of all people, but I guess I was looking for sympathy. She looked directly at me, blurted out "You!" and laughed. It was such an unexpected reaction, like a bucket of cold water in the face. I mumbled something about yeah, maybe it was silly of me to think so, and we soon parted. I knew then that my mojo would soon be working again.

I went to Long Island to visit my family. I wanted them to see that I was alright, and I wanted to see how they were doing. I thanked them for their continuing financial support, which they could barely afford and I felt somewhat guilty about taking. My father's physical infirmity hadn't improved, and he had given up his business. He spent a lot of time watching TV and smoking, the last thing he needed in his condition. It was a habit he once had the discipline to break, but no longer. My mother was still working as a child day care administrator and carrying on valiantly as his caregiver, although at a slow boil at being stuck in that situation. Emotions were raw. After a couple of days I was glad to get out of there.

On the bus ride back I couldn't help but notice a beautiful young blonde in the seat across the aisle from me. It took me a long time to get up the nerve, but before we got to Boston I struck up a conversation with her. Gail was living in Somerville, next door to Cambridge, and gave me her phone number. I went to see her one evening and stayed the night. It felt so good to be making love with a woman, my mind and body freed. She blew me away when she mentioned that she was a friend of The Velvet Underground's manager. They'd be playing in a couple of weeks at The Boston Tea Party, a local rock club like the Fillmore and Avalon ballrooms I'd read about in Ramparts. She said she'd put my name on the guest list.

13. THE TEA PARTY

I'D BEEN TO THE TEA PARTY once before a few weeks ago, with Bob and some of his friends. We drove over from Cambridge in Rodney's van and passed around a joint on the way. The headliner that night was David Blue and his band The American Patrol. He had been part of the folk music scene in Greenwich Village with Dylan before he too went electric. The Tea Party was in an old brick Victorian building in Boston's South End, a pretty rough neighborhood. Members of a motorcycle club were parked out front, dressed in their colors – "Devil's Desciples" (as they spelled it) across the back -- and revving their engines, just in case you didn't happen to notice them.

We went up a short flight of stairs to the front door, over which hung a large sign with stylized lettering reading "Filmmakers Cinematheque and The Boston Tea Party." Then we walked up a long flight of stairs to the ticket window and coat room, and took a left up another long flight to the main floor. At the landing off to the right was a short corridor with black lights which made everyone walking by look spooky. Ahead was the performance space, a big boxy room with a ceiling that must have been forty feet high, a mirror ball suspended over the middle of the hall, the stage at the far end. The Desciples were hanging out in back of the balcony, from where the light show crew projected colorful blobs pulsing with the music onto the back wall of the stage, as well as experimental films and other images. On the wall, large arcing black letters proclaimed, "Praise Ye The Lord," painted there by a religious group which once used the building. With the blasting volume of the band, the kaleidoscopic imagery of the lightshow, the whirling reflections from the mirror ball making the room seem to spin, the ecstatic dancing bodies, and the stoned vibe, this was Boston's psychedelic temple of rock.

I was really excited about seeing The Velvet Underground again, and as a guest of the band no less. It was also a special

Flyer for "Andy Warhol's Velvet Underground" at the Tea Party

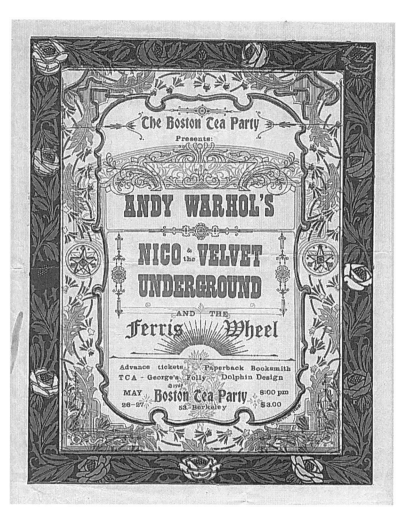

Second flyer for the show listing "Nico & The Velvet Underground"

weekend for me, because on the following Monday, May 29, Memorial Day, I'd turn 26 and become ineligible for military service, ulcers or no ulcers. Since my trip to Fort Holabird, I was no longer in any danger of being called up, but this would make it official. What better way to celebrate than partying on a Saturday night at the Tea Party with the VU. Gail had told me that she thought the guys running the light show might be interested in some of my slides I'd shown her, so I brought along a small box of them. But I decided not to take my camera. Seeing an event through a lens created a distance from it, becoming absorbed in the process of photographing it. I just wanted to surrender to the sounds and sights and energy.

From the Tea Party handbills and posters I'd seen around the Square promoting upcoming shows, most of the bands that played there were local, David Blue being an exception. Now the main attraction was billed as Andy Warhol's Velvet Underground. Even if you'd never heard of the band, Warhol was a famous pop artist and avant-garde filmmaker. His name alone would draw a big crowd, even without him there. The VU was playing Friday and Saturday; I went on the second night. People were talking about what happened the night before. Nico, the band's icy blonde sometime-chanteuse, didn't show up until near the end of the night. Their lead singer and guitarist Lou Reed was already annoyed that a second handbill for the show billed the band as "Nico & The Velvet Underground." Now he was pissed, and there was a scene on stage when he refused to let her perform.

Nico's top billing on that second handbill didn't last long. By Saturday someone at the Tea Party had covered up her name on the remaining copies. She was nowhere to be seen, in print or in the flesh. The band was focused on its music, without any distractions from Warhol world. I'd heard them at the Village Gate and listened to their album repeatedly. But I was hardly prepared for how much more powerful they sounded at the Tea Party. In that big box of a room, with its high ceiling –

unlike the basement of the Gate – their sound exploded in my mind and body. The whole space vibrated with the music, the floor rising and falling, people dancing in a trance. It was the apotheosis of rock 'n' roll, and yet at its most primitive, driven by the relentless pounding of their girl drummer Maureen Tucker.

At the break between sets Gail introduced me to the Velvets' manager Steve Sesnick. When she told me at her apartment that he was a "friend" of hers, I had the feeling that she was sleeping with him too. If so, he didn't show any indication of knowing that I had. Or maybe this was how it was in a new world of free love. I told him that I was a fan of the band from seeing them at the Village Gate. That gave me some status, because it predated his relationship with them.

I also met the guys who did the light show, a Mutt and Jeff pair. "Jeff" the short one was Roger Thomas, disheveled looking, with a bristly little mustache. "Mutt" the tall one was John Boyd, neater, with a spectacular handlebar mustache. They may have looked like laid-back hippies, but when the band was playing, they never stopped for a moment in keeping the light show ever-changing and moving to the beat. They liked my slides and agreed to pay me $25 for them. It was the first time I'd sold my photography, and I was glad to have a little extra money.

When the VU came back on, I hung around the balcony for a while before heading back down into the crowd. From up there I overlooked the whole wild scene in front of me. I thought about a year ago at the Gate when I first heard them, a handsome Harvard Law grad with my beautiful Cliffie girlfriend. Then my whole life collapsed on me. Now I'd crawled out of the rubble. That night at the Tea Party marked my final escape from my war with the draft.

After the show I went to the office to get a check for my slides. I was introduced to one of the owners of the club, Ray Riepen, "you guys are both from Harvard Law School." Since we also both lived in Cambridge, he offered me a ride home in his big black Lincoln Continental. I learned Ray was a former corporate lawyer from Kansas City, in Cambridge for a year taking a Master's in Law degree. It was a gut course compared to the three-year program I'd done. But it was just what he wanted, a reason to be in the Boston area without having to work hard at school. I gave him a little of my background, but without going into any detail, just that I recently beat the draft and was back in Cambridge looking for what to do next.

14. SUMMERTIME

AFTER THE WEEKEND, I started my new job, making sandals and belts at Leather Design. The store had moved from the center of the Square to Mount Auburn Street, about a block from where I lived. Bob had introduced me to Nick Neumann, the owner, who was looking for help. The job only paid $50 a week, and it didn't exactly call on my three degrees from prestigious institutions of higher learning. But it was satisfying to get in a daily routine, earn some money and work with my hands. The store was known for a certain sandal design, which Nick taught me how to make. A customer would come in, take off his shoes, and I'd kneel down and trace the outlines of his feet on pieces of cardboard. Then I'd use that to cut custom-shaped soles, glue them together with straps, and when he came back for a final fitting, make sure they fit right. I even made myself a pair, the first sandals I'd worn since my rubber *llanquis* in Vicos.

On June 1, The Beatles released their new album, *Sgt. Pepper's Lonely Hearts Club Band*. It was an immediate commercial success, going right to #1 on the album charts and staying there all summer. Among the hippies around the Square, it was more than #1, it was a phenomenon. Everyone was listening to it and talking about it. We couldn't believe what we were hearing, there'd never been anything like it. It was only a month or so since I first got high "with a little help from my friends." Now The Beatles got us all high, with or without pot.

The Velvet Underground returned to the Tea Party two weeks after their May gig, but I was out of town that weekend in Woods Hole. Laura Grosch was getting married to another artist from North Carolina, Herb Jackson. It was a hippyish affair, the bride and groom both sporting garlands of flowers on their heads. After the brief church ceremony, the entire wedding party, about fifty of us, paraded down Main Street to the reception. Everyone was having a great time dancing with each other. My brother Peter was there too. Laura prevailed on him to ask her roommate Hillary to dance because, Laura said, she was shy.

For me, the living was easy in the summer of '67. Work at Leather Design during the day, get stoned with friends at night, wander around the Square occasionally with my camera. Gail had moved away, but I still wasn't ready for a relationship anyway. I was living in the present, which was good enough for now, and not thinking about the future. It was being called the Summer of Love, with young people flocking to San Francisco in search of good vibes and good drugs. There was even a hit song about it, the treacly ballad "San Francisco (Be Sure to Wear Flowers in Your Hair)."

The Jefferson Airplane captured the vibe far better with their back-to-back hits "Somebody to Love" and "White Rabbit." A band from New Jersey, of all places, The Young Rascals, got that laid back feeling in their hit "Groovin'"; one of the Rascals, Felix Cavaliere, was formerly with twisters Joey Dee & the Starliters. Two hard-driving singles, Aretha Franklin's "Respect" and The Doors' "Light My Fire," both hit #1. But it was The Beatles who provided the anthem of the summer with their chart-topper "All You Need Is Love." They performed it live on a worldwide television broadcast, with Mick Jagger, Keith Richards, Eric Clapton, Keith Moon, Graham Nash and Marianne Faithful sitting on the floor at The Beatles' feet and singing along with the refrain at the end of the song: "Love is all you need, love is all you need."

15. Words from the Avatar

THERE WAS A COMMUNE on Fort Hill in Roxbury, a white enclave surrounded by a black neighborhood. The group's leader was Mel Lyman, former banjo and harmonica player for the Kweskin Jug Band. Mel had quit music to take on his self-appointed mission of illuminating the people of earth. They were planning to publish an "underground" paper to be called *Avatar*, featuring Mel's writings, an "avatar" being the physical manifestation of a deity, a divine teacher incarnate.

In the spring I'd met one of the writers for the paper, Dave Wilson, who was also the publisher and editor of Broadside, a monthly which covered the Boston folk scene. I was invited up to the Hill and, over a tasteless macrobiotic dinner, asked to write a column of legal advice. This was about the furthest thing from my mind, doing legal research and writing, but I agreed to give it a shot, even though it paid nothing.

My column, "Legal Hang-Ups," appeared in the first issue of the paper in June. By way of introduction I described it as being "about the law, a subject which many of you, often myself included, find to be a drag." I cited the Canons of Professional Ethics to the effect that a lawyer was not allowed to advertise or promote himself, or to engage in any other forms of "self-laudation," such as being quoted in the press. That would "offend the traditions" of the legal profession and be considered "reprehensible." However, a lawyer "may with propriety write articles for publication in which he gives information upon the law" so long as he did not give specific advice. So that's what my column was to be about, general information which might be useful to *Avatar* readers about topics such as drug laws, the draft and discrimination.

For my next column I decided to write about something I was all too familiar with: how to qualify as a conscientious objector. It was hard for me to think about that again, so it slowed me down writing the piece, which didn't appear until Issue #4 in July. I explained that in the U.S. the issue of conscientious objection to military service went back to the time when the Bill of Rights was being proposed in 1789. The version passed by the House of Representatives stated that "no person religiously scrupulous shall be required to bear arms," and prohibited the infringement of the "equal rights of conscience." But the Senate cut those provisions from the final Bill.

I wrote about some changes to the draft law which Congress had just passed in the spring. It eliminated the requirement that belief in a Supreme Being was necessary to qualify as a C.O. That reflected a unanimous Supreme Court ruling in 1965, *United States v. Seeger*, that the Supreme Being test could be met by a belief which "occupies a place in the life of its possessor parallel to that filled by the orthodox belief in God." I remembered Professor Keeton's letter on my behalf, in which he said my beliefs "occupy a position in his personal moral philosophy comparable to that occupied by religious beliefs." Clearly he had read the Seeger case.

I concluded my column by advising would-be conscientious objectors that they would have to make the case about their beliefs to their draft boards. But I warned them that "trying to have a serious and intelligent conversation with them on questions of religion, philosophy, and morality, so as to convince them of your sincerity and qualification as a C.O., can only be compared to preaching non-violence to the S-M crowd." As I had found, trying to have such a conversation was in itself an act of masochism.

16. A NEW EXPERIENCE

I RETURNED TO LEATHER DESIGN one afternoon after a lunch break. Nick said a guy named Ray was looking for you. The only Ray I could think of was Ray Riepen. I asked him, you mean the guy from the Tea Party? I don't know, he replied, he didn't leave a message but he said he'd be back in touch with you. And he was, a day later. We took a walk, and he told me that either he

Ray Riepen

David Hahn

was going to buy out his Tea Party partner David Hahn, or David was going to buy him out. He said that if he bought out David, he was going to hire a manager, since David was more hands on with booking the bands, putting out the posters and other aspects of the business. Ray said that he'd approached Jim Rooney, the manager of Club 47, but he'd decided to stay there. Jim was a pro, and a good acoustic guitar player. But rock 'n' roll wasn't really his thing. It was mine, and that's what Ray was thinking, that he needed someone who was into the kind of music the Tea Party presented. So he asked me if I'd be interested in becoming the manager.

That came out of the blue. I was really excited about the idea, but admitted I'd never run a club, or any business for that matter. But Ray wasn't concerned. He figured that as a lawyer, and someone part of the hippie scene who knew rock 'n' roll, I could handle it. I'd be paid a salary and have use of the Tea Party's company "car," a VW camper bus. He wanted someone who would take over the whole operation, since he wanted to have the time to look into other opportunities which the success of the Tea Party was opening up with the youth counterculture in the Boston area. We shook hands on the deal, pending his buying out David. He said he'd get back to me about that.

Despite what the Canons of Professional Ethics had to say on the matter, I found that self-promotion paid. I hadn't seen Ray since he gave me a ride home two months earlier after the VU show. But he must have been reminded of me when he saw my columns in the *Avatar*. He had his eye on media aimed at young people, and checked out the paper. It was Mel Lyman who had got him into the rock 'n' roll business. Ray had a friend from Kansas City, Jesse Benton, the daughter of the great American painter Thomas Hart Benton. Jesse was living on Fort Hill and wanted to marry Mel. But she needed to get divorced, and called on her lawyer friend Ray.

The Fort Hill people were starting the Filmmaker's Cinematheque (of the same name but not connected to the one in New York) to show "underground" films by the likes of Andy Warhol. They'd rented this old building in the South End, with a big hall, and thought that if they ran dances on the weekends, it would help cover the costs of the film business. So they asked Ray if he'd be interested. He was, and partnered with David Hahn, an MIT grad living on Fort Hill, who had been running a bus line in British Honduras, and buying and selling used military vehicles. Ray and David put up $1500 each to open The Boston Tea Party. It was an immediate success. Mel and the Hill people had nothing more to do with it.

I walked back to Leather Design after meeting Ray, almost in a daze at the prospect of managing the Tea Party, a rock 'n' roll dream I hoped would come true. But I had to wait to hear from Ray. The Velvets returned to the Tea Party for the weekend of August 11 and 12. Warhol himself was going to be there for the Friday show to shoot some film. I wanted to go but decided not to. I didn't know what the dynamic between Ray and David was at that point, and didn't want to be in the middle of their divorce. So I went to Woods Hole for the weekend, happy as ever to be by the sea.

Ray got in touch about a week later. He excitedly told me about the Velvets-Warhol show. A new club, The Crosstown Bus, had opened to compete with the Tea Party. For that August weekend they had The Doors, whom they'd booked before their single "Light My Fire" rocketed to #1 on the charts in late July. The Tea Party put out a handbill playing up the Warhol appearance: "Be Part of What's Happening!! Andy Warhol comes to The Boston Tea Party this weekend to capture the people on film as they explode to the sights and sounds of The Velvet Underground." That pulled them in, girls dressed in their hippie finest, ready for stardom. Ray boasted that the Tea Party outdrew the Doors appearance at the Bus.

Then he got around to business. He was buying out David. Did I still want the job? Yes! I quit my job at Leather Design, thanking Nick for giving me the opportunity when I really needed the money and something to do. I also quit writing my column for *Avatar*, since I wouldn't have time for it anymore. I'd never been that comfortable dispensing legal wisdom in print, and was increasingly uncomfortable being associated with Mel Lyman, his written rants in *Avatar*, and his Fort Hill cult.

Sign above the entrance to The Boston Tea Party

I was to start at the Tea Party on the weekend of August 25-26. I spent a couple of days before that in a purple haze, with the August 23 release of *Are You Experienced?*, the debut LP by the Jimi Hendrix Experience. Jimi had been around the music business for several years, playing with the likes of Little Richard, The Isley Brothers and Joey Dee & The Starliters. But he burst onto the national scene in 1967, fronting his own group, when he burned his guitar at the Monterey Pop Festival in June. We'd all heard about it and were awaiting his album with great expectations. It blew us away. For me it completed a trilogy of The Velvets, Sgt. Pepper and Hendrix as the musical highpoints of my stoned Summer of Love.

Now a new season, and a new experience, was about to begin.

CANNED HEAT

ULTIMATE SPINACH

OCTOBER
6 & 7

the
BOSTON
TEA PARTY

8 PM $3.00

53
BERKELEY

338 - 7026

use Berkeley st. exit
from Arlington st. MBTA station

advance tickets at
paperback booksmiths
leather design   tea

Jerold's
George's folly
dolphin design

SAT. ONLY
The WIZARD EYE PANDCT
and his disciples
meditational harmonics

PART FOUR
Rock 'n' Roll

"She started dancin' to that fine fine music
You know her life was saved by rock 'n' roll."
The Velvet Underground, "Rock 'n' Roll"

1. REPORTING TO WORK

I GOT READY FOR MY FIRST night as manager of The Boston Tea Party. After taking a shower, I fluffed out my hair to dry, so it would curl up more. It had been growing out for months, and by now was a wild mane a la Dylan and Hendrix. I put on a flowered shirt, bell-bottom jeans, a belt I'd made at Leather Design, and boots. I topped off the outfit with my snakeskin vest and a string of beads. I was dressed for work, not all that different from what I wore every day, just much neater. Ray Riepen had a penchant for wearing three-piece pin-striped suits. He looked the part of the lawyer who owned the joint. I was just the hired help. The employees at the Tea Party didn't know what to expect from the new manager Ray had hired, some guy from Harvard Law. When I showed up for work, I could see their surprise, and approval, at what they saw, someone who looked not like a lawyer but more like one of them.

That night, Friday, August 25, the headliner was Country Joe & The Fish. They were one of the bands which came out of the San Francisco music scene and gained national recognition during the Summer of Love. This was their first tour back East, and they were the first of those West Coast bands to play The Tea Party. The handbill promoting the show, with the usual ticket price of $3, quoted a lyric from the band, "I hunger for your porpoise mouth." The labially-shaped design left no doubt what that was referring to. The crowd was hungry to hear the band and the club was jammed, way over the legal limit of 550 people, posted prominently on a wall as required by the city of Boston.

Everyone was buzzing with excitement, most of them buzzed on pot. When the band came on I went to the balcony to survey my new domain. Joe led the enthusiastic crowd in the Fish cheer:

Give me an F!
F!
Give me a U!
U!
Give me a C!
C!
Give me a K!
K!
What's that spell?
Fish!
What's that spell?
Fish!

Then they launched into "I Feel Like I'm Fixin' to Die Rag":

Well, come on all of you, big strong men,
Uncle Sam needs your help again.
He's got himself in a terrible jam
Way down yonder in Vietnam
So put down your books and pick up a gun,
We're gonna have a whole lotta fun.

It was my kind of song. Over in Nam, there were half a million U.S. troops, but the war was going south, literally. North Vietnam continued to flow down the Ho Chi Minh Trail to join the Viet Cong in South Vietnam, despite the unrelenting effort by the U.S. "to bomb them back into the Stone Age," in the words of former Air Force Chief of Staff General Curtis LeMay. We were hearing about a big antiwar protest being organized for Washington in October.

Ray Riepen wanted to be free from the day-to-day details of running the club, which he turned over to me. I was in charge of all aspects of the business: wrote the checks, booked the bands and promoted upcoming shows. I showed up for work on weekdays around ten, and left at five or six, depending on whether I had any calls to California. On Fridays I was there until I closed up after midnight; on Saturdays I came in late afternoon and stayed until closing.

Locking up after a show, I got in the VW bus and drove to the bank a few blocks away, where I did a night deposit of the proceeds from the evening, two or three thousand bucks, all cash. Luckily no one ever figured out that I was carrying that money and held me up. Sometimes after a show Ray and I went to one of the few Boston restaurants still open at that hour, Ken's Steak House in Kenmore Square. Or I'd go to Mondo's, a hole-in-the-wall eatery in the meat market district, where local musicians went after a gig. You could get a big cheap greasy breakfast all night in the company of truckers, cabbies, artists and hookers.

2. AT THE TEA PARTY

THE TEA PARTY BUILDING was a Gothic-looking brick pile with a curious feature, a huge window in the shape of a Star of David high on its front façade. People assumed it was a former synagogue, but in fact it had been built almost a hundred years earlier as a Unitarian meeting house on land donated by wealthy Boston developer John Gardner. His son Jack married Isabella Stewart, a socialite, philanthropist and art collector who founded the museum named for her. The meeting house was established in the memory of Unitarian minister Theodore Parker (1810-1860),a transcendentalist who was an associate of Ralph Waldo Emerson and Henry David Thoreau. Parker was an abolitionist and an early advocate of women's rights. In a speech in 1850 he called "the American idea of freedom... a government of all the people, by all the people, for all the people," words echoed later at Gettysburg by Abraham Lincoln. Had he returned to earth to preach to the Tea Party crowd, Parker would have been welcome. His spirit lived on there. Praise Ye The Lord.

The spirit of Theodore Parker hovered over the Tea Party

Running the Tea Party involved a core group of people working there when I came on board. They knew what they were doing, which made it easy for me to get up to speed quickly. Bob Perlman was my assistant manager, a bright and dependable young guy, but no hippie. Betsy and Debbie ran the ticket window and coat room. We didn't have a liquor license, just a booth at the back of the hall with a soft drink fountain. The sound system was provided by Hanley Sound, a local company run by brothers Bill and Terry who had done the sound at the Newport Jazz and Folk Festivals, including the show when Dylan went electric. The Road lightshow had Roger Thomas and John Boyd, filmmaker Ken Brown and one or two others who joined in. Building manager Mitch Blake kept the old place functional and clean. With his long hair, beard and sandals, Mitch looked the part of the Tea Party house guru that he was, quietly sharing his words of enlightenment.

Two weekends after Country Joe another California group came to town, Canned Heat, from L.A. They'd played Monterey Pop and had their first album out that summer, with covers of classic electric blues. Their great slide guitar and blues harp player, Al "Blind Owl" Wilson, grew up in the Boston area. He came up through Club 47 and the folk scene, and helped rediscover Delta blues great Son House, with whom he cut a record. There was a big audience in Boston for the blues, acoustic or electric, and with their local connection, Canned Heat was a big hit at the Tea Party. For my first booking at the club I brought them back four weeks later. Opening was Ultimate Spinach, a local artsy psychedelic group managed by an outfit in Boston called Amphion, after a figure in Greek mythology. The company was run by partners Ray Paret, an MIT grad who focused more on the business side, and David Jenks, a Williams College alum who handled the creative.

The Boston music business drew in a number of people with elite academic credentials, like Ray and David, and me and Ray Riepen for that matter. The Tea Party was a popular weekend destination for college and grad students. But it also attracted professors and professionals, and not just those in their twenties. They mixed in the crowd with hippies, many of them college dropouts; with white and black working-class high school kids from the Tea Party's South End neighborhood and nearby Roxbury; with Boston brahmins and bikers. Local celebs and media people came to check it out. I got to meet "Woo Woo" Ginsburg when he adventured there one night. It was a crazy cross-section of people, drawn by the music and their desire to be and be seen where "it was happening."

If I were still an anthropology student, maybe I would have done field research in this unique social environment. It was like the festival at Recuayhuanca, every Friday and Saturday night, a mellow crowd bonded by music. But here the leaf of choice was marijuana, not coca. There was no law against tobacco smoking inside, and I'd catch a whiff of grass occasionally, but mostly people got high on the way there, or went outside for a pot break. Not everyone was stoned, just almost everyone. But not me. Lots of people crowded into one room had the potential to be a volatile mix. I had to be totally straight to keep things mellow and be sure we put on a good show.

That's why people went to the Tea Party. No one ever got into a fight, not even the Devil's Desciples. On a rare occasion a kid might try to snatch a wallet left in a purse under a chair along the side wall when a girl got up to dance. I caught one in the act once, hollering for help as I grabbed him heading for the door. Maybe I should have let him go, maybe he had a weapon hidden on him. But my instinct in that moment was to protect what we all valued, a place where we could be together and have a good time. Check bad vibes at the door.

3. THE MUSIC

WHEN MY RESPONSIBILITIES permitted, I joined the audience for part of the performances; I wasn't going to be the only one in the place who didn't get to listen to the music. The Tea Party hosted a lot of local acts. Even with an out-of-town headliner, there was usually a local opener, with some good talent to draw on in Beantown. They got paid very little, but there was no lack of local bands wanting to play there "for the exposure." During my first few weeks I got to hear The Bagatelle, a nine-piece mixed-race R&B band, with three black lead singers – Rodney was tall, Fred medium height, Redtop short -- doing great harmony. They had a fourth singer who wrote some of their material, played keyboards and would handle lead on some tunes, a white guy named Willie Alexander. He'd played the club's opening night in The Lost, now disbanded, as had The Bagatelle's drummer Lee Mason and bassist Walter Powers. It was a tight-knit scene among local musicians.

I also heard The Beacon Street Union, a five-piece rock band with a psychedelic edge. The Sidewinders were another five-piecer in a more Stonesy vein, with lead singer Andy Paley. The Hallucinations were a down-and-dirty quintet which did covers of blues by the likes of John Lee Hooker and Howlin' Wolf, as well as R&B hits and obscurities. They were the unofficial Tea Party house band, playing more gigs there than anyone else. Their lead singer Peter Wolf and I found we had common roots in the Bronx and our love of doo wop. He really knew how to work an audience, and had the charisma to do it. One of their regular numbers was "Funky Broadway." Wolf knew it as a #1 R&B record by Dyke & The Blazers, but it also became a big crossover hit that fall for Wilson Pickett. Wolf would call on a few people in the audience, one at a time, to come up and dance alongside him and the band. I was one of them. Funky Boston.

Like the Fillmore and the Avalon, the Tea Party primarily promoted its shows with posters and handbills tacked up and handed out around town. But most of the Tea Party posters I'd seen couldn't compare to the brilliant work of the artists in San Francisco. I wanted to upgrade our visuals, so when Bob Driscoll asked me if he could design a poster, I said why not. Mostly I knew his work from a few drawings I'd seen and the face paintings for the be-in by the river. But I believed in Bob, that he'd come up with something interesting and original. He quickly evolved a minimalist poster style, with plain block lettering, simple graphics and lots of white space. Unpsychedelic, the stylistic opposite of the swirling West Coast acid art, they were spacey in their own way and gave the Tea Party our own unique image.

I tried my hand at a poster too, for Canned Heat's return engagement. Using an image of a knight in armor I labeled as "Canned Heat," I paired it in stark black-and-white with the lady of his desires, "Ultimate Spinach." I added Old English lettering with information about the show by transferring the letters from thin plastic sheets called Letraset, laboriously rubbing one letter at a time onto the poster layout.

People came to the Tea Party expecting a good show, even if they'd never heard of the performers. They were open to something new, even unexpected, as long as it was good. The Beatles, among many other groups, experimented with the music of India, most recently on Sgt. Pepper's "Within You Without You." Opening for Canned Heat and the Spinach on Saturday-night was The Wizard Eye Pandit and his Disciples, offering "Meditational Harmonics." Later I brought in the Baul Singers and Dancers, a group of mystic minstrels whose roots in Bengal went back centuries.

The weekend after Canned Heat I booked The Luvs, one of the first all-girl bands who played their own instruments. Opening for them was The Grass Menagerie, another local band with the ubiquitous Willie Alexander on drums and Walter Powers on bass, as well as a young musician named Doug Yule.

A month later we took the Tea Party deep into space with the Sun Ra Arkestra. A well-respected avant-garde jazz group, they had a following in psychedelic circles in New York for their cosmic music and costumed performances. At their Tea Party gig,

the luvs
all chicks

and
the grass menagerie
at

the boston tea party

october 13 & 14

eight o clock   three $ 53 berkeley street   four blocks south of
the berkeley street exit of the arlington street mbta station

advance tickets: george's folly tea krackerjack's jerold's ··· dolphin design leather design

Tea Party poster by Bob Driscoll for The Luvs
and The Grass Menagerie

a couple of young black rock fans came up to me in the hallway and asked me why this weird group was playing there. I told them to go back inside and listen. They did, and they dug it. Richie Havens was another but very different black performer I presented. I'd heard him at Club 47, but he was no typical folk singer gently strumming a guitar. He whaled on it, and put out the energy of a folk-rock band, without a band.

One of the Tea Party favorites was the psychedelic New York band Lothar and the Hand People. "Lothar" wasn't the leader of the group, but an instrument called a theremin. It was a box of electronics with a loop-shaped wire on one end and a straight vertical rod on the other. You played a theremin without touching it, moving your hands in its electronic field to control volume with the loop, and pitch with the rod. The result was an eerie sound people might have recognized from the 1950s sci-fi classic *The Day the Earth Stood Still*. The electronic music pioneer Robert Moog credited his interest in the theremin as a high-school student to his later invention of his groundbreaking Moog synthesizer in the 1960s. While the Moog was used in recordings in 1967 by Diana Ross, The Doors and The Byrds, the Hand People were the first band to base their sound on the Moog and the theremin.

In December I booked two more psychedelic rock bands, Clear Light from L.A. and Kaleidoscope from San Francisco. Opening for the latter was a band from New York, Chain Reaction, with lead singer Steven Tallarico [later known as Steven Tyler; his future Aerosmith bandmates Joe Perry and Tom Hamilton went to shows at the Tea Party]. By now my life in the crazy world of rock 'n' roll had settled into a comfortable routine I hadn't known for some time, with a regular job and the company wheels. I had the club management thing down. I found that I had a flair for marketing, even though I had no background in it. Of course, I had to work on Friday and Saturday nights, but that was nothing new to me after working weekends waiting tables at Johnnie's and the San Francisco. But where else would I want to be, when I was at the epicenter of the counterculture earthquake in Boston, the Tea Party.

Chain Reaction, with Steven Tallarico [Tyler] on the right

4. FOUR-LETTER WORDS

WHEN ISSUE #13 OF AVATAR came out just after Thanksgiving, the centerfold opened up to become a vertical poster, which had just four words in large bold lettering with some decorative graphics to highlight them:

FUCK
SHIT
PISS
CUNT

There was no further explanation in the paper about the poster. Maybe it was a cosmic message from Mel Lyman, or a declaration of war against "the establishment." Everyone I knew thought the whole thing was nothing but a provocative stunt, and kind of funny at that. However, the powers-that-be were pissed, and the Boston police began cracking down on the hippies who sold the paper in the street for a quarter but of course had no control over what went into it. But outraged politicians saw the street peddlers as purveyors of smut. Just look at them, with their long hair and weird clothes. They had to be guilty of something.

Thousands of copies of the paper were confiscated from the *Avatar*'s office in Boston. Edward Jordan (aka Beardsley), a graphic designer and the paper's advertising director, happened to be there at the time of the seizure and was hauled into Boston Municipal Court on obscenity charges. Prominent Boston attorney Joseph Oteri argued on behalf of Jordan that the poster was social protest and protected by the First Amendment. The judge Elijah Adlow replied: "Even the French Revolution never evoked such filth and sewerage." He sentenced Jordan to six months in jail [Oteri later got it thrown out].

Earlier that fall, across the river in Cambridge, Mayor Daniel J. Hayes declared war on hippies, saying that "we must rid these people from our city," like they were vermin. He urged landlords not to rent to them and storeowners not to do business with them. Issue #11 of *Avatar* ran a mock obituary of Hayes, as well as an article speculating on whether *Avatar* would be banned in Cambridge, quoting City Councilor Al Vellucci calling it "some of the filthiest junk I have ever laid eyes on." The article went on to wonder "Are fuck, shit and piss four-letter words?," a preview of things to come in #13. Cambridge threatened the newsstands in Harvard Square with prosecution for selling sex magazines unless they stopped carrying *Avatar*. So they did; skin books were too good a business for them to lose. Dirty words no good, dirty pictures OK.

5. THE SODA POP RAID

WHILE THE FIRES OF RIGHTEOUSNESS burned, the Tea Party got singed. We advertised our shows in *Avatar*. After #13 threw gasoline on the flames, Boston City Hall got to thinking that the Tea Party must somehow be involved with *Avatar*, and summoned Ray Riepen downtown. He was able to satisfy city officials that we had no connection with the paper, that we were just an advertiser. Ray put on a convincing performance about how shocked we all were about #13, and promised not to advertise in the paper again. We didn't really need to anyhow, and there was no way we could take a stand on behalf of *Avatar*. With hundreds of stoned long-hairs gathering at the Tea Party every Friday and Saturday night, it would be all too easy for the city to find a reason to shut us down.

That seemed like the end of that episode, but the fire still smoldered inside Albert "Dapper" O'Neill, a city licensing commissioner. He was a right-wing zealot from South Boston, an angry man who hated hippies, blacks and other undesirables. I expected the weekend of January 5 and 6 to be a quiet one at the Tea Party, with the holidays over. Playing it safe, in the face of January weather, I booked two good local bands: Ill Wind, psychedelic rockers with a strong lead singer in Conny Devanney, and Cloud, a bluesy band whose keyboard player Doug Grossman ran a Mexican restaurant in Cambridge called El Diablo ("The Devil") which was a hangout for local musicians.

Cloud was on stage Friday night when suddenly all the house lights went on and a large contingent of cops came charging up the stairs, led by Dapper. They were looking for dope so they could shut us down, but didn't find so much as a roach. However, when Dapper demanded to see our license to sell soft drinks, I couldn't find it. The show went on that night, but Ray and I were summoned to court Monday for not having the $3 license. He did a great "Aw shucks, your honor" routine, telling the judge that we were just trying to give the kids something to do on a Saturday night. The judge not only threw out the charge against us, but made Dapper apologize to us right there in court.

"LET'S SEE THE LICENSE," demands Boston Licensing Comr. Albert L. "Dapper" O'Neil (right) to Steven R. Nelson during raid at Boston Tea Party, a South End psychedelic dance hall.

No Sign of Marijuana

Soda Pop Raid Fizzles

By ROBERT F. HANNAN

My newspaper clipping about the Soda Pop Raid

When he planned the raid, Dapper tipped off *The Boston Herald Traveler*, the conservative daily paper, which sent a reporter and photographer along. The resulting story was headlined, "Soda Pop Raid Fizzles," not exactly the kind of PR Dapper was expecting. It featured a photo of him in his snap-brim fedora angrily confronting me, while I looked back at him oh so innocently from under a wild mass of hair. The article concluded by mentioning an upcoming show with Ultimate Spinach: "But no grass please, said Manager Nelson. The management discourages it." Our crowd understood what that meant: please be so kind as to toke up outside.

6. THE BOSTON SOUND

THE LOCAL MUSIC SCENE was starting to attract attention beyond Boston, in particular a record producer and arranger in New York, Alan Lorber. He'd worked on recordings with '50s and early '60s artists such as Paul Anka, Neil Sedaka, Gene Pitney, Jackie Wilson and Connie Francis, as well as the songwriting team of Leiber & Stoller and the deejay Murray the K. But he had almost no experience with the new generation of '60s bands, other than producing The Mugwumps in 1964, a short-lived folk-rock band whose members split up to form The Mamas and Papas (Cass Elliot and Denny Doherty) and The Lovin' Spoonful (John Sebastian and Zal Yanovsky).

Lorber was aware of the wave of bands coming out of San Francisco, and saw dollar signs in Boston. He signed Ultimate Spinach and soft-rockers Orpheus to record deals with MGM. The Beacon Street Union was signed to the label by producer Wes Farrell, who had the megahit "Hang on Sloopy" by The McCoys. They got promoted by Lorber with Spinach and Orpheus in an ad in Billboard headlined: "The Sound Heard Round the World: Boston!!" If nothing else, Lorber was a good promoter. Newsweek ran a story about "The Bosstown Sound," with a picture of people dancing at the Tea Party, "Praise Ye The Lord" in the background.

Tom Wilson and Nico

Cover of Ill Wind's album Flashes

Ray and I were reported to have once been "proper corporation lawyers," and I was quoted as saying "life is absurd," musing on the strange path which led me to the Tea Party.

The reaction by music critics was not kind. Of the three bands, Orpheus, who had never played the Tea Party, came off the best. Its vocal harmonies and lusher arrangements were more suited to Lorber's musical sensibility. Ultimate Spinach's record was laden with psychedelic mumbo-jumbo, although live they were a trippy and popular act. The rhythmic, jazzy and at times experimental sound of The Beacon Street Union never came across in Farrell's production.

Other Boston bands also got record deals. The Bagatelle and Ill Wind were both produced by Tom Wilson. A tall elegant black guy, he was a Harvard grad and Cambridge resident with an impeccable musical track record. Initially working with cutting-edge jazz acts like Sun Ra and Cecil Taylor on his own label, he transitioned to the rock world, producing several tracks on *The Freewheelin' Bob Dylan*, then went on to produce Dylan's albums *The Times They Are A-Changing, Another Side of Bob Dylan* and *Bringing It All Back Home*. He also produced The Mothers of Invention's first two albums, and The Velvet Underground's second LP, *White Light/White Heat*.

Wilson had initially gained recognition in the pop music business for his work on Simon & Garfunkle's "The Sound of Silence." It was originally a folky acoustic track on their 1964 debut album, *Wednesday Morning, 3 A.M.* When the album flopped, the pair split up. But the single of "Silence" was getting some airplay around Boston. Wilson, who produced the LP, went back into the studio and, without the knowledge or permission of the artists, overdubbed electric instruments onto the track. The new folk-rock version became a huge worldwide hit, and brought Simon & Garfunkle back together.

Wilson must have thought, what worked once will work again. The Bagatelle's album included original material as well as covers of James Brown and Sam & Dave tunes. Without the band's knowledge, he overdubbed strings on some of the tunes in the rocking R&B album they thought they had cut. It didn't work. When Ill Wind went into the studio, young and inexperienced, they were hoping Wilson would be their mentor and exert a strong guiding hand during the recording sessions. Instead, he spent most of the time on the phone, reading a newspaper or welcoming the good-looking women who dropped by to see him. But when it came to working on the mix of what the band laid down for their LP *Flashes*, he took over and excluded them from the process. They were not happy.

Of course, there was no such thing as a "Boston Sound." If anything characterized the Boston-area music scene, it was its eclecticism. Its roots went back to the folk and blues scene at Club 47, and to garage rockers like The Lost and The Remains (aka Barry & The Remains), who opened for The Beatles on their final tour. Still, I wanted to give the "Bosstown" bands their due. They'd played many dates at the Tea Party and helped keep the place jumping musically and alive financially. Now with albums out, they would be even bigger draws for their old fans and for new ones. So on the weekend of January 19 and 20, I put together a "festival" of local bands to celebrate the first anniversary of the Tea Party.

One of the bands was new to the Tea Party, Jessie's First Carnival, just signed by Jimi Hendrix's management company. When they pitched me on booking them, I hesitated. Their piano player was my old roommate Jeff, still living with Beth. She had no relationship to my rock 'n' roll world, and playing the Tea Party meant he'd be working for me. So I put the past aside and gave his band a shot. Jeff was a multi-talented guy, a great piano player and vocal arranger. But he was no rock star.

7. STANDING UP FOR PEACE AND JUSTICE

THROUGHOUT THAT FALL AND winter, opposition to the war continued to grow. The Johnson Administration stepped up its efforts to persuade Americans that the war in Vietnam was winnable. But public skepticism was increasing and support for the war waning. Monday, October 16, marked the beginning of national "Stop the Draft" week. Thousands of young men either "returned" their draft cards or burned them, making their opposition personal by this brave act of civil disobedience. On Saturday of that week in Washington, as many as 100,000 people converged on the Lincoln Memorial to protest the war. Many of them marched on to surround the Pentagon, where Abbie Hoffman, Jerry Rubin and Allen Ginsburg chanted in an effort to "levitate" the building and "exorcise the evil within." It didn't move. A radical contingent of marchers stormed the front entrance, but were violently repulsed by military police and armed troops guarding it. By the time the event ended early Sunday morning, U.S. marshals had arrested nearly 700 people.

On a Sunday evening two weeks later, when the Tea Party was normally closed, we proudly hosted a very different antiwar event: "An Evening with God: A Peace of Bread." God didn't show up and play a set, but a goddess did, Judy Collins. Dr. Harvey Cox, a renowned professor at the Harvard Divinity School, was there as emcee, joined by the artist Corita Kent (a nun also known as Sister Mary Corita), and the poet and antiwar activist Father Daniel Berrigan. The point of the event, called "an evening of beauty, grace and reverence" by The Boston Globe, was to bring together religion and contemporary culture in the name of peace.

The capacity audience was straight and hip, religious and irreverent, drawn together by the message of peace. They were greeted by chanting, drumming and bell-ringing by the hippie collective the Hog Farm, in Boston on its travels around the country. Cox gained fame in 1965 for his international best-seller *The Secular City*, advocating that religious institutions should be leaders of social change. It was a message in the spirit of Theodore Parker. Corita also evoked that spirit with a powerful antiwar multimedia presentation on six screens, accompanied by recorded music ranging from classical to Sgt. Pepper.

Daniel Berrigan, a Jesuit priest well-known as an outspoken opponent of the war, read some of his poetry. He had previously won the prestigious Lamont Poetry Prize, established with an endowment by Corliss Lamont, the actual plaintiff in my Ames final. After a group of college girls distributed bread and wine to the audience, Dr. Cox gave a benediction. Then Judy sang, with everyone joining in for "Turn, Turn, Turn." At Cox's invitation, people put away their folding chairs and danced, forming lines and snaking joyfully around the room. They left the Tea Party that evening as high as any crowd at a rock show.

Mickey Myers, whose Botolph Gallery in Boston handled her friend Corita's work, was instrumental in organizing the evening. In the wake of its success, Dr. Cox asked Mickey and me to do a light show to accompany part of his presentation at Harvard's prestigious Noble Lecture Series the following spring.

At the end of January, Viet Cong and North Vietnamese forces launched the Tet Offensive, named for the lunar new year holiday during which it took place. They attacked over 100 cities and towns throughout South Vietnam, with special focus on Saigon and military facilities in strategic places like Hue, where a bloody battle raged for a month. In the end the offensive failed in its goal of fomenting a general uprising against the South Vietnam government, and the attackers suffered immense casualties. Still, it left much of the South Vietnam countryside in control of the Cong, and shattered any illusion Stateside that victory was in sight.

After a trip to Vietnam in February, the respected newsman Walter Cronkite concluded his report on CBS, "We have been too often disappointed by the optimism of the American leaders, both in Vietnam and Washington, to have faith any longer in the silver linings they find in the darkest clouds…. For it seems now more certain than ever that the bloody experience of Vietnam is to end in a stalemate.... It is increasingly clear to this reporter that the only rational way out then will be to negotiate, not as victors, but as an honorable people who lived up to their pledge to defend democracy, and did the best they could."

Thanks, Walter, but you might have added that among the "honorable people" to "defend democracy" were those of us who tried to dissuade Americans from following our leaders into the disaster of Vietnam. While the supposed "best and brightest" of the generation in power pursued the elusive light at the end of the tunnel in Southeast Asia, millions of my generation lent their voices and bodies to protesting the war. Some of us drifted into a state of alienation from our country, others chased hallucinogenic visions down a road to nowhere. We were all casualties of that distant war.

In late February the Tea Party was honored to host another special Sunday evening event, "A Delicious Difference," sponsored by the Metropolitan Boston Association of the United Church of Christ. It was a benefit for an educational center for Operation Exodus, a program begun in 1965 of voluntarily busing kids from the African-American communities of Roxbury and Dorchester to a predominantly white but underutilized high school in Boston's Back Bay neighborhood. State legislation enacted in the summer of 1966 expanded the busing, still voluntary, to take kids to schools in the posh suburbs of Brookline, Lexington, Newton, and Wellesley.

They weren't always welcome there. The purpose of the evening, besides raising money, was to bring people in from the suburbs to gain a better understanding of the program and to see for themselves the contrast between life in the suburbs and the inner city. Of course there was music, an unpaid performance by The Chambers Brothers, who were in town for a paid gig at the Tea Party the following weekend. They wrapped up their set with the spiritual "A Closer Walk with Thee." That led into a multiprojector slide show with a musical sound track.

Inspired by Sister Corita, I created the show with slides I shot in Wellesley, and then on a walk one afternoon from the Tea Party through the South End into Roxbury. As I wandered along shooting

A family in Wellesley

A family in Roxbury

the cityscape and people, the scene got bleaker and blacker. After a while I was the only white person around, although no one bothered me or tried to hide from my camera. I was shocked by the deep poverty I saw, a result of segregation in a Boston unseen by most of us. I may as well have been in Mississippi.

My slide show opened with sunny images of Wellesley to the sound of upbeat white pop music. About midway through, the Vanilla Fudge version of "People Get Ready," a gospel song of yearning for freedom, segued into the original by Curtis Mayfield and The Impressions. From there on the music was all soul and R&B, with provocative images from my walk. When the show ended, there was total silence in the room. For a moment I thought oh shit, did I blow it? Then slowly people began to clap, and broke into loud applause. The next day The Boston Globe reported: "People came into Boston from pretty places like Newton and Wellesley to be jarred...and they got their money's worth."

President Johnson got jarred on March 12 when he was almost beaten in the New Hampshire primary by antiwar candidate Eugene McCarthy. Many of my friends in Cambridge supported Gene. I didn't. He was a good guy, but I just didn't see how he could win the nomination and the general election, or be an effective President if somehow he did. I was excited when Robert Kennedy declared his candidacy a few days later. Bobby was a star on the stump. He could win, and he knew what it would take to govern and to get us out of Vietnam. Now having to face both Gene and Bobby, Johnson withdrew from the race.

8. THE AMERICAN REVOLUTION

CANNED HEAT WAS BACK at the Tea Party in March. A young group out of Worcester, managed by Ray Paret and David Jenks at Amphion, opened the show: The J. Geils Blues Band. Making its first appearance at the club, the quartet knew their blues, but their stage show was limited with their singer trapped behind the drums he played. Meanwhile, Peter Wolf continued to grow as the jumpin' frontman for The Hallucinations. On March 15 he took on another gig: D.J. on the late-night shift at WBCN-FM.

Back in the early Fifties, cars only came with an AM radio. Then an entrepreneur named T. Mitchell Hastings introduced the FM car radio. He went on to assemble a small group of FM stations, from Portland, Maine to Richmond, Virginia. Their call letters all ended in "CN," for "concert network," like WBCN, the "B" for Boston. Programming which originated at one station could be transmitted to the other stations for them to rebroadcast. Hastings was an eccentric, a follower of the mystic Edgar Cayce and a believer in the lost underwater city of Atlantis. By the mid-'60s his FM empire was sinking. There was no commercial market for classical music. To stay afloat, Hastings switched WBCN's format to easy-listening, hoping that elevator music would lift the station's fortunes. It didn't.

The bands revolutionizing rock, the kind of bands who played the Tea Party, were driving rapid growth in the sale of stereo LPs. In the Boston area some of the DJs at college radio stations were playing cuts from these albums, not just singles. Tom Gamache, known as "Uncle T", cranked up his "Freedom Machine" from midnight to 3 a.m. on WBUR at Boston University. The one commercial radio outlet for the music was at WBZ-AM, on Dick Summer's Sunday midnight show at WBZ-AM. It had a powerful clear-channel frequency reaching dozens of states at that late hour, but it was in mono.

Stereo had been around for years, used for gimmicks like making it sound as if a train were crossing your living room. Then rock bands embraced the technology. But if you wanted to listen to their music in stereo, then you pretty much had to buy their records and play them on your home system. Most cars still didn't come with FM radios, and even if you had one, you might drive out of range of a low-power college station right in the middle of that great new cut you were listening to.

While I was running the club, Ray Riepen was pursuing a vision: to find an FM stereo radio station in the Boston area where he could program rock albums, and attract advertisers wanting to reach the youth market. Out in San Francisco, Tom Donahue, a jock on commercial FM station KMPX, was doing just that. My brother Peter was at San Francisco State and sent me a two-hour tape he made of Donahue's show. After listening to it avidly I gave it to Ray, one more piece of evidence that he was on the right track. Foremost among those potential advertisers were the record companies pressing those albums but with no way to promote them on-air.

By early 1968, Ray found T. Mitchell, who didn't like the music, or the longhairs who played and listened to it, but was desperate. He'd lost most of the network stations, except WBCN and WHCN (Hartford). It was 'BCN Ray had his eyes on, but he and I took a ride in February to check out 'HCN. We couldn't listen to it on the way down, because like most cars Ray's Lincoln didn't have an FM radio. The station was on a mountain overlooking the city. We drove up a winding road, then parked the car and trudged through the snow to the front door. 'HCN was automated, just a shack next to the radio tower with prerecorded tapes playing around the clock. No one else was there. Ray turned the key, then we gave the door a strong shove to get it to open. We were greeted by Christmas music. The tapes hadn't been changed in months.

Ray chuckled at the sound. It was more obvious than ever that Hastings's business was in deep trouble. Although he resisted Ray's entreaties, he was finally persuaded, or at least his Board of Directors was, to let Ray program rock during the graveyard time slot, from 10:30 PM to 5:30 AM, seven nights a week. All was in place for the March 15 debut of the new rock format. For the first shift former college DJ Joe Rogers would be taking the mic under his *nom-de-air*, "Mississippi Harold Wilson."

We didn't have a budget for promoting the launch, other than a flyer designed by Bob Driscoll which we handed out at the Tea Party and around town: "Ugly Radio Is Dead!" So we were trying to come up with a publicity stunt to get some free press coverage. Joe and I and a couple of people were sitting around passing a joint and sharing ideas. We were all familiar with Orson Welles's infamous broadcast of *The War of the Worlds* and the media tempest it caused. We came up with a plan to stage another alien invasion. Listeners, lulled into a soporific state by the current programming, would suddenly be roused by the sounds of a crowd of people breaking into the station, as "alien" longhairs "invaded" and took it over. This would be followed by some weird noises by Frank Zappa and Cream playing "I Feel Free."

Listeners would grab their phones and call the press and the police. In no time the cops would shut down the street and surround the building, demanding with bullhorns that the hippies come out with their hands up. TV and radio stations would go to their reporters on the scene. The story would break not only in Boston but nationwide, a media coup. When we described this admittedly crazy but not improbable scenario to Ray, he quickly put the kibosh on it. T. Mitchell was coming unglued at the prospect of the format change. Ray was concerned that should he even get wind of our plan, he'd back out of the deal, if not have a heart attack.

So the hippie invasion was called off, but Zappa and Cream invaded the airwaves as scheduled on the 15th. That alone caused regular listeners to have fits. And the longhairs who'd heard about the new rock programming tuned in and flipped out. We really didn't need the publicity stunt, word about WBCN spread like wildfire. On a warm day or evening you could walk down a street in Boston or Cambridge where students and young people lived, and you'd hear 'BCN from every open window. Sometimes they put speakers on window ledges, the better to share the music with passers-by.

WBCN's studios were on the fifth floor of a building at 171 Newbury Street, an area of town where many advertising agencies had their offices. Hastings was nervous about the ad guys seeing hippies coming and going from WBCN's building. He was OK with them there for the 2:00 to 5:30 AM shift. But it simply wouldn't do for them to be showing up around 10:00, when ad people might be on the street after a long day at the office or a late dinner at one of the nearby restaurants. So a portable two-turntable console was set up in the back room of the Tea Party, with a connection from Ma Bell to the studio on Newbury Street. And for a few weeks, other than the first night launch at the station, the early shift was broadcast from the Tea Party, the late shift from Newbury Street, where Peter Wolf held court. Just as he was a charismatic front man for The Hallucinations, so too was he a dynamic D.J. He drew on what he'd learned at "the college of musical knowledge," and supplemented the station's LP library with his own collection of rare rock 'n' roll, doo wop and R&B singles. Self-styled as the "Woofuh Goofuh," his on-air patter and musical taste kept the station shakin' all night.

At first the 'BCN record library, provided courtesy of Columbia Records and other labels who wanted airtime for their acts, could fit in a couple of cartons. As the switching hour of 2:00 AM drew near, someone would have to leave the on-air DJ with a few LPs, grab the cartons, drive to Newbury Street, take the elevator to 'BCN's third floor offices, then lug the cartons up two flights of stairs to reach the studio.

One Sunday night I was at the Tea Party, waiting for the jock to show up for the first shift. When airtime arrived, still no D.J. The engineer was at the board, so with his encouragement I got on mic and played a few cuts, at one point fading a Jimi Hendrix solo into one by Albert Ayler, the avant-garde jazz sax player. That was true to 'BCN's "free-form" format, taking the listener on a musical journey, free from the playlists which controlled AM radio. When the jock arrived, I surrendered the mic. That ended the shortest on-air career at the station, making me the George Plimpton of rock 'n' roll radio.

My efforts with WBCN were more focused on marketing the new format. With its connection to the Boston Tea Party, I coined the phrase "The American Revolution" to convey the essence of WBCN's free-form radio. We used it on Tea Party posters to promote the station. In the radio business, spinning those platters on FM stereo was indeed revolutionary.

The schizophrenic broadcast schedule didn't last long. As fan mail and ad buys poured into the station, Hastings finally relaxed, and soon both shifts originated from Newbury Street. By May 1,

T. Mitchell Hastings in his office at WBCN

Sam Kopper, WBCN d.j. and the station's first program director

only six weeks after the new format debuted at WBCN, the station went rock 24 hours a day. With one exception. For years a religious broadcaster had bought an hour of airtime for a Sunday sunrise service. T. Mitchell didn't want to give up the good money, so the service stayed. After a long Saturday night of drugs and sex, radio tuned to rock 'n' roll on WBCN, when you got religion it was time to go to sleep.

9. The Return of The Velvets

On the weekend of March 22-23, the opening act at the Tea Party was an experimental electronic band called The United States of America (really). Their influences ranged from the classical composer Charles Ives, to old-time folk and jazz, to LaMonte Young and the New York avant-garde. Their instruments included an electric violin. The main act had an electric viola, perhaps the only time anywhere two bands featured electric fiddles on the same bill. The headliner, of course, was The Velvet Underground. I'd been looking forward to booking them from the time I became manager of the Tea Party, but their career took an odd course during the intervening six months.

In September they'd played four dates at the Savoy Theatre in Boston, produced by Ray's former partner David Hahn, complete with a light show. It was his first and only foray into concert production since leaving the Tea Party. The Velvets were the opening act, with the main attraction not a band but a movie called *The Happening,* a comedic crime caper in which four hippies kidnap a former mob boss. Anthony Quinn starred, Faye Dunaway made her film debut, and Milton Berle had a featured role. The most noteworthy thing about the movie was its title song, a #1 hit for The Supremes.

Hahn drummed up some publicity for the show in *The Tech,* the student newspaper at his alma mater, M.I.T. VU manager Steve Sesnick told an interviewer from the paper that after the

Savoy shows, "the group would continue to record, but make few public appearances." They were working on their second album, *White Light/White Heat*, which included a 17½ minute track called "Searchin' (For My Mainline)."

In an era of psychedelic excess in LP cover design, the front of the album was all black, except for the title in white and an image of a skull tattoo visible only if you held it at a certain angle. On the reverse side was a picture of the band on the front steps of the Tea Party. Barely visible in the top right corner of the photo were the letters "arty" from the sign over the door, perhaps a sly comment about the band by the cover designer. Their first LP ranged from ironically sentimental (Nico singing "All Tomorrow's Parties") to intentionally cacophonous ("European Son"). Their followup album was an all-out assault on the senses, from the amphetamine-fueled opening title tune to that long track at the end, renamed "Sister Ray." They'd been performing it since the spring of 1967, and when they played it at their Tea Party gig in May, I melted ecstatically into the dancing crowd.

I bought *White Light* as soon as it came out, and loved it. With its release on January 30, the band went back on the road for the first time since the Savoy, appearing at a record release party in Chicago on February 1. Then they snuck into Cambridge with no publicity on the 24th to play a dance and charity benefit at the Harvard student union.

Sesnick had been to the Boston area in January to set up the Harvard gig, and came over to the Tea Party to meet with me. Ray had not been happy about the Velvets playing the Savoy in September, after giving them three weekends at the Tea Party to build an audience in Boston. It took him by surprise, since he didn't expect David to get right back in the rock business. Apparently there wasn't a non-compete provision in their deal.

As between Sesnick and me, I'd gone to bed with Gail, and he'd gotten into bed with David. So I guess that made us even, and was in the past for both of us. Now we were focused on the same thing, to bring The Velvet Underground into the Tea Party. To

Test pressing of A-side of Velvet Underground single

Test pressing of unreleased B-side of the single

schmooze me, he brought me acetates for an unreleased single of "White Light/White Heat." The B-side was "I Heard Her Call My Name," featuring Lou's squealing feedback-driven guitar, an unlikely choice for AM radio play. But so was "White Light." Maybe Sesnick thought some "playola" was needed to get his band into the club. I appreciated the gift, but I didn't need any persuasion to book them. So we agreed on the March dates.

This was the fourth weekend for the VU playing the Tea Party, and they were feeling at home there. It was the place where they first stepped out from under the Warhol shadow. Andy had mentored and encouraged the band, and of course created their iconic banana album cover. He also pushed Nico onto the band. But in no way was he really the producer of that record, as credited. At the Tea Party they were appreciated by the audience as a rock 'n' roll band, not the soundtrack for a freak-out. It made an impression on the Velvets, that people there cared about their music. And the acoustics of the room suited them, like they were playing in the sound box of a giant instrument, vibrating with their energy. Whether walking through the audience to or from the stage, or hanging around the back room, the band was pretty relaxed that weekend, glad to be there again. Lou was approachable and in a good mood could even be chatty. John was a little more remote, but that was John, the avant-garde artist. Sterling and Moe were, as ever, straightforward and friendly.

The Velvets didn't completely leave the New York scene behind. An entourage of arty Manhattanites followed them up to Boston, slumming for the weekend. They stood out in the crowd, more fashionable than the local hippies. One of the New Yorkers caught my eye, a cute blond actress named Joy Bang (her real last name, from her former husband). A one-time Boston University student, she'd made a couple of underground films in Boston before moving to New York to pursue her acting career. It was a pleasure to welcome her back.

10. A New Era, A New Age

Even with **WBCN** taking most of his attention, Ray and I talked about how we could grow the Tea Party. Could we expand beyond our two nights a week? Could we bring in more big-name acts? These two notions came together with a Thursday night series of one-night shows debuting in April, marking a new era for the club. First up was the Muddy Waters Blues Band. The powerhouse lineup featured piano player Otis Spann and the bassist and songwriter Willie Dixon. His tunes "Hoochie Coochie Man" and "I Just Want to Make Love to You" were Muddy classics.

The opening act could only be The Hallucinations. Peter Wolf was friends with Muddy, who used Wolf's apartment as a dressing room when he played Club 47 a few blocks away. The Hallucinations themselves had just played the 47 in March. It was during the week, so I went one night. A few weeks later the club shut its doors for good. It was just too small to be able to continue paying the acts who'd performed there over the years and to compete with new venues like the Tea Party. I felt a twinge of guilt for helping to put them under, having brought old 47 regulars like Richie Havens and Eric Andersen to the Tea Party, and now Muddy Waters. But at the same time, I believed those artists deserved a bigger audience and more money than they could get at the 47.

Before Muddy and the band were to go on that Thursday night, we heard the news. Martin Luther King had been assassinated in Memphis. Everyone was deeply shocked, we'd lived through the JFK assassination, and now this, another great leader shot down. For me it was even more shocking, after the murder of Mickey Schwerner and his fellow civil rights workers in Mississippi. As the manager of the Tea Party, it was up to me to decide whether to close the club for the night. I never got the chance. Muddy and his band came onstage, and started playing.

It was the bluest blues I'd ever heard, not so much a performance as a wake. They were playing for themselves, they had to play, it was how they coped with their sorrow. The rest of us were privileged to be there and share their grief. Tears were shed in the audience. Out in the world of Boston and beyond, raw racial tension led to riots and violence. Inside the Tea Party, a mixed black and white audience sat on the floor and listened, spending the evening peacefully.

One of the kids who worked there, Ravi, of Indian descent, had been pictured dancing in the Newsweek article on the Boston Sound. After we closed up that night, he was headed to his home in Roxbury when he was knocked off his scooter by a brick thrown at his head. He was set on by a group of angry young blacks, who would have beat him to a pulp, even killed him, if one of them hadn't shouted, wait, I know him, he works at the Tea Party.

When Ravi came to work the next night, one side of his face was horribly swollen and discolored from the brick. He probably should have stayed home, but he wanted to be at the Tea Party. Headlining were The Amboy Dukes, led by guitar maniac Ted Nugent. Unfortunately for them many people were afraid to go out in the violent aftermath of Dr. King's murder. It was easily our smallest crowd since I'd been at the Tea Party.

That night James Brown was scheduled to do a show at Boston Garden. There was talk of the City of Boston cancelling it, but also fear of what might happen if thousands of ticketholders showed up. Mayor Kevin White decided that the show must go on, and worked with the management of public TV station WGBH to have it broadcast live, hoping to keep people at home in front of their TV sets. Someone brought in a small black and white set to the Tea Party and we set it up in my office. It was the only time I stayed there without taking some time to listen to the bands I'd booked. After the live broadcast, they reran it. What a show, mind-boggling to see James Brown doing his very black and very sexual performance on the slightly liberal but very stuffy WGBH. They never aired any popular music, except during the innovative weekly magazine-style show "What's Happening, Mr. Silver?" Hosted by the brilliant David Silver, it featured culture and politics slanted to a countercultural audience. Maybe 'GBH tolerated the show because of his native British accent.

After the violence and emotion of the weekend, I needed some relief. I'd always been a sci-fi fan, so on Wednesday night I went to the Cinerama Theater to see the Boston premiere of *2001: A Space Odyssey*. Looking for a seat, I saw Bob Driscoll and Rodney Deming sitting way down front in the middle. Perfect, I took a seat right behind them. The smell of marijuana wafted through the room. Bob and Rod passed me a joint, but I could have gotten a contact high from the smoke in the air. After much anticipation, the curtain pulled back to reveal the giant screen wrapping around us. Then to the dramatic opening music, *Thus Spake Zarathustra*, we watched transfixed as the sun rose over the earth, as seen from space. The film was like nothing we'd ever seen before, one mind-blowing episode after another, peaking with the dazzling visual trip through the Star Gate. It culminated with the awe-inspiring image of the Star Child floating into view above Earth, humankind reborn into the New Age we dreamed of.

11. B.B.

THE THURSDAY NIGHT SERIES continued at the Tea Party with The Yardbirds on April 11. It was their eighth U.S. tour, but somehow they'd never played Boston, where they had a lot of fans and a strong influence on many local musicians. Jeff Beck had left the band, and Jimmy Page moved over from bass to lead guitar. Highlights of the show were "Dazed and Confused" and "The Train Kept A-Rollin'." A big Yardbirds fan, I spent some time afterwards in the back room chatting with him and his latest lady, lovely Lynn, a Tea Party regular. I ran into them coming out of the Tea

B.B. King with his "BB" ring

B.B., after a dip in the Charles River

Party together the next morning, when Jimmy went to collect some gear before the band left for their next gig. She was going with him.

B.B. King headlined the next Thursday show, on April 18. He'd been playing the chitlin' circuit in Boston for 10 years, black clubs and bars. This was his first appearance before a predominantly white audience in Boston. On his left hand he wore a gold ring with "B.B." in diamonds, a gift to himself for achieving success after many hard years. During his set one of the "B"s fell off the ring and into the audience. It would have been all too easy for someone to pocket it and hock it. Instead, it was returned to him. After the set he paused to relax in the ready room just off the stage, and told me how touched he was to get the "B" back.

Before the show began that night, a dog wandered into the Tea Party. Some people riding the Green Line to the show saw the doors of their car open at Auditorium station and a dog get on. When the trolley car stopped at Arlington Street station, people piled out for the walk down Berkeley Street to the Tea Party. The dog did the same and followed them into the club and up the stairs to the ticket window landing. Spotting a cozy corner in the coat room, he snuggled up and dozed off. After the show he wandered around the hall, and I was amused when Betsy told me how he got there. I always liked dogs, except for the wild ones in Peru. This dog was wild too, a stray mutt on Boston's streets, but he knew his way around people.

I was still in the ready room talking with B.B. King when the dog walked in. He went right up to B.B. and began nuzzling him. B.B. was obviously comfortable with him, patting him and rubbing his ears. He asked me what the dog's name was. I said I didn't know, that he was a stray who'd wandered into the club. I added, not really having given it any thought, that I might take him home with me. He said, when I was young, I was a stray too, so why don't you call him King? I told him I already knew a dog named King, a Samoyed who belonged to my grandfather in Monticello when I was a kid. But I did take the dog home, and named him B.B.

I'd booked The Yardbirds through a new agent in New York, Frank Barsalona at Premiere Talent. He also represented The

Steve Miller Band, who opened for them and stayed on to headline the weekend, with Peter Rowan's band Earth Opera as the supporting act. Through Frank I booked more acts for the Thursday series: Procol Harum ("A Whiter Shade of Pale"), Traffic and Blue Cheer (named for a "brand" of LSD). Prior to forming Traffic in 1967, soulful teenage singer Steve Winwood had a big hit with The Spencer Davis Group, "Gimme Some Lovin." Blue Cheer had a hit single with their cover of the rockabilly classic, Eddie Cochrane's "Summertime Blues," and a reputation for playing really loud.

Most of the bands who played the Tea Party had one amp for each instrument, maybe a portable Fender. When Blue Cheer set up for their show, they had a line of 6' tall Marshall amps all the way across the back of the stage. We looked at it in awe. Then they set up another line of Marshalls on top of the first one. The sound was thunderous. Standing in the room during Blue Cheer's set, I felt my body pounded and my guts throbbing with the music. It felt like it might bring the old building crashing down.

I also booked a weekend with blues great Howlin' Wolf. Like his Chess Records label mate and sometime rival Muddy Waters, he too had played Club 47 and used Peter Wolf's apartment as a dressing room. Peter, nee Blankfield, supposedly adopted his stage surname in honor of the Wolf. In his wallet he kept a prized possession, Howlin' Wolf's business card. The Hallucinations often played one of Howlin' Wolf's signature tunes, "Smokestack Lightning" (which had also been covered by The Yardbirds). They opened the show on Friday night, and the two Wolfs rocked the house.

12. ROCKIN' ON

THE ONE-NIGHT SERIES drew big crowds and proved that people would come out to the Tea Party on Thursday night, so I began booking acts for Thursday through Saturday. The first band to headline a three-night run was The Velvet Underground, on May 16-18, followed the next weekend by John Lee Hooker with The Hallucinations opening and also backing John Lee. After one of their shows, I was headed back to Cambridge and gave him a ride to where he was staying. Peter Wolf came along, as did Van Morrison, who attended the show and was living in Cambridge after recently emigrating from Northern Ireland. While I played chauffeur, the three of them sat on the bench seat at the back of the bus having an animated conversation. John Lee spoke in his deep baritone with a Mississippi black accent and a stutter, Van with a heavy Belfast accent, and Peter often lapsed into his New York hipster jive. I could barely understand any of them, but they understood each other perfectly, speaking the language of the blues.

The weekend after John Lee, Van played the Tea Party with his new band The Van Morrison Controversy. They were working out material for his first new album since he'd launched a solo career a year earlier with the hit "Brown Eyed Girl."

With the arrival of warmer weather, the Cambridge Common became the site for free outdoor concerts every Sunday afternoon. The city fathers looked on with trepidation, but allowed the shows to go on. They also looked the other way at all the dope being smoked. You couldn't miss that distinctive aroma of burning pot. By now, hippies were all over the city, there was no getting rid of them, so best not to provoke a confrontation.

Often bands who played the Tea Party over the weekend did a set on the Common on Sunday. I didn't see that as cutting into our gate, the good vibes on the Common were good P.R. for the club. I was there every Sunday, digging the music and getting high right across Mass. Ave. from Hastings Hall, my first-year dorm at Harvard Law. B.B. always came with me. There were lots of other dogs, all wandering around without leashes, so he had plenty to keep him busy, especially with the females. It was spring.

One afternoon I found myself sitting next to a couple of girls and we began talking. They were seniors at Radcliffe, Barbara and Diane. I was really turned on by Barbara, who was tall, curvy, smart and witty. The two of them shared an apartment on Mass. Ave., toward Central Square and across from an old luncheonette called the Elite Spa. My apartment was right behind it, on Hancock Street. But soon I was living with Barbara. Good thing she and Diane liked B.B., because he'd become my constant companion.

The guy who lived across the hall from Barbara and Diane, Ziggy, was a friend of Eric Clapton. Eric stayed with him for a couple of days in early May, on a short break during a long tour with Cream. Jon Landau was a rock critic in Boston, who also wrote for Rolling Stone. Under the headline "The Sound of Boston: 'Kerplop'," he'd panned the Boston Sound but praised the Tea Party as "a consistently well-run outlet" which was "popular with out-of-town groups because of the professional treatment they received from owner Ray Riepen and manager Steve Nelson."

Jon and I were taking Eric to dinner. I suggested El Diablo, because it was a short walk away, and I knew jaws would drop when we walked in with Clapton. We all ordered enchiladas, and conversation turned to Cream. Jon was not hesitant to tell Eric that he thought their act was getting stale, with its interminable guitar, bass and drum solos. I don't think he was telling Clapton anything he hadn't already been thinking himself. And I don't know if was the spicy enchilada sauce or the saucy comments from Jon, but Eric turned green, sick to his stomach, and left the restaurant.

13. GOODBYES

THE BRATTLE STREET NEIGHBORHOOD was the poshest part of Cambridge, and had been since wealthy pro-British Tories lived there in colonial times. I got invited to a garden party on June 4th in the backyard of a large home there. I was stunned the day before by the shooting of Andy Warhol by a deranged feminist writer, but it appeared he would survive. It was a beautiful spring evening and I was in the mood for a party, so I went. Everyone was dressed in their summer clothes, a preppy fashion show, except for me and a couple of other hippie types. People mingled and chatted, enjoying the food and drinks. I got in a conversation with a young woman and her date, they (or at least she) fascinated by the Tea Party. After a while they wandered off but she kept circling back. By the end of the evening she let me know that she wanted to leave with me, not him.

We went back to my apartment and to bed. WBCN was on the radio, the late-night choice of music for sex. Suddenly, a news bulletin: Bobby Kennedy had been shot in L.A. That was an erection wrecker. Shocked, we both quickly dressed. She went home, I walked up the street to Barbara's apartment, in the early light before dawn. I woke her up, she woke up Diane. We were all devastated. Bobby was our hope to get the Democratic nomination and stop the likely Republican nominee, Richard Nixon. We were all so obsessed with following the TV and radio news reports on Bobby's condition as he lingered near death, the subject of where I'd been never came up. I felt bad about cheating on Barbara, and Bobby's shooting made me feel that much worse. He died in the early morning hours of June 6.

The Tea Party was open that night, but it was a small and gloomy crowd for The Group Image out of New York, a Jefferson Airplane-like acid rock band. On Saturday the killer of Martin Luther King Jr. was arrested, capping a weird week of news about three shootings. The next weekend, June 13-15, brought a mainstay of the San Francisco rock scene in their first Boston appearance, Quicksilver Messenger Service. Then the following week we opened on Wednesday for the first time, four nights with The Bagatelle and The J. Geils Blues Band. After their longtime affiliation with the Tea Party, it was The Bagatelle's final performances there before breaking up in the wake of the failure of their record.

The audience for the music we showcased was still growing, in part thanks to WBCN, and the Tea Party was well established as a cool and important venue for rock and the blues, a must-stop for many bands on a national tour. We regularly drew a full house.

People wanted to be part of what was happening there, especially to see the bigger name acts I was booking, with the ticket price still three bucks. Running the club was easy for me, and I was getting that old restless feeling with the approach of summer. Since I'd worked in high school as a counsellor at a sleepaway camp, and especially since Peru, summer had always been a big break from my year-round routine. Last summer I'd been a hippie floating downstream through the Summer of Love.

I'd become friends with Kenny Greenblatt, a former high-school science teacher from the suburbs who'd moved to Harvard Square to be part of the scene there. One day that spring he said to me, let's go to Europe for a couple of weeks. The idea really appealed to me, if I could get away from my job. At the same time, I was having issues with Ray. He was brilliant in foreseeing the opportunities at the Tea Party and WBCN, both of which were by now hugely successful. But his relationships with people were not always stellar. After hanging out at the bar in the flea-bag Hotel Diplomat up the street, he'd show up at the Tea Party toward the end of an evening, maybe a little tipsy, maybe more. He'd strut around like he owned the place – which he did – and knew what was going on – which he often didn't.

I decided we had to have a little talk. I'd gone to work at the Tea Party when I was lost, a Harvard Law grad kneeling at people's feet to make sandals for a few bucks. Ray had offered me $1000 a month, plus use of the VW bus. I was thrilled to take it, saved by rock 'n' roll. At the time I knew nothing about running the club, which was just a local dance hall for potheads and teenyboppers, with occasional out-of-town bands. Now it was famous from California to England, well-regarded among bands and booking agents. I'd had a lot to do with its evolution. True, I was riding a huge cultural wave, but I learned to ride it. And while I did, and ran the club, Ray was able to pursue the radio deal he was after.

We sat out in his car one afternoon and talked. I said I was underpaid, and on top of wanting more money, felt I deserved a piece of the action, not just a paycheck. Ray wasn't buying, he was too much of a control freak to let anyone else own a share of the business. Despite the big crowds we were drawing, he questioned what I was paying the bands. He was particularly annoyed about my paying $2000 for the band coming in for four days at the end of the month: The Jeff Beck Group, on their first American tour. Five hundred bucks a night for guitar genius Jeff Beck, lead singer Rod Stewart, bass player Ron Wood, and drummer Micky Waller. Ray didn't have a clue who they were.

I didn't sign up for the Tea Party thinking it would be a lifetime gig. I loved being there and running it, but I was still trying to figure out who I was and where I was going. Maybe I could have gotten a little more money out of Ray, but I felt my dedication and achievements were underappreciated. I can't remember him ever telling me that I was doing a good job. So I decided it was time to move on, and gave him my notice. I took Kenny up on his offer, and raised it. Let's take off for Europe and hitchhike around for a couple of months, I said. He was down with it.

The appearance of The Jeff Beck Group would be my last weekend managing the Tea Party. I designed the handbill to promote the show, with a great head shot of Jeff. On the reverse side I reprinted a rave review in *The New York Times* about their recent appearance at Fillmore East, where they opened for the Grateful Dead and upstaged them. On the first night of the group's run at the Tea Party, we had about half a house, pretty good for the middle of the week, only the second Wednesday we were open. But just about every rock guitar player in the Boston area was there, as I knew they would be. Word about the band spread like wildfire, like I knew it would. The next three nights the place was packed, we even had to turn people away. The crowds went absolutely wild, more so than at any show I'd ever booked, a fitting finale to my run there.

The Jeff Beck Group: (L-R) Jeff Beck, Ron Wood,
Mick Waller, Rod Stewart

After the show, I drove the band in the VW bus over to Barbara's place. She and I, and B.B. and Diane, were moving to a new apartment two days later, on July 1. The furniture was already gone, all we had to sit on was a bunch of cushions on the floor. We drank wine, didn't smoke any dope, and talked intensely for a couple of hours, about literature, films and such, like a bunch of graduate students. Maybe it was just the English accents, but the band members seemed more sophisticated than most American rockers. Everyone was in a great mood. The band had been a smash at an important gig, and could look forward to more accolades as their tour continued.

I was feeling good about my time at the Tea Party. For the name acts I'd brought to Boston, many for the first time. For the blues greats who got a new home after the demise of Club 47. For the local bands who got to open shows and develop as musicians. For the poster artists who spread the word and image of our shows in the streets. For the people I'd worked with at the Tea Party who made sure everyone who played there and went there had a great time, as they did too. And for bringing The Velvet Underground home to their favorite venue. It was my connection to the Velvets which led to my becoming the manager, and I was grateful to Ray for giving me the opportunity. The Summer of Love had come and gone, and now so had I, but at the Tea Party it was still a love-in for the performers and their audiences.

14. The Urge for Going

The apartment we moved into was on the second-floor of a house on Exeter Park, a quiet dead-end street off Mass. Ave., almost to Porter Square. My old apartment on Hancock Street was where I'd lived while running the Tea Party. Now I'd left it and the club behind. It definitely felt like a new beginning. After getting settled in, we went out for a while one day and left B.B. in the apartment to mind the place. When we came back, he was sitting on the front lawn. Puzzled, we went upstairs, but the front door to the apartment was still locked. One of the windows looked out over a small section of roof above the first floor. It had been left open. It seemed that B.B. went out the window onto the roof, jumped down onto the lawn, and sat there patiently waiting for us to return. He didn't want to be left in the apartment, and he didn't want to run away back to his old street life. He knew he had a good thing going.

Ray hired Don Law to replace me as manager of the Tea Party. He had been producing shows at Boston University, and grew up in the music biz. His father Don Law was a record producer who'd recorded the only sessions of the blues legend Robert Johnson, and worked with Johnny Cash and other country greats like Marty Robbins (his single "El Paso" went to #1 on both the country and pop charts).

It was strange at first not being at the Tea Party, after my life had revolved around it. But I began looking forward to my trip to Europe. Barbara wasn't so keen on my going, but she wasn't standing in my way. I'd be back in a couple of months. She even agreed to take care of B.B. while I was gone. She and I had been together for three months, and now we were living together. I felt guilty about leaving her, but not enough to overcome my urge to go. I really liked Barbara, I enjoyed being with her, and we had great sex. But I wasn't in love with her. I wasn't ready to be in love with anyone, after my relationship with Beth. For me, like many other young people in the "counterculture," it was a time for personal freedom and seeking new experiences.

Kenny and I bought our plane tickets to depart for London on August 7. I decided to wait until then because on August 6 a piece of London came to Boston, The Who, at the Boston Music Hall downtown. Not to be missed. Barbara and I were both into The Who, and for her, especially Roger Daltrey. She looked fantastic that night, in tight black leather pants, and we enjoyed mingling with the rock crowd in the lobby. It was a Tuesday, so the Tea Party was closed, and everyone was at The Who. The opening acts were both local regulars at the Tea Party, Quill and Ill Wind. The Who put on a great performance, and Keith Moon kicked over his drum kit at the end of the show, as he first did at Monterey Pop. After the show Barbara and I went back to the apartment for our last night together for a while. An evening of great rock 'n' roll, plus a couple of tokes, was a sexual turn-on.

Getting ready to fly the following day, I got together with Kenny Greenblatt. We stopped in to see Kenny Gordon, the owner of Headquarters East, the head shop on Mass. Ave. near my old apartment. He was a well-known character around the Square and a regular at the Tea Party. The very existence of his store, selling drug paraphernalia and other hippie goods like black-light posters, was an ongoing provocation to the Cambridge city fathers. Kenny Gordon was someone I could score a bag of weed from, but because of his high profile, he was always low-key about that line of business, dealing only to friends.

He had some advice for Kenny Greenblatt and me. Take these two pieces of hash which he handed us, and when you're waiting at the airport, get something to drink and swallow them before you get on the plane. I'd smoked hash, a delicacy when it was occasionally available, but never swallowed it. We took his advice. We were perfectly straight when we got on the plane, but after an hour or so we were really flying high. All night and across the Atlantic. By time we landed at Heathrow Airport in the morning, we'd come down.

15. RAIN RAIN IN LONDON TOWN

WHEN WE CAME OUT OF the terminal, it was raining hard. We got a cab into London. Through a friend of a friend, Kenny got us the use of a flat while its owner was out of town. There was some confusion with getting ahold of the key when we arrived. By the time we got ourselves and our backpacks into the place, we were soaking wet. Not having had much sleep on the plane, we crashed. Later we tried to take showers, but discovered you needed coins for the hot water, and we didn't have any. That evening we didn't venture far, to a neighborhood pub where we had some food and a pint. We made sure we left with some change.

The next day, it was still raining. We hoped it wouldn't last. London had many great museums where you could spend a rainy day, but that's not why we went there, to go to museums. We wanted to be out and about, taking in the scene, seeing and being seen. It was the place to be. Who wanted to look at some 16th century painting of the Madonna and child when you could be parading up and down Carnaby Street, checking out the birds and the guys? People paraded around Harvard Square in their hippie duds, but Carnaby Street was something else altogether. Of course we went there despite the rain, ducking into the shops and eying the displays. But it wasn't the same as we imagined it would be when the sun came out again. If it ever did.

Late one night we went to a private after-hours club where musicians and music biz people hung out. There was a constant flow of English bands to the U.S., but few Americans from the music scene went to London, Jimi Hendrix being the big exception. The Boston Tea Party was well known to that crowd, and we were warmly welcomed. Someone offered to get us high. But in England and Europe, they didn't smoke grass. Instead, they removed some tobacco from the end of a cigarette and stuck a piece of hash there, twirling the end of the paper to hold it in place. You had to inhale the hash through the tobacco. I never did smoke cigarettes, and I coughed my brains out. I could see this was going to be a non-smoking trip. And that was OK.

After hanging out for a while, I found myself in a conversation with a cute Brit with a bushy head of blonde hair. We talked and danced some to the recorded music in the club, then went back to "my" place. She left before dawn. In the morning Kenny said, Do you know who she is? I said all I knew was that her name was Sandy and she was a singer. We didn't talk much at the club about what she did, because she was so interested in talking about the music world in the U.S. Kenny said, she's the biggest folk-rock singer in England, Sandy Denny. But her band, Fairport Convention, hadn't cracked the U.S. charts, and I didn't know who they were.

It continued to rain, the #1 topic of conversation at the pubs where we spent a lot of time. This was no ordinary London drizzle, but record-breaking rainfall. One evening we were talking with a guy who'd just come back from Germany, where he said the weather was beautiful. By the time we got back to the flat, we'd decided to go there. The next day we bought tickets on the ferry which crossed the North Sea to the port of Bremerhaven, in the northern end of the country. It was an overnight trip, and like many of our fellow passengers, we bedded down in our sleeping bags on the deck.

16. Deutschland

WHEN WE ARRIVED IN the morning, it was sunny. Not having planned to go to Germany, and not knowing much about where we were, we decided just to head south, to follow the sun wherever that led us. Being Jewish, we felt more than a little strange being in Germany. We were concerned about encountering old Nazis, even though World War II had ended almost a quarter of a century ago. We weren't wearing arm bands that said "Juden," so who would know? But we were a couple of longhaired freaks, hitchhiking. That was enough for several cars to swerve far to their right as though to run us over as we walked along the road, or to yell something as they passed. Neither of us spoke German, so we couldn't understand what they were saying, but we got the drift. Hippies not welcome.

After walking along the road for hours, we finally got a lift. With a driver from hell. He liked to play chicken with oncoming cars, staying too far to the left until pulling back into his lane at the last second. He wanted to terrify us, and he did. After each near-miss he laughed and hollered gleefully, only adding to our terror.

We were relieved when he let us off after half an hour of this, but by now were completely lost. Kenny pointed to what looked a restaurant or tavern a hundred yards or so back from the main road, so we walked over to get some food. The place went dead silent when we walked in the door. As we could see with one glance around the room, all the guys had short hair. This was no place to rest and linger over a nice German meal, but we needed a cold drink. Kenny went up to the bar and asked for "zwei bier." Or maybe he was saying "tsvey bir" in Yiddish. Whatever, it worked, we got our beers. But we were still being watched, so we drank up quickly and left.

We continued hiking down the road, but had no luck finding something to eat. When the light began to fade, we bedded down for the night in a ditch off the side of the road. It was a lousy night's sleep, made worse when we awoke at dawn to see "zwei polizei" standing above us. Kenny and I looked at each other. Now we've really had it. The cops spoke some English, and asked us what we were doing there. We explained our unsuccessful attempt at hitchhiking the day before. Rather than run us in, they suggested that we go back to Bremerhaven and take a ferry out of Germany. They even drove us there, whether out of concern for our welfare, or to see us to the border and make sure we left the country. Either way, we were glad for the ride and happy to say "auf wiedersehen" to Germany, goodby!

17. SWEDEN

WE BOUGHT TICKETS ON a ferry to Sweden, where we'd heard the weather was also nice. Four young Swedish guys, looking like blond moptop Beatles wannabes, asked us if we were Americans. They were excited to learn we were and to talk with us. They spoke English very well, but with an English accent, which they learned in school. They were in a band called The Perhaps, on their way home from New York, after spending ten days there at a recording session. They lived in a hotel with a steak house on the first floor, The Cattleman, which provided room service. Steak American style was not something they got in Sweden, so they ordered it for breakfast, lunch and dinner, running up a huge room service bill footed by the record company.

We were amazed when they told us who was producing their sessions, Tom Wilson. They were amazed that we knew him from Cambridge and the record business. That sealed a bond with the band, who invited us to come back and stay with them in Gothenburg, where they lived. It was the second largest city in Sweden (Stockholm being the largest), a nice but rather quiet middle-class place with lots of parks. We moved into a guest room in the house where the lead singer lived with his mother. We were welcome and treated as honored guests. I loved the smorgasbord they ate every night just before going to bed – cheese, sausages and smoked fish. They were a little surprised that Americans liked smoked fish, but I grew up on it. All the smorgasbord was missing for me was bagels.

Our hosts were delighted when we started pronouncing the name of their city, spelled Goteborg in Swedish, as "Yutta-Borry," close enough anyway. Kenny was in paradise there. He had this thing for blondes – his ex-wife was one – and here we were in the blonde capital of the universe. There was a pretty blonde "Svenska flicka," Swedish girl, wherever you looked. We had a preconception of Sweden as sexually open, and maybe it was among the Swedes, or in Stockholm, a far more liberal city than conservative Goteborg. But we didn't find the women there eager to jump into bed with strange-looking Americans. For me, sex was better back in Cambridge.

The days passed pleasantly enough, and we enjoyed the long evenings of a Swedish summer. Our idyll was shattered when, on the morning of August 21, we awoke to the news of a massive Soviet invasion of Czechoslovakia. That put an end to the Prague Spring, a period of political and cultural liberalization that became intolerable to the Kremlin. It was the largest military operation in Europe since the end of World War II. Many people in Sweden remembered well the Nazi invasions during that war, and it sent a chill down their collective spine. As Jews, Kenny and I felt it too.

On September 15, a couple of the band members took us to an afterhours club. As I was walking around, who do I see heading toward me but Jimmy Page. He immediately recognized me from the Tea Party, and we stopped to chat. What are you doing here, we each wanted to know. He was on a short Scandinavian tour working out his new band, The New Yardbirds, before debuting them in England. Of the "old" Yardbirds, he was the only one left and had the right to use the name. He introduced me to the chap with him, his lead singer, who had a mop of curly blond hair and was named Robert. They'd just played at a local amusement park which presented "popband" concerts. If Kenny and I had known, we would have been there. We'd just missed one of the very first performances of Led Zeppelin.

18. MEDITERRANEAN DAYS AND NIGHTS

NO ZEP, NO SEX, the days were growing shorter, the nights cooler. It was time to move on to somewhere warmer. We thanked our host family; we all expressed the hope that we'd see each other again if the band returned to the U.S. Kenny and I got a super cheap round-trip airfare on a tourist package to Spain. We had no plans to use the return ticket, but the round-trip fare was cheaper than a one-way commercial flight.

After the flight landed in Barcelona, we took a ferry to the island of Majorca. It departed just before midnight and arrived early in the morning. A guy with a guitar was sitting in the prow playing Beatles songs. That attracted a group of a dozen or so listeners, including Kenny and me. Soon we were all singing along, as the ferry chugged its way across the Mediterranean on a warm starry night, trailing Beatles tunes in its wake.

We only stayed in Majorca for a few days, too touristy for our taste. But before leaving, we went to a shop which made custom leather jackets. Kenny got a classic brown one. I had them cut one like the Levi's denim jacket I was wearing, but out of cowhide, with black, brown and white hair on the outside. We took another ferry, this one to nearby Ibiza, an island getaway for young hip Europeans, uncrowded and unspoiled. We rented a simple little cottage and settled in. During the day I caught a bus which went to a beautiful beach. In my skimpy swimsuit, I fit in with the Europeans, some of whom wore even less, or nothing. In the evening Kenny and I promenaded around the streets of Ibiza Town, then had late dinners of Mediterranean seafood and sangria at open air restaurants. I loved the easy living on the island, beach by day, bistro by night.

I had a brief affair in Ibiza with an English hippie who was living on Formentera, a small island just a few miles off the Ibiza coast. It lacked any of the civilized aspects of its larger neighbor, a far-out and funky outpost, "beyond beads" I called it to Kenny's amusement. I was thinking of going with her when she returned to Formentera, but changed my mind at the last moment. It felt like a step too far, and I was beginning to feel the pull of home. Kenny was feeling the pull of a blonde he'd met in Gothenburg. So we decided to use our return tickets after all and flew back to Sweden.

Big mistake. It was early October, but snow was falling as we landed. I decided to part company with Kenny, leaving him to chase his Svenska flicka, and got on a train headed south, back toward Spain and the sun. In Paris, I had a few hours to wander around the city before my connecting train left. No doubt attracted by my cowhide jacket, a stylish young Parisienne approached me. She didn't speak any English. I didn't speak any French. We tried but just couldn't communicate. With a shrug and a knowing "oh, well" smile, we parted ways.

The train to Spain was a long overnight run, followed by the ferry ride to Ibiza. I spent a week or so back on the beach. But the sun was growing weaker, the pull of home stronger, and my money running low. It was time to return to Cambridge.

19. You Can't Go Home Again...
Or Can You?

BARBARA GREETED ME COOLLY when I arrived at her apartment. No wonder, I'd been gone 2½ months, without writing a letter or even sending a postcard. I'd treated her badly, and she was pissed. I'd left her B.B. in her care. He remembered me and was glad to see me, but would be staying on with her while I looked for a new place to live.

There was a bar near Central Square which was the hot new hangout. I went over there and was greeted across the room by a loud "Ste-vie!" in Kenny Greenblatt's familiar baritone voice. Things hadn't worked out with his flicka, so he'd beat me home. I saw a lot of old friends from the scene, and felt at home again.

The big news from the local music world, which happened while we were gone, was the demise of The Hallucinations. Peter Wolf and drummer Stephen Jo Bladd had left to join up with The J. Geils Blues Band. I wondered why they kept J.'s name for the band, when Peter was going to be the natural leader of any band he was in. But the band's management, Amphion, had insisted that if Peter and Stephen were to become part of the band, the J. Geils name would not change. Peter was O.K. with that, not laying down some star trip. He knew he'd be the man out front when they took the stage.

I'd also missed a lot of national news. The Chicago police had gone crazy attacking antiwar protesters outside the Democratic Convention. But despite the left's opposition to Hubert Humphrey, he got the nomination. Richard Nixon became the Republican nominee. I was back in time to hear Johnson announce on Halloween the ceasing of all bombing of North Vietnam. A treat for Humphreys' campaign, giving it a last-minute boost just before Election Day. Tricky Dick won anyway.

Amy Tosi, a Tea Party regular and a friend, couldn't wait to tell me about a new club that was opening, I had to come see it right away, they need me to do the booking, she said. During my travels I hadn't given a moment's thought to getting back in the music business, but she wouldn't drop the subject. So I went with her where the club was going to be, on Lansdowne Street behind the famed left-field wall at Fenway Park. The space was an old taxi garage, and there were oil spills on the concrete floor. It was hard to imagine it becoming the cool new music venue she kept rhapsodizing about.

She persisted, so I agreed to a meeting with the club owner, a successful businessman named Charlie Thibeau, from the very WASPy Boston suburb of Groton. He pulled up in his Excalibur, a limited-edition modern replica of a classic 1930s Mercedes roadster, ivory with gold trim, and a Corvette engine. Charlie badly wanted to be cool, but the car was gauche. And to be cool, he was prepared to throw hundreds of thousands of dollars into creating the club, to be called The Ark. He hired the Boston multimedia design firm Intermedia to create a "total environment." This would supposedly bring in the crowds and lure them away from that old dump, the Tea Party. The Ark would also have bands, and Charlie assured me that I would be totally in charge of the club bookings.

I needed the job, so I went to work and started lining up acts. One band I did not try to book was the VU. They were solidly in the Tea Party camp, having played a couple more three-day weekends there while I was in Europe. I was not confident enough about the future of The Ark to try poaching the Velvets from the Tea Party. It would have put the clubs in a state of war, and The Ark would have lost. Ray and Don had too much pull in the music business.

For the launch in January, I booked the jazzy psychedelic California band Spirit, who had a major hit album. That's when I started to get flak from Charlie, who was running way over his construction budget. He questioned why we had to spend so much money on bands when it was the multimedia environment of The Ark that would be the big draw. But I knew well that people would go where the performers they liked were playing. Maybe you could book a couple of unknown local bands and pack the Tea Party in early 1967, when the music and the light show were a

Poster for final performance by Cream

novelty. But WBCN was turning people on to a lot of good music, and their tastes were growing more selective when it came to how they spent their entertainment dollars on shows and records.

His carping about the cost of talent did not sit well with me, reminiscent of Ray's complaining about paying two grand to Jeff Beck. I decided that I'd had enough, that I didn't want anything more to do with Mr. Charlie Cool, and bailed. Amy was apologetic about the situation, but I brushed it off as just a bad trip I'd get over. One night I went over to the Tea Party and made my peace with Ray and Don. I told them Thibeau didn't know what he was doing, and that I'd shared that opinion with some of the booking agents I'd worked with, endorsing the Tea Party as still the best club in Boston. They knew that people in the music biz would hear my message.

20. Old Friends

BACK IN THE RIEPEN camp, if only on the fringes, I got some freelance work doing marketing for WBCN. Steve Segal had recently been brought in from California, where he worked as a jock in L.A. under the tutelage of Tom Donahue, the freeform radio pioneer. I went over to the alternative weekly *Boston After Dark* to place an ad promoting his show, on which he was known as "The Seagull." The new art director at B.A.D., Charlie Giuliano, saw me walk in with my aviator shades, cowhide jacket and a briefcase. He was taken aback when I asked for a space to work at, and opened the briefcase to reveal not papers but art materials, including sheets of my beloved Letraset. Taking an image of a seagull I had in my briefcase, I whipped up an ad and handed it to Charles. He was aghast. The look on his face said, "Who is this asshole? I'm the design guy."

On November 4th, the night before the Presidential election, I "went down to the crossroads" of Providence, Rhode Island to see the last-ever performance of Cream. The arena, normally home

My backstage photo of Eric Clapton in Boston After Dark

to a minor league hockey team, was a dump, the audience local rowdies, not the kind of a crowd Cream would draw in Boston. Backstage, guitar cases replaced hockey sticks leaning against the wooden benches. I was surprised to see Steve Stills noodling around on a guitar. Then a smiling face stopped in front of me and simply said, "Hello." I didn't recognize him for a second, Eric Clapton, with a new English rock star haircut.

He quickly brought up our dinner at El Diablo. "Do you know what made me sick?," he asked, and then answered his own question, "That magazine article." He was talking about Jon Landau's critical review in *Rolling Stone*, saying in effect that the band had become a caricature of itself. Eric was more blunt. "He said we were shit." After its publication Jon regretted the tone of what he wrote, but Eric insisted that Jon was right, and that reading it ultimately led to the breakup of the band. He added with a laugh, "I'll get my revenge."

Their final set proved Jon's point. It was just two long and largely instrumental versions of the Cream classics "Spoonful" and "Toad." While Ginger Baker pounded away in perhaps the longest "Toad" drum solo ever, Clapton and Jack Bruce stood out of view behind the banks of Marshall amps, looking bored. When the set was over – no encore – and the houselights came up, their road manager came on stage and to mark the end of the band, passed around paper plates heaped with whipped cream. They started throwing them at each other on stage, then down the corridor back to the dressing room. Inside, Eric stuck his head under a faucet, chuckling while he washed away the last remnants of cream.

With The Velvet Underground booked for the Tea Party on December 12-14, I did the poster for the show. Going against their stereotypical dark image, I drew them as smiling kids in a band. Actually, I couldn't draw. They were depicted by simple stick figures as though drawn by a kid, me, a kid who couldn't spell very well, writing their name as "Unerground" with the first "d" missing. When I showed the poster to Lou Reed on opening night of their gig, he said, How'd you know that's who we really are? I knew. They were just four people having fun playing in a rock 'n' roll band. Lou asked

"Kids" poster for Velvet Underground gig at the Tea Party

Wayne Kramer of the MC5 opening for The Velvet Underground

me to send them my artwork, because he was intrigued by the thought of using the drawing on their next album cover.

The opening act that night was the MC5 from the Motor City, where they played regularly at the Grande Ballroom, Detroit's Tea Party. They were infamous for their on-stage rallying cry, "Kick out the jams, motherfucker!" They played at high speed and high volume, their influences ranging from Chuck Berry to Sun Ra. They were also politically radical. Their manager John Sinclair was a founder of the militant White Panther Party, styled after the Black Panthers. On stage after their set at the Tea Party, he called for people to burn the place down, music should be free, not controlled by bloodsucker promoters. But I didn't hear him offer to forego the band's fee for the gig.

The atmosphere was tense. When the Velvets took the stage, Lou, who was ordinarily not publicly political, denounced what Sinclair said as "very stupid." He called the Tea Party "our favorite place to play in the whole country." That calmed everyone down. The band was now without John Cale, who'd left after his final performances with them at the Tea Party in September. The split between Lou and John was a long time coming, but inevitable. To replace him they added Doug Yule to their lineup, a talented young musician who'd played the Tea Party in The Grass Menagerie. Doug grew up on Long Island, as did Lou, Sterling and Moe.

December 12 was the Velvets' first gig at the Tea Party since the personnel change. This was an audience into their music and not about to accept some watered-down substitute. Lou knew this full well, and opened the set defiantly by doing "Heroin," the VU song most closely identified with John's electric viola. Then they went on to play several other VU classics, including "I'm Waiting for the Man," "White Light/White Heat," and of course "Sister Ray." The crowd loved it. The band also did some songs they were working on for their next album. One was the country-ish lament "Pale Blue Eyes," which they'd been playing live for some time and was requested by a shoutout from someone in the knowledgeable Tea Party audience.

Another new song they did was "I'm Set Free." In it Lou sang of having "been bound to the memories of yesterday's clowns" – John and Nico – but "set free to find a new illusion" in his vision for the band. He even put his manager in his proper place. Steve Sesnick was a manipulator of the band members and a teller of tales. "The prince of stories ruled / walks right by me / And now I'm set free," no longer under Sesnick's domination, and the indisputable leader of the Velvets. He was so amazed at his new freedom that it was as if "I saw my head laughing / Rolling on the ground / And now I'm set free." His *cri de coeur* was underscored by some of Moe's most incisive drumming and a soaring guitar solo by Sterling. It was still very much The Velvet Underground, but it was Lou Reed's Velvet Underground.

21. GO WEST YOUNG MAN

I BECAME GOOD FRIENDS with John Boyd, of The Road light show, and his wife Barbara, hanging out after shows in their South End apartment. They always had good weed. One night at the Tea Party, after I'd left The Ark, John took me up some stairs behind the balcony to the floor above. I'd never been there, even when I ran the place, and found myself standing in front of the Star of David window. It was over six feet in diameter, and lights from the city shone through. This was the secret retreat of The Road's crew, where they went for a quick toke for creative inspiration. John lit a joint and passed it over. It was the first time I got stoned at the Tea Party.

In early 1969 the Boyds and I began kicking around the idea of opening our own club in western Mass. The Connecticut River flowed through the Pioneer Valley, which stretched from the Vermont border up north down to Connecticut. It was home to many colleges, including Amherst, Smith, the University of Massachusetts, and super-liberal Hampshire College. Up in the gentle hills rising from the river, hippies lived a back-to-the-country lifestyle.

With its mellow vibe, the area was fondly known as Happy Valley. There were bars in the college towns with bar bands, but aside from an occasional college concert, no place to hear the kind of music played at the Tea Party.

To open a club, we needed to find the right place. Ken Brown, the filmmaker who worked with The Road, knew the area and told us about an unoccupied old building that might work. It was in South Deerfield, several miles up the road from Northampton. Back in the 1930s the building was a road house called The Gables Ballroom, which held dances with touring bands like "New England's Waltz King" McEnelly & His Orchestra, and Helen Compton and Her 42nd Street Girls, "Gorgeous Young Princesses of Rhythm." It was owned by a local businessman who was a jukebox distributor, but not like the guys upstairs at Johnnie's Steak House. Looking around the building I noticed a beautiful old Rockola jukebox, with glowing brightly-colored plastic panels and loaded with old rock 'n' roll 45s. That was it for me, the place felt right. It already had a stage, could hold 400 people or more, and the rent was cheap. So we decided to go for it.

Before moving to western Mass. to run the club, I went to see one of my favorite bands, The Byrds, at the Tea Party in February. They were into country rock with their latest album *Sweetheart of the Rodeo*, but the shift from their classic psychedelic sound was embraced by the Tea Party audience. The album was recorded with a lineup including Harvard dropout and country rock pioneer Gram Parsons. Since then he and original Byrd Chris Hillman had left the band and formed The Flying Burrito Brothers, who were opening the show. All eight members of the two bands were either present or former Byrds, and during the evening they all came on stage to do a few numbers together. I had my camera with me and took some shots. Jon Landau was there covering the show for Rolling Stone, and wanted to use one of my pictures for the story. He asked me to send the undeveloped film roll directly to the production department of the magazine. I did, and dug

*Byrds and Burritos on stage at the Tea Party; emcee Charlie Daniels,
a.k.a. "The Master Blaster," in silhouette with hat on the far left*

it when one of my photos ran as a half-page in Rolling Stone. But I was not pleased when they never returned my film.

The Boyds and I rented an old farm house in Conway, a neighboring town up in the hills from Deerfield. It had a couple of extra bedrooms, which could come in handy for putting up guests. I bought a well-used VW microbus, not nearly as nice as the Tea Party camper, but suitably funky. In the morning we'd hop in and drive over to the club, me in my cowhide jacket carrying my old briefcase. I looked totally out of place in the country, but was ready to do business.

Now I could run a club without having to answer to a Ray or a Charlie. Barbara would work with me on the business side, while John would put together a light show and be a general handyman. To give the place a hipper image, we renamed it The Woodrose Ballroom. That had a nice country-sounding ring to it. And for those in the know, the seeds of the Hawaiian Baby Woodrose plant contained an ingredient closely related to LSD and could get you high. Or so I'd heard.

Not everyone in the valley was happy to see us longhairs arrive in Deerfield, especially the owners of the restaurant across the road. It was a longtime family business with a straight middle-class clientele and the usual fare of steak, chicken, fried fish and the like. They feared our presence would drive away business, and certainly didn't expect any of our crowd to be reserving tables for dinner. They tried to prevent us from opening.

In the early 18th century, the frontier settlement of Deerfield was the victim of an infamous massacre during the French and Indian Wars. French troops and native tribesmen raided it, burning most of it to the ground, killing several dozen people and taking the remaining hundred or so inhabitants as captives to Canada. This was still a sensitive subject in town after more than 250 years. Commenting on the effort to kill the club, we posted "Deerfield Massacre" on the marquee along the main road in town. That didn't win us any friends at the restaurant, or elsewhere in town. But there was no way they could legally prevent us from operating the same kind of business as The Gables Ballroom had at that location, only with more hair.

Me in Deerfield in my cowhide jacket

22. Rockin' the Valley

To LAUNCH THE CLUB, we brought in some of our friends from the Tea Party: The J. Geils Blues Band on opening weekend, March 14-15; The Velvet Underground the following weekend; Van Morrison a month later. We were all struggling with money issues, so the Geils band camped out at the club in sleeping bags ["slept in the Woodrose Hall," as they later sang in "Hard Drivin' Man" on their debut album] but hung out with us at the house. The Velvets stayed over the house on Friday night and for breakfast on Saturday, before driving back to New York after the Saturday show.

For the VU, that most urban of bands, it was odd being in the country. But it also took off the pressure they were always under from the misperception of who they were as artists, and as people. Their reputation didn't bother the Woodrose audience, many of whom didn't know much about them but quickly became fans. They were grateful to finally have a place to go to hear bands like Geils and the Velvets. As one guy said to me on opening weekend, "Thank God you finally came," as though our arrival had been sorely awaited, if not preordained.

The VU had just released their third album. It was eponymously titled *The Velvet Underground*, as though it was a debut record, which in a sense it was, with Doug Yule replacing John Cale. It went in a very different direction from the previous two, opening with the ballad "Candy Says," sung by Doug, and including soft tunes such as "Pale Blue Eyes," "Jesus," and "After Hours," Moe's singing debut. The Woodrose was where, away from the critical rock press, they could sharpen live performances of the songs in the new album and develop material for the next one. I was a little disappointed that my kids poster drawing did not make it onto the album; instead it had photos by longtime Warhol factory photog Billy Name, a good friend of Lou's. But I got a consolation prize when Sesnick gave me a test pressing of the album, which was not yet available in stores out in the sticks. It didn't even have a label, just "Velvet Underground"

Woodrose Ballroom poster for Van Morrison

written in grease pencil in that blank space. I played it once and stashed it away.

On our third weekend we featured two local bands, Bold and FAT. They were the real pioneers of the music scene in the Valley. Bold was formed by some students at UMass Amherst in 1966 and had just released an LP on ABC, blending psychedelics with folk rock. FAT were five Valley hippies who lived together in a big house near Amherst. They played psychedelic blues rock with a terrific lead singer, Peter Newland. As at the Tea Party, I wanted to expose local talent. Likewise, Bold and FAT had big local followings who came with them to the Woodrose and exposed us to the audience we needed. It was the start of a beautiful friendship.

Since Van played the Tea Party when he was living in Cambridge, he'd moved to Woodstock, New York, and his new album was released, *Astral Weeks*. It was a remarkable and uncategorizable work, with elements of rock, jazz, blues and soul. Naturally, his record company, Warner Brothers, didn't know what to make of it, so it got little promotion from the label and languished saleswise. But it was great to hear where Van had taken the material he tried out at the Tea Party, not only live during his Woodrose gig, but on the record which got a lot of play at the house.

Opening for Van was a band from L.A., Country Funk, who showed up at the Woodrose one day, moved into the house for several weeks and became regulars at the club, either as headliners or opening for bigger name acts, like when The Velvet Underground returned in May. They were a talented group of guys, good songwriters and singers, although their name was misleading. Their sound was reminiscent of Buffalo Springfield and Crosby, Stills and Nash. Not funky, just nice 'n' easy L.A. harmonies, yet they could crank it up and really rock.

Shortly after they arrived, John and I were up in the attic of the club, checking on some wiring. I spotted something over in the corner, and walked over gingerly along the joists. Tucked between them were some old Gables Ballroom posters. As I was picking them up, I heard John yell and turned around to see him disappearing through

John Boyd, a.k.a. "Captain Video"

the attic floor into the performance space below. There was nothing under the joists but wallboard, which gave way when he stepped on it. He might well have broken his back, or worse, from the fall. But somehow he just sprained it badly, requiring a lengthy hospital stay to recover.

Barbara and I carried on with the rest of the crew we'd hired to work with us. When John came back to work, our poster hailed the return of "Captain Video," the show biz moniker he'd adopted. Back that weekend for a return engagement were The J. Geils Blues Band, with The Flying Burrito Brothers opening. This was not the Gram Parsons Burritos, but an East Coast group with guitarist/lead singer Barry Tashian and keyboardist Bill Briggs, former bandmates in The Remains. It was said that Gram copped the Burritos name from them after they opened for him at a gig at Harvard.

23. TO THE MOON AND BACK TO EARTH

THE VELVETS, GEILS AND FAT were back in June, and again in August. In between, on Sunday, July 20, John, Barbara and I took a trip to her family's summer home on one of the Thousand Islands, in the St. Lawrence River. That night we were part of a huge international TV audience as Neal Armstrong took "one small step for a man, one giant leap for mankind" onto the surface of the moon. John had scored some capsules of mescaline, which the three of us and Barbara's hippie sister Carol tripped on the next night. I'd never done anything more than grass and hash, and experienced a crazy ride of emotions and hallucinations.

I became obsessed with the beautiful half-moon above. After gazing at it in wonder for tens of thousands of years, human beings were standing on it. JFK had posthumously delivered on his pledge to land a man on the moon before the end of the decade, thanks to the brilliance of the project managers and engineers at my old employer, NASA. After the moon set around midnight,

Sign at entrance to the Woodrose, with hole on the other side

The Woodrose Ballroom

Carol took me aboard a sailboat tied to the dock, where we spent the night rockin' and rollin' on the river.

The Apollo mission brought back samples from the lunar surface. They may have just been rocks and dirt, but they were the most remarkable treasure ever brought back by a voyage of discovery. By then John, Barbara and I were back on planet Earth at the Woodrose. To celebrate the Apollo mission and its cargo, we posted "MOONROCK" on the marquee. When we came in to work the next day someone had thrown an earth rock at the sign and broken a hole in it. We were annoyed, but didn't feel threatened. However, we were threatened by the hole in the club's financials. We were surviving, but drawing smaller crowds than we'd hoped.

Everyone was talking about the upcoming Woodstock Music & Art Fair in White Lake, New York. It was going to be held on the farm of Max Yasgur. When I was a kid, my grandfather in nearby Monticello was in a summer tourist business with Yasgur's father Sam. I would have loved to go to the festival, same for John and Barbara. But we had to keep the Woodrose open, to keep revenue flowing. We couldn't risk bringing in a name act that weekend, since many of our potential customers would be off to the fair. But we figured there were people who weren't going to Woodstock but might want to gather together and listen to music. So we booked Bold and another local act, and got a decent-enough crowd. The following weekend we had an act you couldn't see at Woodstock, The Velvet Underground.

24. A Crazy Idea

NIXON WAS IN The White House. The war in Vietnam dragged on and on. The Chicago Eight were indicted and facing trial for allegedly causing the riots outside the 1968 Democratic Convention. Major antiwar demonstrations were being planned for the fall. The U.S. was trapped in a cycle of troops fighting in Vietnam and protesters fighting the war at home, with no resolution in sight. Nixon had the power of the government and the Armed Forces. Those of us against the war had no real power other than rallying public opinion.

To change the direction of the country, I came to believe that we couldn't just rely on winning the Presidential election every four years, a strategy which had not been going too well. More young people needed to vote. We also had to take our power in the streets and turn it into actual power in city halls, not just supporting candidates for national office, but being candidates for local office. It wouldn't stop the war overnight or bring about instant change on so many critical issues we faced, but it was a necessary step in a long trek.

Maybe it was the lingering aftereffects of the mescaline, or a couple of tokes off a joint one evening at the house in Conway. But it dawned on me that I could be such a candidate, and run for Cambridge City Council in the election coming up in November. It kind of made sense. After all, wasn't I a graduate of Harvard Law School and the Kennedy School of Government? Wasn't I a successful business manager serving the youth market? Wasn't I a skilled media maven capable of delivering a message to that audience? Wasn't I still a legal resident of Cambridge?

Still, at first it seemed like a crazy idea. I never had any ambitions to be a politician. But then, neither did I ever have any ambitions to go to Peru, to go to law school, to run a rock club. Until an opportunity arose and I caught the wave. So the more I thought about it, the more sense it made. Except for one little catch. I really did not want to be a City Councilor, to live my life in public, to be answerable day and night to people and their needs from City Hall. Nor did I have any desire if elected to use my visibility in Cambridge as a springboard to higher office. That would be a natural career path for a politician, but it was not one I wanted to take, to be a politician. I didn't want that kind of a life.

But I couldn't shake the idea. I knew I could get the message across to apathetic young people to get involved with local government, and to vote. The very fact of who I was, and what I looked like, would reinforce that message. So I decided to do it, but on my terms. Deliver the message, but don't go around day and night knocking on doors and asking people for their votes. If I won, of course I'd serve. But if all went right, I could make my point without getting elected. That was a strategy I didn't talk about.

25. CAMPAIGNING

DURING THE TIME I'D been out in western Mass., I'd been able to hang onto the apartment in Cambridge which I'd moved into when I split with Barbara. It was on Mass. Ave. upstairs from Headquarters East, and appropriately halfway between Harvard Square and City Hall, a perfect location for my campaign headquarters. I was soon joined there by an old friend. Barbara had moved into a new apartment with B.B. but it was small for the two of them. She'd been extremely generous in taking care of him all this time. And I'd been thoughtless in leaving him with her for so long, unfair to her, unfair to him. So I went over to her place and picked him up. He was happy to come with me, and I was happy to have him back. I was also glad to have a watchdog around the apartment, not knowing who might take offense at my candidacy, in an era of political assassinations.

One day who walked in the door but Stanley Mouse, as if he'd just stepped off the cover of that Ramparts magazine which had so intrigued me. He was accompanied by his partner in art Alton Kelley. Together they'd become well known for their great psychedelic San Francisco music posters, especially for shows with the Grateful Dead, for whom they'd created the now-familiar skeleton-and-roses motif. They were spending some time in Boston. Although they'd never done an election poster, that's what they proposed to do for me. It was not really a campaign contribution, because in return I gave them an ounce of grass.

B.B. and me on the back porch of my apartment in Cambridge

They set up a photo shoot with me, in a very hippie setup with a Tiffany lamp, ferns, and all sorts of odd stuff in the backgound. I was wearing a suit I bought in the Square at Krackerjacks. It was white with dark blue pinstripes, the reverse of a lawyer's suit, dark blue with light pinstripes. It reminded me of a Yankees uniform. I thought of sewing a number on the back, maybe a 7 like Mickey Mantle wore.

Mouse and Kelley came back a few days later to show me the artwork, a circular red-white-and-blue star-spangled design with "VOTE" in bold letters across the top and "Steve Nelson, Cambridge City Council" below. I was surprised to see in the center of the poster not a photo of me a man but a mouse, a hippie cousin of Mickey, with a lit joint in his mouth. Was he my cartoon alter ego? Would I be accused of running a Mickey Mouse campaign fueled by pot fantasies? Maybe so, but it was a very cool poster using hip imagery to deliver that simple message: vote.

I did put out another poster which did have my picture on it, sort of. It was shot by Henri ter Hall, a young Dutch photographer living in New York while apprenticing to fashion photog Bill King. Through art connections in New York he got friendly with The Velvet Underground and accompanied them to their first gig at the Woodrose. Henri and I became friends and he came back to visit, staying at the house. After taking some portrait photos of me in my cowhide jacket in a country setting, he asked me to lie down on the grass and close my eyes. I became aware of his Hasselblad and its wide-angle lens very close to me. The resulting black-and-white photo showed my face in an extremely tight horizontal profile, wearing steel-rimmed round glasses, looking up at the sky as though imagining a better world.

What little campaigning I did was limited to walks around Cambridge by day, talking with people I'd run into, and by night hanging out at The Plough and Stars. It was a new bar which had opened in the space formerly occupied by the Elite Spa, catering to longhairs, and the first place in America where you could get Guinness on tap imported from Ireland. Its name was from a play by Sean O'Casey about a group of Dubliners caught up in the 1916 Easter Rising

Detail from contact sheet for my Mouse/Kelley photo shoot

*The Mouse/Kelley poster for my
Cambridge City Council campaign*

STEVE NELSON
CAMBRIDGE CITY COUNCIL

Campaign poster with Henri ter Hall's close-up profile of my face

against British rule. Much of the action takes place in a pub. The Cambridge bar was started by several local Irish-American guys, among them Tom Hargadon, a 1962 grad of Harvard Law with whom I became friends. So the Plough had a revolutionary legacy and spirit. There were rumors, never substantiated, that some of its revenues were being ploughed into the Irish Republican Army.

I got great coverage in local newspapers and the college press -- *The Harvard Crimson, The Heights* at Boston College, and The Tech at MIT, which dubbed me "Cambridge's radical rock 'n' roll candidate." I wasn't saying anything terribly radical, but I looked the part. A new alternative weekly *The Cambridge Phoenix* launched to compete with *Boston After Dark*. The front page of its first issue featured a lengthy story about my candidacy, with a photo by a young up-and-coming photog named Peter Simon. The cover of the music paper *Broadside* was a caricature by Cambridge cartoonist David Omar White depicting me as a knight in armor slaying the dragon of "Sin Evil and Corruption." [A short while later Omar, as he was known around the Square, painted murals in The Casablanca bar on Brattle Street of Bogey and Bergman et al. in scenes from the movie.]

A high point of the campaign for me was a benefit concert I produced, complete with a light show by "Captain Video," at the Harvard Square Theatre, a classic movie house which had never hosted rock before. Among the performers were local musicians Willie Alexander, Peter Ivers, Peter Malick and Peter Rowan, plus my friends Country Funk. The headliner was The New York Rock & Roll Ensemble, who played a fusion of classical and rock, and had been taken under the wing of famed conductor Leonard Bernstein (a Harvard grad). Making an unbilled appearance was The J. Geils Blues Band. Reviewing the show in Broadside, Charlie Giuliano wrote, "Well, Steve, you get my vote."

Under Cambridge's complicated system of proportional representation, it took several days to count the votes after the November 4 election. Of 26 candidates for nine seats, I finished 15th, a respectable showing. I was closely bunched in the results with

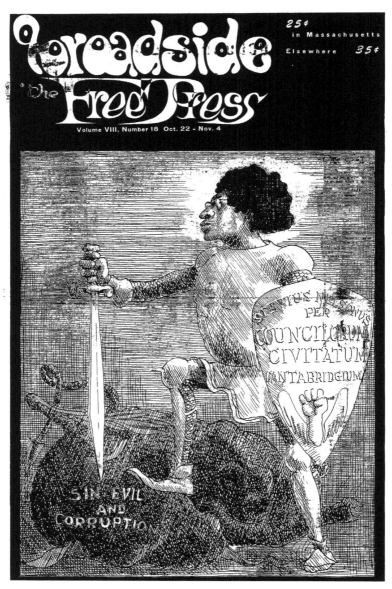

Cover of Broadside with "Stevius Nelsonus" slaying the dragon

two other young also-rans whose fathers were well-known figures in Cambridge politics, while I was a newcomer. Some people speculated that if the voting age were 18, not 21, and if students were not discriminated against when they tried to register to vote, I would have won. A close call.

I was satisfied that I'd accomplished what I set out to do, making it cool to vote and run for local office. I had fun conducting a media event and performance art piece in which I played the role of "candidate." As I was closing up my campaign office, a guy who'd been a regular volunteer let me in on his secret. He was a plant sent by the feds to infiltrate my "radical rock 'n' roll" campaign. I can't say I was shocked, since I was sure my phone was tapped. I'd put on a convincing enough performance, but as he found out, I was no leftist radical.

26. STILL ROCKIN'

WHILE THE CAMPAIGN WAS going on, I still kept a hand in running the Woodrose, going back and forth on weekends. Barbara Boyd, a.k.a. "Auntie Gravity," was playing a bigger part in running the club. The regulars continued to make appearances: J. Geils, The Velvets, FAT, Bold, Country Funk. We did a great blues night with Charlie Musselwhite and Magic Sam, even brought in old Tea Party favorites Lothar and The Hand People.

I was in Cambridge for a few days the week after the election. On the evening of November 12th I went over to the Plough and Stars. At the time I was having a brief affair with a recent University of Michigan grad, Ann, who was living in Boston. She told me that a woman friend of hers from U. of M. was going to be there that night and she'd like to introduce us, since her friend was living near me in western Mass. while going to graduate school at UMass Amherst. I left B.B. at the front door, his accustomed spot, and went inside. The place was packed as usual. After the campaign

*Horsing around before a Woodrose show: (L-R) Kenny Greenblatt,
me and Peter Wolf with his girlfriend Edie*

Magic Dick (legs), Peter and J. Geils in my house in Conway

I was pretty well-known at the Plough, unmistakable in my cowhide jacket, and greeted some friends and supporters over the din of the crowd.

Ann waved me over to a table where a group of people were eating and drinking. As I approached, she gestured to a woman sitting on the far side, Jan Lewis, this is Steve Nelson, Steve, this is Jan. I pulled up an extra chair opposite her, and we talked off and on, drinking draft Guinness, enjoying our conversation and laughing. She was striking, with long thick auburn hair, freckles and hazel eyes. Over my years living in Cambridge I'd come to appreciate that Irish look. But if I had happened to be at the Plough sometime and saw her there sitting at the bar by herself, I might not have approached her, not the kind of "hip chick" I ordinarily would have been attracted to. Quiet in demeanor, not flashy looking, yet still, Jan had a certain *je ne sais quoi* that intrigued me. I invited her to come by the Woodrose, see what I do, and enjoy the music. When I left the Plough, B.B. was still outside waiting for me.

I was a little surprised when she showed up at the club that weekend. The J. Geils Band (they'd dropped the "Blues" from their name) was headlining and put on a great show as always, Peter Wolf hopping and bopping in a yellow jumpsuit. Jan was there with a date, so there was no question of spending time with her after the show. At the Plough she'd told me about this fantastic place down the street from her apartment, the Miss Florence Diner. I loved old diners. So date or not, I managed to take her aside at the Woodrose and asked her to go to the diner with me. She would be glad to, she said, wanting to show me the Miss Flo and, it seemed, to see me again.

Meanwhile, protests against the war continued to escalate. On October 15 millions of people around the world participated in the Moratorium to End the War in Vietnam, with the largest single crowd in Boston, 100,000. On November 15 some 500,000 people gathered near the White House for the Moratorium March on Washington. Pete Seeger led the crowd singing "Give Peace A Chance." Nixon didn't give a

Jan

The Miss Florence Diner

damn, declaring that "under no circumstances will I be affected whatever" by antiwar demonstrations.

About a week later I picked Jan up at her apartment. She was wearing something simple and purple, an interesting color combo with her auburn air. Arcing over a wide doorway between two rooms was a graphic she'd painted on the wall, which she explained was Nut, the Egyptian sky goddess typically depicted in ancient Egypt in just such a pose. Hmm, I was thinking, graduate student in English, Egyptian mythology, is she some kind of academic who wouldn't click with a rock 'n' roller like me?

We walked up to the Miss Flo, which was aglow in the cool autumn evening. A giant neon sign shaped like an arrow pointed down at a perfectly preserved classic Worcester diner car, with its original porcelain exterior and wood interior. Some of the waitresses seemed to have been there since the place opened in 1941, the year I was born. There was a jukebox at every table, with rock 'n' roll and country oldies, three plays for a quarter. It was nice to discover that Jan and I had similar tastes in music.

As she'd promised, the diner had a great menu at very reasonable prices. I ordered the roast beef dinner for six bucks, she had the turkey croquettes. We lingered over dinner and talked. I liked listening to her, not only for what she said, but for her mellifluous alto voice. She told me that she was a descendant of Pocahontas, who married an Englishman, John Rolfe, and had one son. The best part of the meal was at the end, a choice of six or eight different homemade pies. We walked back to her place and talked some more. No sex, not even a kiss goodnight. But I was still intrigued. I told her I'd call her, and I meant it.

The Rolling Stones were playing Boston Garden on November 29, and Debbie Ullman, the first female jock on WBCN, invited me to the show. I loved the Stones, owned all their albums, but had never been to a live performance. What seats, third row center. And what support acts: B.B. King and Ike & Tina Turner with the Ikettes. The Stones did some of their iconic tunes – "Satisfaction," "Sympathy for the Devil," "Street Fighting Man," and

"Jumpin' Jack Flash;" two Chuck Berry oldies – "Carol" and "Little Queenie;" and some material from their about-to-be released new album *Let It Bleed*. 'BCN had been playing cuts from it prior to release, as they often did for hotly anticipated new records. So in "Midnight Rambler" when Mick sang, "Well, you heard about the Boston…" and slammed his heavy belt buckle on the stage, the crowd was primed for that moment and went wild with hometown fervor. After the show I went with Debbie over to her place, where we went wild with some fervor of our own.

A news item from Cambridge caught my attention. Back in September a group of the Weathermen invaded Harvard's Center for International Affairs. One of its founders was Henry Kissinger, and it did contract work for the federal government, including the Defense Department. The invaders caused a melee during which several professors and secretaries were shoved or punched. Now in late November Eric Mann, the leader of the incursion, was sentenced to a year in jail on assault and battery charges. It was the same Eric Mann who was one of my tormentors from ZBT at Cornell. The onetime fraternity poohbah and tweedy asshole had become a radical leftist and convicted felon.

Back at the Woodrose, we had two not-well-known but up-and-coming blues rock acts booked for December. One was out of Georgia, The Allman Brothers Band, who'd played a number of gigs at the Tea Party and on the Cambridge Common, and had their first album out. The other was from Wales, Love Sculpture, with lead guitarist Dave Edmunds, also with one album and another due in January.

Things were coming to a head financially. We realized we were getting more kids driving up from Springfield and Hartford than from the nearby college towns. So we began thinking about moving our shows closer to our market. That's when we saw the shuttered Paramount Theater in Springfield, a classic 1920s art deco movie house in pristine condition, a big room with a high ceiling and a balcony. We loved the place, and had to do it. So on New Year's Eve 1969 we put on our first show there, rebranded as "The

Woodrose Presents at The Paramount Theater." The headliner was Cold Blood, a blue-eyed R&B band out of San Francisco with a horn section and a lead singer, Lydia Pense, who belted them out like Janis Joplin. Opening were Bold and another Woodrose regular, Far Cry, who'd played my Harvard Square benefit. It was a great night to say "Auld Lang Syne" to the 1960s.

27. A New Decade

The calendar read 1970, a new decade. But it still seemed like the '60s. Nixon was still President. The U.S. was still hopelessly mired in Vietnam. And it still sounded like the '60s. On the new Billboard 200 chart for January 3rd, The Beatles had the #1 album, *Abbey Road*. Led Zeppelin was at #2 with *Led Zeppelin II*, and the Stones were at #3 with *Let It Bleed*. And I was still producing rock concerts in the Pioneer Valley.

But there was something new: Jan. I hadn't forgotten her, and invited her over to dinner at our house. I showed her around, and we went down to check out the basement. Watching her hips sway as I followed her back up the stairs, I couldn't stand it any more. When we got to the landing, I put my arms around her and kissed her, really kissed her. She had such beautiful lips, what a kiss. She'd been waiting for me to do that. We held each other close and smiled, but said nothing. There was nothing that needed to be said.

Not long after, I went over to her place one evening. We both knew what was going to happen that night. Jan was slender and small-breasted, unlike the women I'd typically been attracted to. When we were lying naked and entwined, it was a revelation. Our bodies fit together like two pieces of a puzzle, as if we'd once been separated but were now reunited. I didn't want to be separated from her again.

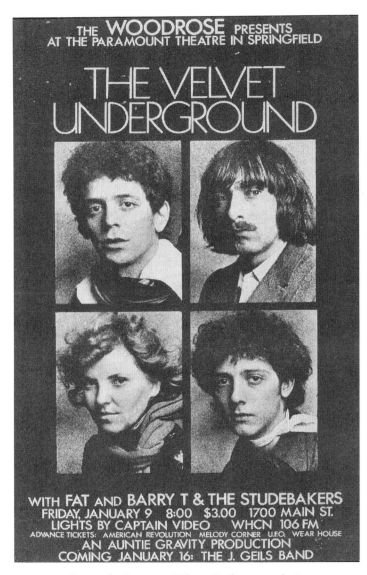

Poster for January Velvet Underground gig
at the Paramount Theatre

Jan began staying over the house regularly. It was so cold in the bedroom that by morning, there was ice on the inside of the windows. B.B. slept at the foot of the bed to help keep us warm. One night after making love, Jan and I lay there, our bodies and minds quiet and content. Suddenly I felt what seemed like a giant spark leaping between our heads, like you see in the laboratory of a mad scientist in a horror film. Did you feel that?, I said. Yes, what was it? Neither of us could really explain it. The result was like a mind meld in a Star Trek episode. We were now one.

The next show at the Paramount was on Friday, January 9. FAT and Barry T & The Studebakers opened for The Velvet Underground. But there was an unexpected and unbilled pre-show performance. Jonathan Richman was a huge Velvets fan, and an aspiring musician. He went to just about every show they played at the Tea Party, and became friends with the band, who respected his offbeat musical talent. He must have got a ride out from Cambridge to Springfield with Barry Tashian and Bill Briggs of the Studebakers. Jonathan and I were friends and I was surprised to see him out in western Mass.

Shortly before showtime, I was up in the balcony with Jan and B.B., where they were going to sit for the show. Jonathan came over to tell me that Sterling Morrison of the Velvets told him he could use his guitar and amp to play a few solo numbers. This was news to me, and I explained to him that no one was going on stage and playing anything without my say-so. But I quickly added that if it was OK with Sterl, it was OK with me. So he went out there, in front of the closed curtain, and played. The audience was puzzled by this guy with short hair in a white vinyl jacket. But Jonathan was never afraid to express himself musically, no matter how quirky he might seem to some people. He'd often busked in the entryway of the Harvard Coop, where there was a natural echo to amplify his acoustic sound. His appearance that night at the Paramount was his first-ever plugged-in performance at an indoor venue.

The shows at the Paramount, a space much larger than the old Woodrose, were generally for one night only. Over the next few

Poster for Chuck Berry show at the Paramount

weeks I brought back J. Geils, with NRBQ opening, and on successive weekends in February, MC5 and The Stooges from Detroit. The 5 had a new album out, produced by Jon Landau, and had dropped the radical politics to focus on being a kickass hard rock band. The Stooges kicked ass too, with wildman Iggy Pop on the mic. In a nostalgic moment, I'd booked Chubby Checker to open for them, the Twist and the twisted.

We ran into a bit of trouble a couple of weekends later, when The Kinks were due in. As a big fan, I was excited about seeing them for the first time, but they cancelled a few days beforehand due to an injury. Barbara Boyd was able to get Van Morrison to come over from Woodstock on short notice. Then we brought in one of my rock 'n' roll heroes, Chuck Berry. He traveled solo and counted on having a local band back him up. True to his reputation, he demanded to be paid in cash up front before he went on. No dough, and he'd be gone like a cool breeze. But it was a thrill to present a show with Chuck.

Then we ran into big trouble. Spirit was booked on Saturday, March 21. With people already starting to line up outside the theater, I got a call from their booking agent. They would not be playing. He'd booked them into two different venues for that night, the other in New Jersey. He admitted they'd be keeping that date, where I guessed they'd make more money from the gate. With its insanely rapid growth over the past few years, I could see that the music biz was spinning out of control. Maybe I just had bad karma with Spirit. We sent the crowd home. The cancellation didn't help our karma with them.

28. BACK TO THE SQUARE

BY NOW JAN HAD DROPPED out of grad school and moved in with me and B.B. in my apartment on Mass. Ave., where I was spending most of my time. We were deeply in love, and all I really wanted to do was to be with her, to stare into her hazel eyes, to

*Video stills from April Velvet Underground show at the Paramount:
(top to bottom) Sterling Morrison, Lou Reed, Doug Yule*

"make love, not war." With the Woodrose struggling, I turned it over to "Auntie Gravity." We had no debt, so if Barbara could make it work, she could keep it.

A big antiwar march in Boston was coming up on April 15. Jan did a Betsy Ross, sewing a cool flag with a green peace sign in the middle, and a red-white-and-blue stripe on either side of it, like it was some military insignia. I'd become friends through mutual acquaintances with a guy in Boston, Michael Pitkow, who had a Sony Portapak mobile video recorder, maybe the first one in the Boston area. He loaned it to me, and I taped Jan making the flag. On the 15th, a contingent of marchers came from the Cambridge Common down Mass. Ave. to join up with the demo on Boston Common. As they came by, I stood on our stoop waving the flag, and shooting video of the people flowing past.

That weekend, on April 17th, Barbara had booked the Velvets, and Michael and I drove out to Springfield in his Porsche to see the show and videotape some of it. On the way out we listened to WBCN as long as we could pick up the signal. Among the hot new albums were *Santana, Sweet Baby James, Blood, Sweat & Tears* and *The Band*.

When we got to the theater, VU drummer Moe Tucker was not there, too pregnant to go on the road. The band had just been in the studio for two days beginning to work on their next album. They'd been playing some of that material at Woodrose shows for several months, and that night did "Sweet Jane" and "New Age." They played as a trio, with Doug jumping onto a drum kit when a song, like "Heroin," needed a propulsive beat. When Michael and I got back to Cambridge and looked at the tape, we discovered that there was no audio. I hadn't remembered to turn on the camera mic.

The following Thursday, April 22, Michael and I took the camera to Soldiers Field at Harvard. It was one of many locations across the country part of an event called Earth Day, peaceful demonstrations and speeches in support of the environment. It was a beautiful spring day, which helped draw a big and mellow crowd. A group of us, including Jan, Bob Driscoll and several hippie friends, kept in touch with the earth by sprawling on the ground and passing around joints.

Video still of me at the first Earth Day at Harvard's Soldiers Field

That weekend Michael and I were back on the road to shoot the J. Geils Band in a Woodrose show at the Paramount Theater. This time we got good audio, including one of their signature numbers, John Lee Hooker's "Serve You Right to Suffer." I was standing on stage with them, and the low-res black-and-white single-camera video captured the essence of the band. We also got some short clips of The Allman Brothers, but not as successful. When I left the Paramount that night for the ride home, it was for the last time.

During the VU gig, their manager Steve Sesnick had mentioned to me that they would be appearing in late June and early July at Max's Kansas City, the infamous New York watering hole which was the hangout for Andy Warhol, artists, writers, musicians, celebrities and wannabes. It would be their first real gig in New York in three years, while Sesnick played hard-to-get. I decided to do a poster, for my own amusement if nothing else. Using the promo photos from the black-and-white poster I did for their January 9th show, I cut out all their faces. Then I bunched them closely together, inspired by the famed black-and-white group photo of The Beatles by Richard Avedon in *Look* magazine.

I laid it out in a long horizontal shape to evoke an ad in a NYC subway car, the Underground underground. Jan, B.B. and I drove down to the city to show the design to Mickey Ruskin, the owner of Max's and patron of struggling artists. He loved it, and paid me $1000 to print him 1000 copies. It was good money. I shipped them to him in advance of the show, then Jan and I went down for opening night. It was quite a scene, the return of New York's prodigal sons (Moe was still sidelined). The Velvets never sounded their best in a small room with a low ceiling. And people in the audience talked all the way through the show. In their eyes they were the show, the band merely the musical accompaniment. Maybe Sesnick had been right in staying away from New York. That's why when the VU first played the Tea Party it was such a revelation for them. People listened, and they cared.

I was still a regular reader of *The New York Times*. In the morning I'd usually walk down to the Square with B.B. and maybe Jan,

"Subway" poster for the VU's return to New York at Max's Kansas City

to pick up a copy of the paper. Then we'd head over to the Patisserie Francaise on Boylston Street, where I'd have a French coffee (or two) and one (or two) of owner Maurice LeDuc's incomparable ham and cheese croissants. The space was partly underground, and pretty much everyone there was part of the cultural underground. It was the hangout for the hip crowd, and I had a lot of friends and acquaintances I'd see and chat with. It was easy to while away a couple of hours, watching to see who came in or passed by on the street above.

After leaving the Patisserie, I often wandered around Cambridge, with a camera hanging around my neck. Harvard Square was at the center of the '60s youth counterculture, and I was part of it. Yet sometimes I felt like an anthropologist, an outsider observing and photographing the natives, their customs and their costumes. On my walks I became visually fascinated by the icons of corporate American culture which were everywhere, even as we rejected the values they represented, the Coca-Cola logo and the red Pegasus flying above Mobil gas stations.

On June 1, I got the *Times* and folded it up under my arm before going to the Patisserie. I didn't get around to reading it until I got back to the apartment. When I opened it up, a small item at the bottom of the front page leaped out at me: "Earthquake Rocks Half of Peru; Nearly 200 Are Reported Killed." The worst hit city was Huaraz, near Vicos. The next morning I ran out early to get the paper for the latest news on the damage. The earthquake was now the top story, the true extent of the catastrophe becoming clearer: "Peru Estimates 30,000 Died In Quake That Wiped Out Scores Of Towns In North." I was stunned. The quake, centered 12 miles off the coast at Chimbote, was estimated at 7.75 on the Richter scale. Among the dead were two young American women who were volunteers with the Peace Corps in the Callejon de Huaylas.

When all the facts of the disaster became known, it was even worse. The quake broke loose a piece of the Huascaran glacier half a mile across and a mile long, which roared downhill at over two hundred miles per hour. Yungay, a village neighboring Vicos,

Patisserie Francaise in Harvard Square

Mobil station in Harvard Square

was in its path. The 20,000 people who lived there were instantly buried under forty feet of ice, rocks and mud, although Vicos escaped with minor property damage. With total casualties of some 70,000, the landslide was the deadliest ever in the world.

I was horrified and helpless. I wanted to go and help somehow. Paul Doughty, our group leader in Vicos, did go, but he had long been involved in the Callejon. My Spanish was too rusty, my rescue skills too minimal for me to be useful. I'd just be a gringo getting in the way. My idyllic memory of Huascaran gleaming white against a deep blue sky was forever marred. As Mary Poppins author P. L. Travers might have said, on Huascaran "beauty and death were two sides of the same coin."

One afternoon I ran into Kenny Greenblatt in the Square. Stevie! He was really psyched. John and Yoko had visited WBCN that day, where he was working in sales. Afterwards they'd come over to his apartment, in the big building at University Road and Mt. Auburn Street, a few blocks from the center of the Square. Kenny still had one of my campaign posters on the wall, the one with Henri ter Hall's tight profile shot of me. He told me that John and Yoko kept looking at it, and thought it was really cool. [When John's album *Imagine* was released in 1971, the front cover featured a Polaroid of John taken by Andy Warhol. On the back was a photo by Yoko, a tight horizontal profile of John's face, wearing steel-framed round glasses, looking up at the sky as though imagining a better world.]

That building was home to many members of the counterculture, including Peter Wolf. It was also the scene of an infamous murder by Albert de Salvo, the Boston Strangler. Charlie Giuliano had a corner apartment in the basement, crammed with his art, weird artifacts and a jungle of plants. Since giving me his endorsement in Broadside during the election, he'd become the rock and jazz critic for *The Boston Herald Traveler*, and we'd become friends. Often on a Saturday morning, cruising the Square with B.B, I'd drop by his place. When Charlie would come upstairs to the lobby to let us in, "Mr. B," as Charlie affectionately called him,

Charlie Giuliano in his basement apartment in the Square

would scoot downstairs ahead of us to his accustomed spot under the kitchen table. Charlie and I would talk for hours, maybe have a toke. In July he mentioned that he'd coined a word which he used in his review of a Ten Years After concert at Harvard Stadium: "gonzo." That was our life in the '60s underground, real gonzo, man.

Things were gonzo above ground too. On May 4, students at Kent State University protested the recent U.S. invasion of Cambodia. Ohio National Guard troops fired at the crowd, killing four students and wounding nine. The campus immediately shut down, as did 400 colleges and universities across the country in sympathy with the victims and their cause. On May 9th 100,000 demonstrators converged on a barricaded White House to protest the killings and to demand the withdrawal of U.S. forces from Cambodia. By the end of June the troops were pulled out.

By then the U.S. Senate had voted on June 24 to repeal the Gulf of Tonkin Resolution, passed nearly six years earlier as the legal basis for President Johnson to conduct the war in Vietnam. But it was a sham. It exaggerated the supposed attack by North Vietnamese patrol boats against U.S. destroyers, whose deliberate presence so close off the North Vietnam coast provoked their response. The Senate may have repealed the Resolution, but it couldn't repeal the death, destruction, pain and suffering it had unleashed. The war was a waste. Now the only real question was how to get out, and how soon.

29. Mt. Massaemett

JAN AND I WERE GOING to spend August in a cabin we rented in western Mass., on Mt. Massaemett above Shelburne Falls. With the lease coming due on my Cambridge apartment, I couldn't afford to keep it and had to let it go. For the first time since moving back to Cambridge while I was fighting induction, I no longer had a physical foothold there. We left in Jan's VW Beetle with

Jan at a window in the fire lookout tower on Massaemett Mountain

what we decided to keep from the little we owned. B.B. rode along in the back seat.

We kept the radio on while we could still pick up a decent station. Even AM radio reflected the turmoil in the country. The Temptations had a giant hit with their psychedelic soul tune "Ball of Confusion (That's What the World is Today)." Eric Burdon had a new funk group called War; a single from their first album was rapidly climbing the charts, "Spill The Wine." So was a record by Edwin Starr, a runaway hit destined to reach #1, "War." It was co-written by Barrett Strong of "Money" fame: "War, huh, yeah / What is it good for? / Absolutely nothing." We headed west on the Mohawk Trail, to The Beatles #1 and final single, "The Long and Winding Road." As we reached the hills of western Mass., the radio faded away. We rode in silence, with only the sound of the summer breeze blowing through the open windows.

The cabin was owned by a farming family with a maple sugaring operation. A dirt road from their place went uphill to the cabin, and ended there. The space itself was very spartan, basically one big room, but it did have electricity. We were totally isolated. It was hot and we wore very little, sometimes nothing. From the cabin a footpath led up the mountain through the woods to an old stone fire lookout tower at the top. Except for the mortar between the stones, it wouldn't have looked out of place in the Andes. It provided a spectacular panoramic view of western Mass. Every evening we walked up its stone steps to watch the sun set behind the rolling hills. Every night we made love.

When we moved into the cabin we noticed two books that had been left behind. One was of no interest, a collection of condensed stories from Readers Digest. But the other was remarkable, called *American: The Life Story of a Great Indian: Plenty-coups: Chief of the Crows*. Published in 1930, it was the first autobiography of an Indian chief, as told orally to a writer from Montana. The name Plenty Coups was the English translation of his Crow name *Alaxchiiaahush*, signifying his many acts of bravery ("coups") in battle.

Crow Chief Plenty Coups

As a boy and according to Crow custom, he went to seek a vision, spending several days and nights in the Crazy Mountains. In his vision he saw buffalo coming out of a hole and spreading across the plains before disappearing. Then strangely-colored buffalo came out of the hole and remained on the plains. Interpreting his dream, tribal elders said it represented the conquest of Native Americans by the white man, whose cows replaced the buffaloes. Accepting the inevitability of his tribe's fate, Plenty Coups led them through that transition, counseling them on how to adjust to the dramatic changes they faced. He said, "Education is your most powerful weapon. With education, you are the white man's equal; without education, you are his victim, and so shall remain all your lives." It was a message that many years later and thousands of miles away, Nestor and Urbano Sanchez understood well.

Thinking about Plenty Coups's vision while at the cabin, I knew from an anthropological perspective that the buffalo was fundamental to the way of life of the Plains Indians. It provided food, clothing, shelter (tepees) and more. Without it, that life was not sustainable. I thought about the "buffalo" of the modern American way of life: oil. How much of our "buffalo" could come out of the holes of drilling rigs before disappearing? Someday we'd need a new source of sustenance for our civilization. Like the Incas, I was a sun worshipper. It made all life on earth possible. We would have to turn to the Sun to survive.

Jan and I spent a lot of our time typing poetic fragments, simple plays on words, sometimes just arrangements of words or letters on a page. They were about love and sex, they were about the past and the future, they were about time and space, they were about A vision of a globally interconnected human consciousness. Crazy words on a crazy mountain.

The entrance to the tower

30. THE TOWER

I WANTED TO SPEND one night on the tower alone, to savor the serenity of that isolated aerie under a starry sky, and to seek my vision. Jan kissed me goodnight and held onto B.B., so he wouldn't follow me up the trail. She and I always came down from the tower right after sunset so we could get back to the cabin before dark. Now I entered the tower alone and climbed the stairs. At the top I watched the sky in the west, glowing after sunset and then fading. As darkness settled over the land, a darkness settled over me. I began thinking about how I got here, on a journey in which I'd been blown far off course from the life I once knew. It was something I really hadn't given much thought since my exile and then being caught up in my life in rock 'n' roll.

I knew my legal career was long over. Given my success in the Ames Competition, it could have been a brilliant one. "I coulda been a contendah," as Marlon Brando said in *On The Waterfront*. A contender for achieving personal success, of course, while using my legal powers to do good. But I'd been too burned out by my fight with the draft, a casualty of the war. I didn't have it in me anymore to contend at the highest level of the legal profession. Yet I'd learned I could fight, not just to win a competition at school, but to survive.

I'd always had a lingering doubt from my one law case, representing myself against the Selective Service System. Was I a conscientious objector as I'd claimed to be, or just trying to save my skin? I was sincere in my belief at the time, that I could not and would not kill Vietnamese in a wrongful war.

Yet as my lawyer, I asked myself tough questions, and the toughest was about the Nazis. Adolf Eichmann was on trial as I was leaving for Peru, and I believed he deserved to die. If I'd been of age during World War II, would I have fought and killed Germans? At the time of my draft ordeal, my answer as a conscientious objector would have been "no." But after battling the government, pushing myself to the edge and beyond, maybe at the risk of my life, I had to admit that my answer now was "yes." I learned that I was a fighter, not a conscientious objector.

The night grew black. It was as if I were floating in space, the ground invisible far below me. I realized how easy it would be to jump off into nothingness. And there were times in that long and lonely night when I really thought I might, overwhelmed by confronting my painful feelings of loss and failure.

But if I'd lost so much, I'd gained much. First and foremost, Jan of course. I'd found the love of my life. Growing up in the middle of a bad marriage, I always had doubts whether I could find long-term happiness in a relationship. But I had no doubts about Jan, I wanted to be with her forever. How could I leave her behind now, and cause her such pain?

I'd discovered a new creativity in myself. I'd lived the excitement and pleasures of sex, drugs and rock 'n' roll. I'd been on that thrill ride called the '60s, and played a small part in making it happen. And I had more than memories from those times, I had a living reminder in B.B. Maybe as a result of living as a stray, he was an unusual and perceptive animal. He took life as he found it. He was a fighter too, every now and then around Cambridge taking on a bigger dog in a burst of growling and scuffling, and coming out on top. B.B. was loyal and protective of Jan and me. But he couldn't protect me from myself.

I thought of my family, especially my mom. She would be devastated. I'd seen what the loss of her son had done to Annie Schwerner. She hadn't gotten over it and never would. With my mom having to be my dad's caregiver while working full-time, she already was carrying a greater burden than most people could bear. She was strong, but losing me might be more than she could take.

No, I couldn't jump. I was no longer the person who opened that first "Greeting" letter from the President, I barely looked like him. But I was a survivor. I was a new person with a new life and too much to live for, especially Jan. By dawn I accepted what I'd lost, and was at peace with who I'd become. I walked down the stone steps in the tower and headed back down the trail.

B.B. waiting outside the cabin

Nearly 3,000 years ago, the Greek poet Homer wrote the epic poem *Odyssey*. The hero Odysseus (called Ulysses by the Romans) tries to return to his home on the island of Ithaca after fighting the Trojan War. He faces trials and tribulations on a decade-long journey. When he finally gets home, his old blind dog recognizes him but dies from over-excitement.

My odyssey began in Ithaca, when I left for Peru. I faced trials and tribulations on a decade-long journey. When I emerged from the trail that morning, my dog was waiting and came running over to greet me excitedly, wagging his tail, very much alive. I was excited to see him too, hiya, B.B.! Hearing the fuss we were making outside, Jan came to the screen door of the cabin. We looked at each other and smiled.

I was home.

Encore

"You can't always get what you want,
But if you try sometime, you might find,
You get what you need."
The Rolling Stones,
"You Can't Always Get What You Want"

Jan and I were married on July 4, 1974. At the time we were living in Plympton, Mass. in the house where Deborah Sampson was born in 1760. She was a young woman who, dissatisfied with her lowly station in life, disguised herself as a man and served in the Revolutionary War for a year and a half. It was only when she became ill and required medical attention that her true gender was revealed. Clothes made the man.

On January 22, 1977, coming up from the subway at Park Street in Boston, I glanced at the headline of The New York Times on the newsstand: "Carter Pardons Draft Evaders." It was his first official act as President. I had nothing to be pardoned for. But walking through the Boston Common, the site of major antiwar demonstrations, I felt a weight lifted. In fighting against the war I considered myself to be a patriot, and my patriotism was no longer in question. By now, if people associated my name with anyone, it was not the Steve Nelson of the American Communist Party, but the star linebacker for the New England Patriots, Steve Nelson.

After my rock 'n' roll days I was an entrepreneur in solar energy, computer magazine publishing and software, and video production, doing management and business development, public affairs and communications, and sales and marketing. I never got rich but I rode some great waves.

On June 6, 2003, Jan and I went to see Lou Reed play the Calvin Theatre in Northampton, just a few miles down the road from the old Woodrose. He left us tickets and backstage passes. I'd recently issued a limited edition reprint of my VU at Max's poster, and in the dressing room after the show he told me he wanted to sell it on his web site. Of course I agreed. Then he introduced me to his band and explained my involvement with The Velvet Underground: "We couldn't have survived without him."

The Boston Tea Party became legendary. On January 20, 2007, the 40th anniversary of its opening night, the Music Museum Of New England celebrated with an event that brought together many of the people from back in the day. The Bostonian Society unveiled an historic marker to be installed on the former Tea

Party building, now redeveloped as condos, although the exterior is largely intact. MMONE is a virtual archive at mmone.org, which I co-founded and run with old friend and Orpheus drummer Harry Sandler. The beat goes on.

Over the years I've been asked many times, "You're a lawyer, aren't you?" This was usually a lead-in to wanting my opinion or help on some legal matter. I demurred, "Well, not really, but that's a long story." And it is.

In 2011, I was appointed to the Board of Directors of WiredWest, a cooperative of many small rural towns in Western Mass. Our mission was to connect people with a fiber-optic network in order to bring them broadband internet service where there was none. We often compared our lack of broadband in the 21st century to people in rural areas not having electricity in the 20th century. I knew what that was like.

The chair of the WiredWest Board knew I'd gone to Harvard Law. "You're a lawyer, aren't you?," she asked. I demurred, "Well, not really." But despite that she appointed me Legal/Governance Chair. It was the first time I held a legal position since NASA. That's one giant leap for a man.

In 2016, fifty-five years after living in Peru, I donated my Vicosino suit to Cornell. I'd kept it in mothballs all those years and it was in excellent condition, a rare artifact. Looking through my field notes and photos, which I also planned to give to Cornell, I thought to myself, "There's a story here."

The author

ACKNOWLEDGMENTS

Jan, for her support, understanding, patience, editing and love.

My son Nate, my brother Peter and my old friend Michael Pitkow for reading the draft manuscript and encouraging me to keep going.

Professor Allan Holmberg, who enabled this journey to begin; my Ames teammates and Ray Riepen, whose faith in me allowed it to continue to places I could not have imagined; and my friends around Harvard Square and everywhere who welcomed me when I arrived.

My parents, alternately proud and bewildered by the twists and turns of that journey, but always happy to see me when I needed them, whether for parental love, a little cash or a bowl of chicken soup.

Susie, Szusza, Beth and Barbara, for helping a boy to become a man. "Though we're apart, you're part of me still." (Fats Domino)

And B.B., not just a dog, but a unique being with smarts and soul.

Throughout this book I've lapsed here and there into lyrics from songs, sometimes consciously, sometimes not. I haven't always cited the sources of the words I sampled. But I used them with deep appreciation for those who wrote and sang them, so I could listen. They're part of me, words of wisdom, even if it's only rock 'n' roll.

Much of the factual basis of this book is based on documents, artifacts and images I saved over the years, including my field notes from Peru, Ames Competition briefs, and Selective Service records. Some background facts are from online research and published sources. The rest of the book is from memory, some of it vivid, some of it hazy and, for better or worse, all of it mine.

CREDITS

Front cover and interior design: James McDonald
Front cover photo: David Laing
Back cover concept: Steve Nelson
Back cover and interior production: Carol MacColl and Davin Pasek
Back cover images:

    The Andes: Allan R. Holmberg Collection on Peru, Cornell University
    Summer of Love: courtesy Laura Grosch
    The Draft: Uncle Sam by James Flagg Montgomery
    The Judges: Frank R. Parker
    The Velvet Underground: Promo photos, from Woodrose poster
      by Steve Nelson
    The Boston Tea Party: Photo of Jeff Beck by Peter Simon, courtesy of
      Special Collections, UMass Amherst Libraries
    B.B.: Steve Nelson

Page:

    2   David Barkin
   10   Steve Nelson
   11   (top) Steve Nelson
         (bottom) Paul Doughty
   14   Steve Nelson
   16   Family photo
   20   (top) Polly Doughty
         (bottom) Allan R. Holmberg Collection on Peru, Cornell University
   22   Steve Nelson
   28   (top left) Unknown
         (top right) Allan R. Holmberg Collection on Peru, Cornell University
         (center and bottom) Steve Nelson
   33   Allan R. Holmberg Collection on Peru, Cornell University
   38   Steve Nelson
   50   Steve Nelson
   58   Steve Nelson
   63   Steve Nelson

66 (top) Steve Nelson

(bottom) Allan R. Holmberg Collection on Peru, Cornell University

70 (top) Steve Nelson

(bottom) Allan R. Holmberg Collection on Peru, Cornell University

72 (top) Unknown

(bottom) Allan R. Holmberg Collection on Peru, Cornell University

(captioned "Two Vicosinos in traditional black outfits")

76 Steve Nelson

78 Steve Nelson

81 Steve Nelson

85 Allan R. Holmberg Collection on Peru, Cornell University

88 Old postcard

94 Family photo

96 Promo photo, from the collection of Donna Halper

101 Yearbook photo

109 (top) Promo photo

(bottom) Promo poster

114 (top) Scopitone

(bottom) Johnnie's Steak House

122 Old postcard

132 (top) Family photo

(bottom) Promo photo

134 Yearbook photo

140 Family photo

146 Family photo

151 Federal Bureau of Investigation

152 Unknown

156 Steve Nelson

162 Harvard Law School

165 Frank R. Parker

178 Bain News Service

185 Promo photo

190 James Flagg Montgomery

192 Steve Nelson Archive

197 Promo photo

202 Ramparts Magazine

206 Steve Nelson

213 Club 47 calendar copyright James Rooney, used by permission, all rights reserved; image courtesy of Folk New England

215 Steve Nelson

216 (top) Steve Nelson
(bottom) Unknown, courtesy Laura Grosch

220 Unknown, from Steve Nelson Archive

221 David Hahn

228 (top) Michael Dobo / Dobophoto.com
(bottom) Unknown

231 Steve Nelson Archive

234 Steve Nelson

240 Collage by Steve Nelson, images unknown

245 Bob Driscoll

247 Promo photo

250 Boston Herald Traveler clipping from Steve Nelson Archive

252 (top) Unknown
(bottom) Courtesy Dave Kinsman, Ill Wind

258 Steve Nelson

264 (top) Sam Kopper
(bottom) Leslie Parmiter, courtesy Sam Kopper

267 Steve Nelson Archive

272 (top) Promo photo
(bottom) Steve Nelson

280 Promo photo

292 Mad Peck Studios

294 Boston After Dark clipping from Steve Nelson Archive

296 (top) Steve Nelson
(bottom) Michael Dobo / Dobophoto.com

300 Steve Nelson photo, from Rolling Stone clipping

302 Henri ter Hall

304 Steve Nelson

306 Steve Nelson

308 Steve Nelson

312 David Laing

314 Stanley Mouse and Alton Kelley

315 Stanley Mouse and Alton Kelley

316 Photo by Henri ter Hall; poster design by Steve Nelson

318 Broadside cover art by David Omar White, courtesy David Wilson, all rights reserved.

320 (top) Sam Kopper
     (bottom) Henri ter Hall

322 (top) Steve Nelson
     (bottom) Unknown

326 Poster by Steve Nelson, courtesy Jeff Gold, recordmecca.com

328 Tom Kuchenski

330 Steve Nelson

332 Michael Pitkow

334 Steve Nelson

336 Steve Nelson

338 Steve Nelson

340 Steve Nelson

342 Rodman Wanamaker

344 Steve Nelson

347 Steve Nelson

350 David Jenkins

356 Jan Nelson

In Memoriam

Laura Herrmann Couallier
1965-2017

For some 25 years Laura was my go-to graphic designer for the many projects I worked on. A good friend and trusted colleague, she always delivered great work and never missed a deadline. We were looking forward to collaborating on the design for this book after the holiday season.

She and her husband Christophe were on vacation just before Christmas. They were traveling in a bus on a narrow road to see Mayan ruins in Mexico. When the driver lost control, the bus went off the road and rolled over, killing Laura, Christophe and ten other people. A tragic ending, ironic in the light of how my journey began in Peru.

Made in the USA
Middletown, DE
19 May 2018